Do You Want to
WORK in
BASEBALL?

Inside Baseball Operations

BILL GEIVETT

© Bill Geivett 2016

ISBN: 978-1-48359-093-6

Dedication

To my mother Amanda. Even as a youngster, she supported my love for baseball every way possible. I love you, Mom.

To my wife Bonnie, who has been with me since Highlands High School supporting my baseball career in the good years and the bad. I love you, Bonnie.

To Rachel and Sam, the two best kids anyone would be happy to call their own. You make me and your mom proud. I love you.

My Mom, Amanda Geivett   **My family, Rachel, Bonnie and Samuel**

Contents

CHAPTER 1:

AN INTERVIEW WITH TOMMY LASORDA

Tommy Lasorda and me

WHEN ONE "DOES" LUNCH WITH TOMMY LASORDA, IT'S A TREMENDOUS exhibition of human consumption—multiple courses and huge portions. Tommy and I finish one such enormous lunch and head to the lobby of the Marriott Hotel in Anaheim, California, site of the 1999 Major League Baseball Winter Meetings. Everyone who's either in baseball or trying to get into baseball comes, pilgrimage style, to these annual gatherings.

The hotel lobby at every MLB Winter Meetings brims with staff members from all 30 clubs— front office executives, field

*managers, scouts, coaches, trainers, and clubhouse person-
nel—plus player representation (agents), and national and local
media. Job-seekers occupy any remaining open floor space. It
teems with energy. Every club sends staff members to sniff out
possible trades or free-agent acquisitions. A quick glance over
the crowd yields clues to the business at hand. At all Winter
Meetings, one typically sees MLB club officials huddled together
in groups of five or six discussing the rapidly changing rumors
of the hour. Large groups of baseball friends engage in light-
hearted banter with more serious discussions confined to a
smaller group. If two staff members from one team are meeting
with one or two from an opposing team, it's typically a "trade
discussion." When a club official meets with an agent one on
one, it's usually a "free-agent/player negotiation." These serious
meetings take place on the periphery of the room—off to the side
away from the earshot of others. If any of these negotiations gain
traction in the lobby, they are continued upstairs in a club suite
with the executives. Yes, with the rumor mill churning, multiple
MLB trades and free-agent acquisitions have their genesis in the
hotel lobby at the Winter Meetings. It is almost impossible to
keep secrets in Major League Baseball, and information, including rumors, is shared vigorously in the lobby. Valuable information obtained in the lobby is taken to club executives who
combine it with data analysis and scouting reports. These then
influence the style or the posture a club assumes in trade or free-
agent negotiations.*

Tommy and I traverse through the crowded mass of baseball human-
ity filling the hotel lobby. We slowly make our way to the elevator, headed
for the fourth-floor suite occupied by the Los Angeles Dodgers' staff during
the four days of the Winter Meetings. *MLB clubs turn fancy suites into*

headquarters for staff meetings, interviews, trade discussions, player contract negotiations with agents, and more.

But before we reach the elevator, Peter Gammons, the era's best-known baseball writer, stalls our progress. He asks Tommy his opinion about the skyrocketing free-agent player salaries. Tommy *(acting uncharacteristically un-opinionated)* ignores the question and describes in great detail our most recent lunch. *(Did I mention the lunch was enormous?)* Because I had just watched Tommy eat all five courses of his lunch while keeping pace forkful-by-forkful, I skip listening to the bloating details so as not to relive the experience.

Diversions

Looking for a diversion, I scan the hotel lobby for someone to talk "baseball business" with. I casually join a group of officials from various teams discussing the most recent events and rumors in MLB. Some rumors seem farfetched, but "you never know," which is why I tuck them away in my mind as "possibilities." Discreetly, I get the attention of a member of another club's front office and engage him one-on-one about a potential trade for a player the Dodgers want to acquire.

The discussion doesn't last long—a disappointing dead end. His organization has no interest in trading the player we like *(trades for good players are not easy to consummate).* So I look for other groups that might consider the trades we have in mind, but it's a tough day on the trade market. Moving on, I bump into a couple of player agents who are eager to remind me of how *great* their players are *(as if they would ever let you forget).* We set up meetings for later that evening upstairs in the suite, as we have serious interest in their free-agent players *(until later when the agents tell us how much money they want).*

Suddenly, I hear a roar of laughter. Across the expansive room I see Tommy in the middle of a crowd of 20 people or so, performing as if on stage. He's recounting his greatest baseball stories *(there's no funnier man in our sport).* I can hear his distinctive voice from across the lobby and see more people moving toward the assembled crowd. He has his audience laughing hysterically. It was obvious how much everyone was enjoying Tommy's stories. *It would have been more productive for us to go up to the suite, but admittedly, I have little chance to steal Tommy from his admirers.* I know they are having a great time, and nobody enjoys telling funny baseball stories more than Tommy Lasorda. I keep walking.

Shifting away from the Tommy show, I see a group of six young men overdressed in their business suits. *These guys look like kids.* I usually know the faces of everyone attending the Winter Meetings, but they are strangers to me. Their youthfulness affirms their lack of MLB experience, and their un-pressed shirts expose their need of employment. They're carrying satchels that contain an extraordinary number of loose white sheets of paper—résumés most likely. In direct contrast to the boisterous, fun-loving Tommy, the young men stand stiffly minding their own business. *Definitely job-seekers.*

As I walk in their direction, I notice their eyes tracking my progress. *No doubt they believe I am someone who can help them get a job in MLB.* Presumptively, I ask if any of them has lucked out getting an interview with a team. Without hesitation, all except one respond that they have interviewed. *I deduced their situation correctly.* So I directly ask that one, "You haven't interviewed yet?"

"What's your name?" I ask.

"Jon."

"Well, Jon, you have one now. I'm Bill Geivett with the LA Dodgers. Let's go; Mr. Lasorda and I are going to interview you."

The Celebrity

Immediately, I turn my back to Jon and head in the direction of Tommy's sideshow. With Jon, I act as if it's normal procedure to include

Tommy in interviews, but it isn't. My intention is to add Tommy to the process this one time to make it memorable for Jon—and, deviously, to raise the young man's anxiety level by having Tommy present. I wear a sly grin as I walk across the room to retrieve Tommy, the celebrity. There is nobody in that lobby this day more popular or famous than Tommy.

Another roar of laughter explodes from the crowd as I walk closer. I can see the glee in the faces of those listening to Tommy. *I feel bad for these 50 people now surrounding him for I'm about to end their wonderful time with a baseball legend.*

I make eye contact with Tommy and motion to the elevators, letting him know "it's time" to go upstairs. In response, Tommy excuses himself and meets us outside of the ring of disappointed onlookers, who enthusiastically thank him as we walk away. I inform Tommy we have an important interview to conduct upstairs, then I introduce Jon to Tommy.

At the Winter Meetings, I'd interview a few job-seekers every year, whether our club had openings or not. Knowing some may not get even one interview with an MLB front office executive during the entire four days of meetings, I make sure someone who hasn't interviewed gets the chance. It gives the applicant valuable experience and shows our club the talent available to hire when a position opens up. These job-seekers spend their own money to travel to the Winter Meetings in hopes of employment; it was the least I could do.

Jon understandably seems nervous but under control. *I have seen much worse.* He repeatedly addresses us respectfully as Mr. Lasorda and Mr. Geivett. While in the elevator, Jon informs us he's scheduled to meet with Allard Baird, general manager of the Kansas City Royals, later that day. *(I guess that's why he didn't respond to my question in the lobby.)* I feel happy that Jon has an interview he's excited about. At the same time, I'm confident this interview with Tommy is more than he could have ever expected.

Jerry's Meeting

As we enter the Dodgers' suite, we realize we are interrupting a Player Development staff meeting led by our farm director, Jerry Weinstein. I ask Jerry if Jon might sit in and listen to their discussion and, when finished, would the team interview Jon for a Player Development office job? Jerry says "yes" but looks at me as if I am crazy. *Everyone in the room (except for Jon) knows we don't have a job opening.*

I sense Jerry is a bit perturbed by my spontaneity and lack of communication, but he acquiesces, and Jon sits down to join the meeting. Tommy and I grab a few snacks *(that's a joke)* and go into the next room to wait for Jon to complete his interview.

Tommy and I discuss how surprised and thrilled Jon must be to have this experience. We congratulate each other for the benevolent gesture bestowed on this young man as if we're the saints of professional baseball.

Then we hear a knock at the door.

Our delusional moment of self-congratulation abruptly halts as I open the door to see Jon standing there. To our surprise, Jon's interview with the Player Development team must have been the shortest in recorded baseball history, for his knock came only four minutes after we'd left him. *Jerry was never one to waste time.*

Candidate Interview

I tell Jon, "Come in. Tommy and I will interview you now."

My approach to interviewing a candidate is to get him or her to talk as much as possible. I give applicants a chance to discuss what's important to them and what they feel passionate about. They are usually nervous and on edge, a perfect emotional state for the interviewer to gain insight into their abilities. Asking general questions allows candidates to speak of what they know best. When an interviewer asks too many questions or talks too much, it decreases the chances of truly learning about the candidate. Applicants—be prepared to talk!

I proceed with basic questions about Jon's family and upbringing, then I allow him to explain how he thinks he could assist the LA Dodgers organization. From his answers, I can tell Jon is close to his family and loves his parents deeply. He talks about his baseball background and how he has studied the game. He speaks of his passion for the profession and how seriously he desires to have a career in Major League Baseball. Judging from his impressive answers, Jon conveys that he would be a tireless worker. Clearly, he is an intelligent young man who is eager to begin a career in Major League Baseball—a prospect for the future and a person to keep in mind.

Still, we aren't hiring. Cruel? Maybe, but as I said, this mock interview helps Jon gain valuable experience.

I glance over at Tommy during my questioning to assess whether he's engaged, but I can't tell. He sits silently. Maybe the big lunch has rendered him groggy? I know it has made me groggy. Or maybe he's tired after his comedy routine in the lobby. Either would have been understandable. *Normally, Tommy would have participated in any conversation or meeting to a great extent. After all, he'd been excited about celebrating our delusional benevolence.*

As I finish, I ask Tommy if he has any questions to ask Jon. "No, I don't have any questions. But, I have something to say."

I'm suddenly excited (and relieved) when Tommy announces he has something to say to Jon. Tommy will probably give Jon sage advice he would hear nowhere else. He will tell him something so significant, it will influence his entire career—a poignant positive uplifting message to inspire Jon to great heights.

"Go ahead, Tommy," I say.

In a soft tone, Tommy says he has been watching Jon the entire interview and has listened to all of his responses. He believes Jon has answered all of the questions satisfactorily. Tommy then speaks about his years in baseball, saying he has met hundreds of scouts and front office staff members who have influenced him. Tommy fondly mentions some of their names—emphasizing Branch Rickey and Al Campanis—two of the greats who shaped his knowledge and success. He praises their great work ethic and passion for baseball.

Tommy talks about starting out as an area scout, not making much money to bring home to his wife Jo and their children. He didn't know if the Dodgers would ever recognize his true potential as a professional baseball man. Slumped in his chair, he then quietly states he has only a few things to say to Jon.

Tommy's Tirade

In an abrupt motion, he straightens up, points his crooked finger squarely at Jon, and screams, "YOU'RE NOT TOUGH ENOUGH!"

Still screaming, he adds,

"YOU CAN'T HANDLE THE LONG HOURS."

"YOU CAN'T LIVE WITH LOW PAY."

"YOU CAN'T TAKE THE DOWN TIMES."

"YOU'RE JUST NOT TOUGH ENOUGH!"

Whoa! What the hell is Tommy doing? I'm shocked and alarmed by Tommy's loud, disdainful shouting. I feel terrible for Jon. Why is Tommy attacking this respectable young man with the aggressive fervor he normally reserves for umpires? This former Major League manager, baseball icon, legend of the game, and Hall of Famer has just crushed Jon's dreams. . . .

But I'm incorrect.

Jon fires back, "YOU'RE WRONG, TOMMY!"

I guess that, since Tommy screamed at him, Jon feels there's no longer a need to use "Mr. Lasorda" when addressing Tommy.

"I AM TOUGH ENOUGH, AND I WILL BE IN BASEBALL!" Jon shouts.

Tommy slowly sits back into in his chair and smiles. He has used inappropriate screaming and an extreme level of emotion to evaluate Jon's true conviction about a career in MLB. Brilliant! Jon has shown his toughness and confidence by defying Tommy. He has won us over. Jon will not be denied his place in Major League Baseball.

After Jon departs the room, we reflect on how much we like this convincing young man—until Tommy brings up our next item of business, DINNER!

By the way, Jon eventually acquired a job with the Kansas City Royals and made a steady rise in the hierarchy of MLB as an accomplished, seasoned front office executive.

Are You Tough Enough?

Professional baseball is a tough gig. From the outside, it looks like great fun filled with good times and glamour, travel, and excitement. From afar, one typically sees only the celebrations and the winning team players spraying champagne on each other. On the inside, though, a career in Major League Baseball is filled with defeats and a never-ending supply of "punches in the stomach." No television crew is filming other teams' employees who didn't qualify for the post-season. Instead, the "losers" are answering tough questions posed by their club owners. They're taking a beating in the media and alerting their families about the real threat of the possibility of selling their homes if the team has another losing season.

Statistically, the majority of MLB clubs fall into the "loser" category.

Ask yourself: *Can you withstand the job's negative aspects? Only the toughest can take it and persevere. Can you?*

Can You Handle the Long Hours?

When you take employment in most other industries, appropriate questions to ask are "What are my hours?" and "How many days a week will I be required to work?" Major League Baseball has only one answer to those questions:

"AS MANY AS IT TAKES TO GET THE JOB DONE!"

Therefore, you had better be passionate about a career in this game because you won't punch a time clock. If working all day, every day, all year is not desirable, then pick another career. Those who have worked in MLB can tell you about all the family gatherings, funerals, Little League games, birthday parties, dance recitals, band performances, school plays, and graduations they have missed because of their work in professional baseball.

If you dedicate yourself to a baseball career, let me caution you: *You are not choosing a job in baseball; you're choosing a LIFE!*

Can You Start with Low Pay?

Entry-level jobs with high salaries don't exist in Major League Baseball. Expect long hours for low pay. An organization will hire you in your first position because club officials see you as a "prospect"—someone with the potential to grow into higher positions in the distant future. They're investing in your "future ability." The club is paying for your education in the game of professional baseball. Your first job should be taken for *the experience*, not for the rate of pay. Let me give you a heads-up: *Don't compare starting salaries with your buddies who work in other industries; it will be painful. Instead, think of your first job as a scholarship.*

Can You Survive the Down Times?

Pittsburgh Pirates Manager Clint Hurdle has this great saying: "Baseball is filled with humble people—AND THOSE WHO ARE ABOUT TO BE!"

You learn to survive the down times by exercising your humility very quickly. No matter what position you hold, it seems the entire world knows all of your unfortunate mistakes. Detractors are everywhere: media, fans, neighbors, and sometimes even members of your own organization. You take potshots (some fair, some not) on a regular basis, making it mandatory to have thick skin.

Do this: *Learn to "shower off" the criticism and prepare to take a lot of showers. Be humble.*

Do You Have a Realistic Perspective?

Thinking back to Tommy's tirade with Jon, here's his message: *Believe in yourself and your ability to withstand the pressures, long hours, travel, and defeats. It's the only way you can sustain a long career in MLB.*

Just as you must be tough to the core, you must also be realistic. Know that the good times don't last long, but the bad times seem to last forever. If you can take crushing blows, defeats, and disappointments and still keep showering them off, only then are you destined for a successful career in baseball.

Most of all, have a *realistic perspective.* I won't ever sugarcoat this career choice by saying it's a bunch of fun. My 28 years in the game have taught me that the most successful MLB staff members are truly passionate about the game. No matter how much criticism is thrown their way, those who succeed don't feel they're working a job. They absolutely love the game!

One of Tommy's favorite pieces of advice is: *Choose something you love, and you will never work a day in your life.* It doesn't appear to be complicated. Sage advice from a wise man.

That said, Tommy Lasorda emphasizes the need for toughness. Clint Hurdle advises humility. These great baseball men speak from the experiences of their long careers. Yes, baseball brings a lot of good, mixed with a lot of bad. Only the most talented, resilient, persistent, fortunate, humble, and tough will enjoy a long career in professional baseball.

Will you be one of them?

CHAPTER 2:

DO YOU WANT A JOB OR A CAREER?

Times Have Changed

BACK IN THE OLD DAYS IN 1995 WITH THE MONTREAL EXPOS, OUR Baseball Operations front office staff consisted of General Manager Kevin Malone, Director of Player Development Bill Geivett (me), Assistant Director of Player Development Neal Huntington, Scouting Director Ed Creech, Assistant Scouting Director Gregg Leonard, and International Operations Director Fred Ferreira. We did not employ an assistant GM *(at present, all MLB clubs have at least one AGM, and some have multiple AGMs)*, nor did we have a Director of Professional Scouting or a singular department dedicated to professional scouting *(every club has a Pro Scouting Department today)*. Prior to the June Draft, Expo Advance Scout Bob Johnson was the only staff member watching Major League games, but he wasn't evaluating players. He was designing strategies against Expo opponents for the coaching staff.

With the 1995 Expos, Ed Creech coordinated all scouting assignments, and the scouts evaluated the professional leagues in the summer following their June Draft duties. No formal professional evaluation scouting took place until the June Draft was completed. *(Today, an entire department is dedicated to scouting professional games starting with Spring Training and continuing through winter ball.)* We employed no Special Assistants to the GM *(most MLB clubs currently have three or four; some have more)*. Having an Advanced Analytics Department was unheard of. Front office members would review player personnel decisions based on statistics, but compared with today, we had less depth and detail and no sophisticated software, technology equipment, or tech-savvy staff.

The Expos Minor League teams in 1995 each had a manager, a pitching coach, and an athletic trainer. Today, teams at this level carry a hitting coach, a strength and conditioning coach, and sometimes another coach. Our 1995 Expos Minor League Head Athletic Trainer Sean Cunningham also served as a strength and conditioning coordinator. In fact, Sean was the entire Strength and Conditioning Department.

Those days, we struggled to have an operable video camera *(video equipment was not as widely used as it is today)* and no video staff. By today's standards, we operated with a skeleton crew.

If There Are Jobs, People Will Come

To prospective employees, a career in MLB is considered exciting, and landing a job with a club is quite a coup. As mentioned, the growth in the number of positions within Baseball Operations has been impressive. However, the growth in the number of applicants wanting one of these "dream" jobs is staggering. Competing with more enthusiastic, passionate, prepared, and talented applicants than ever makes it extremely difficult to gain employment in MLB today. Applicants often have bachelor's degrees in sports management or coursework related to the study of the sports industry, which includes statistical analysis. This type of focused study has become commonplace at most universities.

In addition, applicants can now tap into a wide array of relevant information online. They study to understand specific aspects of the industry before they ever pursue practical experience. Altogether, this growth of capable, energetic, and knowledgeable applicants spells extreme competition for the highly coveted MLB employment opportunities.

A Competition for the Anonymous

For prospective Baseball Operations staffers, acquiring their first job in Major League Baseball presents a tremendous challenge. They aren't regarded as well-vetted and valued assets to MLB organizations; rather, they are anonymous. Despite having played and studied the game, most have no close, influential contacts in management to assist them in gaining employment with a club. To guys like Jon and his cohorts at the Winter Meetings, getting a simple introduction to decision-makers in professional baseball is great progress.

Exceptions to being anonymous include: former Major League players who have name recognition throughout baseball; former players who have built good reputations in a particular MLB organization; or a helpful friend or family member of someone in the industry. In the grand totality of MLB employment data, however, these exceptions are extremely rare.

For the most part, the anonymous must compete with all of the other unknowns in a huge mass of applicants. These applicants churn out an endless stream of cover letters with attached résumés and emails to all of the 30 MLB teams. With their applications buried in the sea of others, candidates must find ways to separate themselves from the masses. It's a competition!

How Do You Start?

Most applicants begin their quest by executing every common strategy of contacting executives of MLB clubs. They: send résumés *(usually filed away after a form letter reply)*; send emails *(forwarded to an assistant for a form letter reply and saved in a never-again-seen inbox folder)*; make phone calls *(unreturned because people are too busy)*; and (much dreaded) show up at the offices asking to speak with a Baseball Operations executive *(to be told staff is in a "meeting" or "not at the stadium")*.

TIP: Only use the first three examples; never show up unannounced at the stadium offices. (It's not smart to be a stalker.)

Rather than address these common rituals, let's focus on the mindset of a successful applicant.

Job versus Career Mindset

Are you looking for a job or a career? This is a very important question. If you choose professional baseball as a future career, then enter the industry as soon as possible. If no job is available to you in Baseball Operations, look for employment in another department of the organization—or in any capacity that's open. You have to get your foot in the door *(and it doesn't matter which door)*. Ultimately, your first job in *any* area of the organization can be instrumental to building a pathway into Baseball Operations. Do not lose sight of your goal: a career in Major League Baseball *(not just a job)*.

Your First Job is Secondary to Your Career

While interviewing candidates, I'm told that certain jobs aren't what they're looking to do. If they seek a Baseball Operations office job, they would not consider taking a job in the Ticketing Department. Some want to be a Major League coach but have no interest in a Minor League coaching position or a scouting job.

But working *anywhere* in a club puts you in a position to learn. Employment in a department other than Baseball Operations enlightens you to a different perspective than what you gained from your past experiences. It can steer your insights into other important components of an MLB organization. With a sincere goal to achieve a career in Major League Baseball, be on a mission to learn all aspects of a professional baseball club. It's not about where you start; it's about how much you can learn!

Truly understanding how an MLB organization operates only comes through years of experience and study. You don't have to begin in your most-desired position to start your career.

TIP: If you're struggling to acquire your "dream first job," then attempt to land whatever position the club has available. Start your work experience in the industry as soon as possible.

How They Got Started

Let's look at high-ranking personnel with MLB clubs in the game today and note their positions at present compared with their first jobs in baseball. (See Figure 2.1.)

Figure 2.1

NAME – POSITION	CLUB	ENTRY-LEVEL JOB
Jean Afterman- AGM	NYY	Sports Agent
Rob Antony- AGM	MIN	Public Relations Asst., MIN
Gord Ash- VP Baseball Projects	MIL	Part-Time Game Day Staff, TOR
Al Avila- GM	DET	Asst Coach, St. Thomas Univ.
Billy Beane- PRESIDENT	OAK	Advance Scout, OAK
Jeff Bridich- GM	COL	Commissioner's Office Intern
Ned Colletti- SR. ADVISOR	LAD	Public Relations Asst., CHI
Jon Daniels- GM	TEX	Intern, COL
Theo Epstein- PRESIDENT	CHC	Public Relations Asst., BAL
Bobby Evans-GM	SF	Commissioner's Office
Derek Falvey – EVP, CBO	MIN	Intern, CLE
John Farrell- MANAGER	BOS	Pitching Coach, Ok. St. Univ.
Freddie Gonzalez- MANAGER	ATL	Grad. Asst. Coach, Univ. of Tenn.
Rick Hahn- GM	CWS	Sports Agent
John Hart- PRESIDENT	ATL	HS Baseball Coach
Neal Huntington- GM	PITT	Intern, MON
Walt Jocketty- PRESIDENT	CIN	AAA Affiliate Office Staff, Iowa Oaks
Matt Klentak- GM	PHI	Intern, COL
Tommy Lasorda- SR. ADVISOR	LAD	Area Scout, LAD
Thaddeus Levine- GM	MIN	Business Development, LAD
Joe Maddon- MANAGER	CHC	Minor League Coach, CAL
Dayton Moore- GM	KC	Asst Coach, George Mason Univ.
John Mozeliak- GM	STL	Clubhouse Staff, COL
AJ Preller- GM	SD	Intern, PHI
Mike Rizzo- GM	WASH	Asst. Baseball Coach, Univ. of Ill.
Zack Rosenthal- AGM	COL	Business Intern, BOS
David Stearns- GM	MIL	Intern, PIT
Farhan Zaidi- GM	LAD	Data Analysis, OAK

This chart tells you that your first position may not resemble the role you'll eventually attain in your career. These people didn't prioritize their starting jobs over their careers; their beginning job titles were secondary.

The first jobs of these highly regarded MLB staff members helped shape their careers.

TIP: If you want a career in MLB, who cares what your first job might be? They didn't and you shouldn't!

Delay is Not Denial

When I was with the Colorado Rockies, I had the pleasure of working with Clint Hurdle, a Major League manager and one of the best in the game today. Almost everyone who knows Clint agrees he's an even better person than merely a great baseball manager.

Clint could be tough and stern when needed, but he always showed compassion toward others. When we worked together, we had to send players down from the Major League squad to the AAA team at the end of Spring Training, as they were not going to make the 25-man roster. This makes the last week of Spring Training a stressful time for players *and* staff. The majority of veteran players feel confident they've made the team, but the others sit squarely on the "bubble," knowing their fate could go either way.

When a player was deemed headed to AAA, one of the coaches would send him to Clint's office. There, we'd break the unfortunate news gingerly, knowing the player's feelings were already hurt. *No need to throw salt in the wound by being too negative.* Clint would handle the situation as well as I have ever seen. He got the departing player to understand he was an important part of our club that season and could eventually rejoin the team at the Major League level. If that return was likely sooner than later, Clint used a particular statement that struck me as perfect for the situation. He'd say, "Delay is not denial."

It's so true. We knew many of the players sent to AAA would be playing with the "Big Club" soon, but our immediate task required building the "collective" best 25-man squad to begin the year. "Collective" meant constructing our roster in a way that might dictate a player wasn't a fit *at that point*. We may have needed a left-handed reliever instead of a right-handed one or a left-handed hitter on the bench instead of a right-handed one, for example. For that player, not making the club out of Spring Training didn't mean never playing at the Major League level in the future. We *delayed* his participation, but we weren't forever denying it.

Delay Not Deny Applies to Staff, Too

Theo Epstein made the most of his opportunity in public relations. Imagine if he'd only wanted to work in Baseball Operations and turned down the position in PR. It would have been a different story for him personally and for the Boston Red Sox and the Chicago Cubs. Some could even argue that, if Theo had never agreed to the PR job, the Boston Red Sox and the Chicago Cubs might still be looking for their first World Series Championship in 86 years and 108 years respectively. By building a pathway to working in Baseball Operations through a different door, he became General Manager of the Boston Red Sox and then President of the Chicago Cubs.

Theo's job in Baseball Operations may have been *delayed*, but he would not be *denied*.

What about John Mozeliak (Mo), Senior Vice President and General Manager of the St. Louis Cardinals? He worked as a clubhouse and equipment staff member to get into professional baseball. Longtime Colorado Rockies Executive Assistant Adele Armagost remembers Mo raking leaves outside the Spring Training offices in Tucson, Arizona. The fact that Mo was raking leaves wasn't what made his story remarkable. Adele emphasized his impressive work ethic and great attitude. Mo has been dedicated to his career in MLB from his first day at his humble job. Today, Mo is GM of one the most successful baseball franchises in Major League history!

Take another look at the list in Figure 2.1 and notice where some of those MLB hotshots started their careers. For you, too, delay does not mean denial.

TIP: If you don't find a job in Baseball Operations with a Major League team to begin your career, it doesn't mean you've been denied a career in Baseball Operations.

Building a Pathway to Additional Experience

You might find it difficult to even acquire an interview for a Baseball Operations position. In reality, you might not possess the perceived skills or reputation to acquire a job interview. You need documented experience to convince club decision-makers you are a worthy candidate. That might mean building a pathway to Baseball Operations through another position within the industry.

What are these possible pathways? Let me offer my opinion on six employment options that have most reliably led to jobs in Baseball Operations.

The Commissioner's Office

Many current MLB club front office members started their professional baseball careers in the Major League Baseball Commissioner's Office and transitioned to Baseball Operations with an MLB club. The Commissioner's Office has positions in the Labor Relations Department and the Baseball Operations Department. In Labor Relations, the daily focus of research and study of the MLB Player Arbitration System helps to develop expertise in the field. Analyzing player contracts and extensions to player contracts provides a tremendous amount of specialized knowledge. In Baseball Operations, focusing on the rules and regulations by which MLB clubs must abide leads to understanding a club's responsibilities in this area. Learning intricate aspects of what's allowable for MLB clubs and players also provides valuable specialized knowledge.

Every role in the Commissioner's Office requires interacting with club officials from all 30 Major League teams, often resulting in strong relationships. Members of the executive team in the Commissioner's Office can help ambitious staff members move to an MLB team's front office. How? These executives work with high-ranking officials of every club and can be influential in the hiring process. Imagine the positive effect of getting a recommendation from an executive in the Commissioner's Office.

TIP: Having a law degree is held in high regard by people everywhere but especially by those at the Commissioner's Office.

Business Operations Department

The "business" arm of an MLB team can provide a solid pathway to a career in Baseball Operations.

Business Operations include public relations, broadcasting, marketing, promotions, accounting, ticketing, grounds keeping, and more. Currently, dozens of MLB front office members in Baseball Operations started their careers in Business Operations, and it has proven to be a successful route.

Simply working in the same building offers opportunities to gain understanding of the Baseball Operations Department and a sense of its everyday duties and issues. Building strong relationships with employees in Baseball Ops leads to better understanding of daily departmental procedure and information exchange. These employees often make known their ambitions for working in Baseball Ops as they seek advice about developing the necessary skill set to qualify for a position.

One cautionary note: Being too candid about wanting to join the Baseball Ops staff can set up a dangerous situation for an employee in Business Operations. People in Business Ops might think you aren't paying enough attention to your present business duties. You must prove you're a valued employee on the business side first. You're not building a reliable pathway to the Baseball Operations Department if you get fired from your ticketing job!

College Baseball

Before my employment as an area scout with the New York Yankees years ago, I was an assistant baseball coach at Loyola Marymount University (Los Angeles, California) and Long Beach State University (Long Beach, California).

Coaching college baseball provides a strong training ground for a job in professional baseball scouting. Recruiting at the collegiate level offers a basic indoctrination into amateur scouting. While evaluating potential college recruits, I'd sit with some of the best scouts in the game. Quality interactions between scouts and college coaches occur often. I still owe a debt of gratitude to Larry Corrigan (Minnesota Twins), who explained a "team scouting card" to me during the 1988 Area Code Games. Larry mentored me in amateur and professional scouting the entire time I coached in college (and also while I scouted for other Major League teams).

Seasoned college coaches spend time with their less experienced counterparts to help them learn to teach and coach. Being teachers at heart, they love to share their information. The annual ABCA convention of college coaches offers valuable networking opportunities for attendees as well as a full program of lectures on the art of coaching various aspects of baseball. Many college coaches have professional experience as players or staff members, which makes them a valuable source of information and relationship. It's quite a fraternity.

Administrative skills and budgeting are part of the learning experience at the collegiate level. All college programs require their coaches to handle aspects of the administrative duties: recruiting, teaching, budgeting, conducting camps and clinics, and more. Most universities assign a

Director of Baseball Operations to their program. This position requires coordinating administrative duties designated by the coaches.

This first step into the professional baseball world provides many opportunities to learn aspects of both the administrative and on-field sides of baseball. Plus, those in college programs with consistent MLB-prospect-level players constantly communicate with MLB scouts. These contacts can lead to employment opportunities. They did for me.

TIP: Look to the collegiate level to gain practical experience. Even as a student, you can find employment opportunities.

Sports Agents

Sports agents use a combination of expertise and experience for acquiring a position in MLB. They spend time with MLB scouts at high school and college games looking for prospective players to advise for the draft. Most agencies have an evaluator *(usually a former scout or player)* on their staff of agents. Duties at the Major League level include contractual negotiations, making agents formidable foes for club officials.

To successfully represent their clients, agents are required to understand all aspects of Major League Baseball affecting players: MLB player salaries, MLB player service time rights, MLB player arbitration, MLB contractual player rules, and more. Do you see how experience as an agent provides expert training for many administrative front office positions in Major League Baseball?

Agents interact regularly with club officials regarding the players they represent. This frequent contact gives them the chance to exchange ideas and engage in meaningful conversations about the club's perspective on certain issues. As a result, many close ties have been forged between agents and club personnel. If the agent desires to switch to working for an MLB club, this closeness can only help.

TIP: Do not view working for an agency as going to the dark side. Knowledge is key.

Minor League Affiliate

Initiating your career with a Minor League affiliate team can pave another path to MLB Baseball Operations Department. You can gain tremendous knowledge at an affiliate club, especially in the area of player development. Forging friendly relationships with the coaching staff can lead to conversations about player development philosophies and coaching techniques.

You might also interact with professional scouts and gain valuable practical knowledge of scouting procedures. In addition, you have the chance to learn the business aspects (reimbursements, player transactions, travel) of an MLB club's Player Development Department. As a Minor League staffer, you're also in a good position to learn an MLB club's perspective on the Minor Leagues.

To be honest, your most realistic opportunity would be with your parent organization. But, MLB clubs may shy away from stealing an employee from an affiliate club. The risk of upsetting the affiliate owner by taking a prized employee may be too great to justify the reward. However, if the affiliate club is owned by the parent MLB organization, your chances improve significantly.

TIP: Look to apply to an affiliate team owned by a Major League club.

Baseball Research Websites

Websites which offer advanced baseball study are great training in the modern analytical processes of the game. The collection of data and its analyses are prominent in every organization. Statistical analytics is here to stay. The sites that have MLB teams as clients would be the most beneficial to work for. Their employees will be in contact with team officials and learn the current perspective of front office executives. Additionally, employees will be at the forefront of innovations in the analytical study of the game.

TIP: For the prospective front office employee, practical experience in the analytical study of baseball is a necessity if you have mediocre educational credentials.

Summary

☐ It is critical to possess the mindset of someone who will not be denied a career in the competitive world of Major League Baseball.

☐ Your first job is exactly that—your first job. It will not define your career.

☐ You likely won't be able to choose your preferred pathway. Sometimes the least desirable route is the only one available.

☐ Delay is not denial. Have patience.

☐ Learning other perspectives of the industry will enhance your knowledge and your future opportunities in the game.

CHAPTER 3:

UNDERSTAND THE MODERN MAJOR LEAGUES

Design Your Career

ACQUIRING YOUR FIRST JOB IN MAJOR LEAGUE BASEBALL TAKES SUBSTAN-
tially more than *dressing* for success. In the competitive hiring process, you
need to *plan* for success.

Every action begins with a thought. *I want a career in Major League
Baseball.* This chapter helps you develop a plan of action. Building a house
is not initiated by pouring cement for the foundation. Rather, it begins with
the architect's vision transformed into drawings of the finished product.
Whenever we look to build something, we should know the desired result
first. Then the design plans dictate which tools and skills are necessary for
construction. You design a career in professional baseball in a similar way
as you shoot for a Major League position.

Consider Others' Perspectives

The first step in designing your career plan is to understand the
perspectives of top decision-makers *(isn't that where you want to go?)* in
the organization. Studying the highest level first helps you gain an "upper-
level perspective" that can guide you. How do the highest-level employees think? What's important to them and how could you help in these
areas? This knowledge aids in developing the kind of perspective and decision-making they appreciate from their subordinates. Also, by exhibiting

perspectives that align with their roles, you show them your *potential* to be one of them someday.

You also begin to develop a framework regarding organizational decision-making. After all, club decisions aren't made by the general manager or Baseball Operations staff alone. They involve various departments and personnel who offer a variety of perspectives.

Let's look at Major League characteristics of the upper levels of an organization through the perspective of the club owner.

Minority Owner

In 2009, the Colorado Rockies purchased the Casper Ghosts of the Pioneer League. Believing it was a good investment, I expressed my opinion to Rockies Owner Dick Monfort before the acquisition. He said that because I thought it was such a good investment, he expected me to buy a stake in the Ghosts. I should have kept my mouth shut! Because of my well-honed ability to speak before thinking, I'm presently a minority owner in the Grand Junction Rockies (the club moved to Grand Junction, Colorado, from Casper, Wyoming). I proudly own one percent of the team. (Don't laugh; it's a lot to me!)

My first duty as an infinitesimal minority owner included attending the Pioneer League Owners Meeting with Hal Roth, CFO and Legal Counsel for the Rockies. We voted on formal league affairs and offered opinions on current issues from an ownership perspective.

As foreign as this role was to me, I had to put myself in the owner's chair and believe it was truly my money at risk. To be honest, I found it boring to discuss strategies on sponsorship agreements, radio promotions, and souvenir sales. Being an executive in a few Major League clubs, I had attended meetings about the business of professional baseball that were enlightening, but I was never truly engaged in matters discussed by the Business Operations side. Trained as a player, coach, and scout, I was focused on Baseball Operations. Could I think of strategies better than someone trained in marketing and promotions? I trusted they'd figure out the best ways to proceed and didn't need me to chime in on aspects of their "turf."

This time, my mindset was different. I brought the acute focus of an owner whose bottom line would be affected by decisions made at this meeting. So I tried hard to get engaged. I had never given much thought to how many bobble-heads a half-season Minor League team should order before a July 4th promotion. Frankly, I couldn't wait for this meeting to end. As the talk of promotional souvenir items laboriously continued, one owner told the others about a new company that had decreased the club's costs for novelty items by five percent. The savings helped fund other promotions the club otherwise couldn't afford. The amount of money saved didn't appear substantial to my "high-falutin" Major League standards, so I was unimpressed with his glee over sharing this resource. In similar meetings I'd attended, the financial impact of decisions was measured in millions of dollars, not hundreds. "Pompous-ass" described me perfectly.

Then he made a statement that forever changed my appreciation of having an ownership perspective. He said, "It may not seem like a lot of money, but a dollar saved is a dollar earned." (This is widely attributed to Benjamin Franklin's "A penny saved is a penny earned," but this guy had acknowledged the cost of inflation.) Before then, I had always related this saying to saving my personal money for a rainy day. But wearing my ownership hat gave it a greater meaning—that is, saving a dollar is no different than having earned another dollar to be used in another capacity to create additional revenue. Until that moment, I had viewed owners as either cheap and greedy or appreciative and gracious. I had never thought beyond their tight budgets.

Owners have hundreds of employees to worry about and many departments to fund. They manage a high-stakes balancing act of prioritizing dollars throughout their organizations. Additional money allocated to Baseball Operations is less money for the Marketing or Promotions Departments. From the perspective of an owner, every dollar counted more. This meeting wasn't so boring after all.

This story reminds you that money in an MLB organization is a finite commodity with spending held to the highest degree of scrutiny. The club's money should be seen as sacred. As an employee, showing an ability to care about every dollar can elevate your potential from an average employee to an executive *prospect.*

Executives are concerned with wasteful spending of precious club dollars. Unfortunately, it's uncommon for them to see employees who show that kind of mindset regarding the sanctity of the club dollar. Just as a high batting average is important to a professional baseball player, *fiscal responsibility* is important to a professional baseball executive.

TIP: Any research, study, or recommendation you propose in an interview should include the financial impact of your decision-making. While working for an MLB club, decide to spend every company dollar as if it were your own.

Get Out of Your Box!

Try applying a new perspective by understanding various roles within an MLB club.

General Manager (GM)

As the architect of the Baseball Operations Department, the GM typically focuses on two main areas: 1) Philosophy and/or function, and 2) RESULTS!

GMs ask themselves questions like:

☐ Is the Major League staff *function* consistent with *organizational philosophies*?

☐ Does the Major League team embody our *organizational philosophies*?

☐ Does the Player Development Department *function properly* to build the foundation of our *organizational philosophies* in our younger players?

☐ Does the Scouting Department *function properly* to acquire players consistent with *organizational philosophies*?

☐ Do the Scouting and Player Development Departments *function cohesively*?

General managers live in a *bottom-line* world in which they're personably held accountable for the club's failure *(credit for success is typically bestowed upon the players and field staff)*. They have no acceptable excuse for failure. When team results are deemed unsuccessful, leaders in the Baseball Operations Department shoulder the blame from the owner, media, and fans.

Regrettably, they can wear it like a bad suit. For example, GMs have a tendency to judge as they are judged—*strictly by the results*. They evaluate Baseball Operations employees by the personal and baseball characteristics of the young players who show up; *they* are the results! If new players have characteristics inconsistent with organizational philosophy, the GM scrutinizes the *function* and expects to locate the *dysfunction* within the department. Staff members often view GMs as unrealistic, hardheaded, stubborn, micromanaging, and too emotional when unfortunate situations occur.

Why? The responsibility of accepting the blame for an entire organization is a heavy burden.

Employees should appreciate the immense pressure GMs endure. GMs want to see successful accomplishments by the Baseball Operations Department. They don't want to hear theory, explanations, and excuses of why a particular player hasn't progressed.

Whatever the expectations for a particular season at the Major League level, the General Manager wants and needs positive results to show the many detractors palpable evidence of a well-run organization. It's about bottom-line accomplishments, not excuses.

Giving an eloquent oral dissertation in pitching mechanics helps the GM gain respect for your knowledge. Yet showing how a pitcher has improved and the positive results of your work enables the GM to assess your true value to the club. Both tangible *evidence* and *results* are critical to your future career. High-level executives demand them.

TIP: In an interview, it is not enough to state you have completed exhaustive research on the game. Be prepared to show the results of your studies. What information have you gathered? What is your plan to apply the information you have gathered? What's the financial impact of that information?

Club Executive

Professional baseball has evolved to a point of advanced study. Specific aspects of the game and their *practical applications* have become more cohesive at the Major League level. Therefore, today's MLB front office executive must have a well-rounded baseball background to help direct the philosophy of an entire Baseball Operations Department.

The duties of a front office executive involve making *value judgments and decisions* regarding individual players or the team itself. Baseball Operations executives must design and develop their organization's scouting processes aligned with their respective league and ballpark factors. Front office executives aren't required to be the best scouts in the world but will need to understand fundamental scouting processes to assess a player or team. They must be able to form their own opinions, because they are held accountable for the personnel decisions of their club. That means as the game changes, executives must have the ability to alter their scouting processes in response to the latest trends.

Because many executive-level decisions affect the activities of the coaches and players, executives must also have a good understanding of the game's on-field aspects. Then the success of their *executive direction* will directly correspond to the field staff's ability to implement that direction *(both in the Major and Minor Leagues)*. Undesired consequences can arise if executives don't completely understand the on-field aspects of the issue.

An abundance of front office applicants have a strong understanding of, for example, advanced statistical analytical research or the MLB player arbitration process. However, they might fall short regarding scouting or on-field professional baseball activities. For "brainiacs", crunching numbers and forming hypotheses is relatively simple, but they must have some understanding of on-field realities to successfully apply proper strategies.

TIP: If you are comfortable with advanced statistical analytics but don't have much personal on-field baseball experience, get out of your box!

Major League Field Staff Member

Similarly, the modern Major League *field staff member* (including scouts) must understand the use of advanced statistical analytics and the type of processes used for player evaluations, player acquisitions, team payroll, player arbitration, and so on. They must form their own *balanced opinion* to assist front office decision-makers. Granted, they don't need to be an expert in statistical analytics, but having an understanding of them helps maintain cohesive, productive relationships with people in the front office. Everyone in all areas of Baseball Operations must speak a *common language* to better comprehend differing perspectives. For example, because *field staff members* assist the front office in player personnel decisions, they should have a solid understanding of the professional player evaluation process. At the same time, they must have an appreciation for specific issues that face front office executives, such as configuring a team within the limits of the available payroll and player contractual control.

Applicants who are former players might have excellent on-field attributes but limited experience and knowledge of scouting procedures or front office decision-making processes. To be an *impactful* Major League staff member means developing a strong understanding of the front office perspective. They must get out of their box!

Strengths and Lesser Strengths

No one person has it all. Realistically, we have *strengths and lesser strengths*. You can build up your lesser strengths by studying and developing areas you lack experience in. As products of their experiences, some people have a *special ability* in one area but not so much in another. Your job? Understand your strengths and lesser strengths, and get to work.

Especially, start examining all aspects of Baseball Operations and push yourself to study your areas of lesser strength. Doing so might help you land that first position because you'll be a more qualified candidate in your interview. Once hired, the more you improve your lesser strengths, the greater probability you will exhibit the characteristics of a future Major League executive or field staff member.

A Modern Major League Professional

Major League front office members are required by their organization to attend regular meetings with the organizational Business Operations Department heads. They speak at season ticketholder and sponsor events; they attend fan fests and charity events; they scout amateur and professional players for the team.

Major League managers and coaches may be required to perform the same duties. Because of their recognition in the community, they get involved in many aspects of the Business Operations Department. The public often sees the manager as the "face of the franchise." If you plan to spend your career in Baseball Operations and occupy a position at the Major League level, seek to understand key aspects of both Baseball and Business Operations.

Any candidate who desires a career in Major League Baseball must be willing to possess an *organizational appreciation* for the various departments. Good decision-making in the highest positions involves having well-rounded perspectives of people in all departments. Having an appreciation for other departments will help you rise through the department and eventually rise to the Major League level.

TIP: Consider the definition of an organization: an institution or entity that has a collective goal and is linked to an external environment. Having a "collective goal" is the key to success.

"We Need a Left-Handed Bat Off the Bench"

In 2009, I was working as Vice President and Assistant General Manager of the Colorado Rockies. As the season unfolded, we were contending for a Wild Card spot in post-season play. To present "danger" to the opposition toward the end of the game, we needed to add a left-handed bat off the bench. Jason Giambi had just recently been released by the Oakland Athletics. As a Baseball Operations group, we discussed Jason as a possible addition to our club. Jason was always a great hitter with power. He was older, but he still represented an imposing threat with the bat. His career history had been interesting, to say the least. Jason had testified before a grand jury regarding his alleged connection to BALCO, a laboratory reputed to be involved with performance-enhancement substances. At the time, a negative stigma was placed on all players with such allegations. All this aside, Rockies GM Dan O'Dowd and I had confidence Jason could add something special to our bench against the best late-inning relievers in the game. Every opposing manager would have to think twice before replacing a pitcher if he knew the Rockies had Jason Giambi in its dugout.

I had no reservations about Jason or his background. I had coached him in college at Long Beach State University. Knowing his close-knit family for almost 20 years, I had great respect for his parents and how he was raised. I stayed in touch with his career through his agent, Joel Wolfe. I thought he would be a great addition to our ball club. The highest levels of the Rockies organization were involved in the decision whether to make Jason Giambi a Colorado Rockie. There were concerns over Jason's history and how our fans would react if we signed him. Would he be viewed as a positive representative of the Rockies? Sue Ann McClaren, Rockies VP of Ticketing, was involved in the debate and discussion, eventually becoming the deciding voice on signing Jason. Sue Ann's view was that our season ticketholders and fans in general would happily welcome Jason to our ball club. Her perspective from knowing the fans eased the other decision-makers' fears. Decision made; meeting adjourned. We signed 38-year-old Jason Giambi.

After a short time with the AAA Colorado Springs Sky Sox, Jason reported to the Colorado Rockies in Denver. Late in his first game as a Rockie, manager Jim Tracy summoned him to pinch hit. As he took one step out of the dugout, the entire crowd gave him a tremendous standing ovation. Jason hadn't even made his first plate appearance, and he'd already received a standing O! Sue Ann got it right.

That post-season, Jason was a big part of our playoff run and advancement to the 2009 post-season. He became such a beloved performer and clubhouse leader with the Rockies that he continued to play through the 2012 season. He was so well respected that the Rockies interviewed him for the Major League Manager position prior to the 2013 season. (Walt Weiss was eventually offered the job.) During the 2013 season, Jason continued playing and helped the Cleveland Indians get into the playoffs. To this day, Jason Giambi stands as one of the most popular players in Colorado Rockies history.

In a healthy MLB organization, decisions are made collectively with a voice from all departments. Every department affects the others. If you gain an appreciation for other perspectives within an organization, you increase your potential to discern what's best for the organization as a whole.

TIP: Always remember, the fans have a perspective that needs to be respected, too. They pay the bills.

Summary

Take on a higher level of thought as you prepare for a career in MLB. Apply these key points from this chapter:

☐ Plan your career by understanding the *perspective of the highest level.*

☐ Adopt the *Major League perspective* and act accordingly.

☐ Spend club dollars as if they were your own.

☐ Appreciate other departments in Baseball Operations, and you can rise in the Baseball Operations Department.

☐ Appreciate other departments throughout the entire organization, and you can rise to the Major League level.

☐ Identify your strengths and lesser strengths.

☐ Develop your lesser strengths the best you can.

☐ Get out of your box!

CHAPTER 4:

HOW TO GET AN INTERVIEW

Entry-Level Positions in Baseball Operations

BEFORE DETAILING HOW TO OBTAIN AN INTERVIEW FOR EMPLOYMENT IN Major League Baseball, let's examine the jobs that may be reasonable to acquire: entry-level positions in the front office and in the field.

Just as you considered the perspective of the executive level when determining your career potential, also understand the perspective of mid-level executives who hire entry-level employees. *What are they looking for in this job?* Many applicants attempt to rely on personal characteristics *(e.g., hard-working, passionate, etc.)*, believing those attributes can qualify them for employment. However, you'd be better served by studying the *position* and then tailoring your *presentation* to show skills that fit the specific duties of the job. *Know where you are going!*

FOR FRONT OFFICE STAFF:

Knowing specifics about a front office position benefits how you prepare to gain an interview. Interns in the front office typically assist with player salary arbitration research, statistical data study, and special projects involving research/study/conclusion. That means you must have a reasonable level of foundational competence in these areas to acquire an interview. Internships can also be dedicated to one specific department *(e.g., Major League, Amateur Scouting, Player Development, etc.)*, providing other opportunities to position yourself for an MLB career.

In fact, having an internship is almost a *prerequisite* for acquiring a full-time position. An applicant who has no work experience in professional baseball has a difficult time competing for a full-time position against an intern who has previously worked with an MLB club.

TIP: The successful front office applicant tends to have a solid academic background with a high level of understanding in advanced statistical baseball research.

FOR FIELD STAFF:

Field positions include associate scouts, area scouts, professional scouts, athletic trainers, hitting/pitching coaches, and managers. The associate scout position is typically the only part-time position; other entry-level positions are full time. These positions are at the direction of a regional supervisor in the Scouting Department or a player development coordinator in the Player Development Department.

Scouting is especially difficult for a rookie. Area scouts typically travel to games by themselves, learning their craft without regular guidance or advice. They must maintain a productive level of performance. A staff member in Player Development has more contact with veteran staff for advice than a scout would have, but in many instances, they too are faced with player issues on their own without guidance. You must be able to perform immediately in these full-time critical positions in the organization. *There is no grace period.*

TIP: A field staff applicant's present skill level will be assessed on the applicant's ability to demonstrate the skills necessary to perform in the job immediately.

How Do You Get an Interview?

First, understand the basics of what it takes, which include:

☐ Commit to a master level

☐ Have a defined strength or specialty

☐ Use your specialty to compete

Commit to a Master Level

To acquire the knowledge worthy of employment means wholeheartedly committing to the craft. Due to fierce competition, you may never be considered a potential hire without *extraordinary* focus on your area of expertise. It cannot be an ordinary study; your lofty goal calls for becoming a *specialist* in the subject matter. So you need a voracious interest in your field of study to understand the most detailed aspects.

However, becoming a specialist is problematic in the face of constant changes in professional baseball that require flexible responses. The nuances of sabermetrics, coaching, and scouting shift depending on the individuals being compared, coached, or scouted. In short: players change, the game changes, and so do your beliefs.

To acquire a specialty means committing to a *master-level approach—an on-going, thorough study and advanced analysis of your subject matter.* Master-level sabermetricians, teachers, or coaches believe they will never arrive at *a total* understanding of their subject. They dedicate themselves to never-ending research and study to learn and adjust to the current circumstances.

Have a Defined Strength or Specialty

How do you separate yourself from the masses of applicants? By showing specific abilities through a *defined strength* related to the position available. It is akin to a major in college. It's the single most important attribute a prospective applicant can possess to get an initial interview in Major League Baseball. Although well-rounded applicants are attractive, they still have to possess a *defined strength or specialty* to interest MLB mid-level hiring executives. Duties are aligned to the main tasks the employee is asked to perform in a specific area of expertise *(e.g., player arbitration research, statistical study, pitching/hitting coach, scout, etc.)*. Having a *tangible demonstration* of a specialty with specific skills elevates an applicant to a serious candidate.

Use Your Specialty to Compete

Applicants with the *most advanced specialty* will rise from the masses and become serious candidates for a particular position. It's important to grasp this aspect of competition. Remember, this is a competition of *you* versus the *masses* vying for the same position.

FOR FRONT OFFICE APPLICANTS:

Having a defined strength *(e.g., mathematics, statistics, uber-smart, etc.)* alone may be enough to get hired. However, it's not likely if you don't also have some baseball knowledge. Show competence in the on-field aspect of professional baseball; most clubs want to see knowledge of the sport.

TIP: A deep awareness of the sport of baseball is required to make your research strengths applicable.

FOR FORMER PROFESSIONAL PLAYERS:

For the prospective coach or scout, the defined strength is either teaching or player evaluation.

It's easy to assume former players who are prospective coaches or scouts have acquired a defined strength through their experiences. But do they know all there is to know to coach or scout? Not likely. A prospective coach needs the defined strength of teaching or coaching. Your baseball knowledge is less important than the knowledge you're able to implant into your students. It's about what students know *eventually*, not what the coach knows *presently*.

Having baseball knowledge and/or extensive playing experience doesn't mean you'll get hired. The back of your bubble-gum card will only get you so far. And guess what? Hundreds of former players also want to land one of those coaching or scouting jobs. Their extensive playing experience may place them in high esteem with an MLB club as a prospective "candidate," though, that doesn't mean they will be hired. What's the determining factor? You're hired when the organization believes you possess the appropriate characteristics, work ethic, and skills to *apply* what you know.

TIP: Don't attempt to rely solely on your playing experience to acquire a job.

Brand Yourself with Specific Skills

I've been fortunate to conduct hundreds of entry-level professional baseball employment interviews in my career. In these interviews, striking similarities arise as candidates offer their reasons for getting hired. I've heard the *exact same responses* to my interview questions even from people of sharply differing backgrounds. Every candidate tends to use one or more of these phrases:

"I was born to be in baseball. It's my life."

"Nobody will work harder than me."

"I've dreamed of working in MLB all my life."

"Baseball is my only passion."

"Nobody wants this more than me."

"I'm the best candidate out there; I just need a chance."

These are quotes from the masses. As an applicant who has this as your only strategy, you have no separation from the other candidates.

Instead, determine what makes you different from all of the rest of the candidates *(your defined strength, your brand)*.

If you had to describe your brand, how would you define yourself? Let's explore your answers to these questions:

- ☐ If you were packaged as a product, what would be written on the label?

- ☐ What are the ingredients contained in this product?

- ☐ What does this product do?

- ☐ Why is this particular product better than others someone might buy?

In essence, when they make a hire, MLB executives are purchasing a product—a future employee who has particular *skills and talents* on the open market. Remember, this market has no shortage of highly qualified candidates. So brand yourself consistently with the specific skills and/or duties of the job. Your label should reflect the ingredients desired by the club for the position. If the label appeals, they'll want to learn more about the product. The more advanced your specific skills and talent, the more likely the MLB club will hire you. Your specific skills help define you and your brand.

TIP: Define your brand clearly.

Branded

Joe Maddon was a Major League coach for the California/ Anaheim/Los Angeles Angels of Anaheim from 1994 to 2005. A consummate student of the game, Joe studied every phase of professional baseball during his long apprenticeship, first as a player in the Minor Leagues and then as a Minor League coach, manager, and roving instructor. As a Major League coach, Joe dug heavily into statistical information to help the Angels gain an advantage over their opponents. Remember, the mid-'90s were like the "stone-age" compared to today's standards of statistical research.

In my recollection, Joe became one of the first data-driven field staff members in professional baseball. He embraced the computer and used it without fear of scorn or ridicule at a time when most people in Major League Baseball relied on their "gut" or their "eyes" to make decisions. Joe relied heavily on statistical analyses to do his job and prepare the Angels to compete against their opponents. The media, always on the lookout for the next story, heard about Joe's new-age data-driven approach and wrote articles about the coach who was helping the Angel teams succeed. By the way, Joe wore thick, black-rimmed, geeky-looking glasses—part of his brand.

Needing a manager to succeed Lou Piniella in 2005, the Tampa Bay Devil Rays went looking for suitable candidates. Andrew Friedman, the 29-year-old GM of the Devil Rays, had a progressive mind and a background in finance. He saw great potential in the analytical study of the game, and it became part of his strategy to level the playing field with the high-payroll teams in the American League Eastern Division. He needed a manager who wasn't hung up on the traditional way of decision-making and could use statistical evidence as well as baseball instincts. Because of Joe Maddon's branded reputation, it didn't take Friedman and team President Matt Silverman long to find and hire him.

Joe managed the Tampa Bay Rays from 2006 through 2014, winning the 2008 American League pennant. Following the 2014 season, he joined the Chicago Cubs, led them to the 2015 National League Championship Series and the 2016 World Series Championship. Today, nerds are cool!

Building a Presentation

Organize Your Evidence

To show evidence of your specialty through your prior work requires you to systematically organize it into a presentation. You have identified the desired entry-level job. You understand the duties involved. You have tailored your brand or defined strength to the specific duties of the job. Now, you must show tangible evidence of your defined strength.

If you haven't achieved this quality already, become a good self-evaluator. Your ability to determine your strengths and lesser strengths can be key to a successful career. Honestly analyze your abilities from the perspective of a potential boss. Release yourself of any ego/pride/over-confidence and perhaps delusion.

Next, organize your experiences and beliefs into a coherent presentation that highlights your specialty. Three questions can guide your answers:

1. What are the formative steps to develop your specialty?

2. Which examples show it's a specialty?

3. What are the major tenets of your specialty?

1. What are the Formative Steps to Develop Your Specialty?

Understand the Language, Resources, and Role Models

FOR FRONT OFFICE APPLICANTS:

You will need a basic understanding of advanced baseball statistical analytical research *(sabermetrics)* and the use of statistical analytics as it pertains to MLB. *(Use the same protocol for studies in MLB Player Salary Arbitration.)* Begin by studying baseball-related formulas and respective abbreviations *before* reading related articles or research. That's because most resource material on sabermetrics assumes a certain intermediate level of understanding and won't explain every single formula or abbreviation.

Start with MLB.com and ESPN.com or similar baseball websites to begin your journey into advanced statistical analytics. These websites offer a solid base for understanding primary baseball statistical terms. From there, you can progress to the more sophisticated websites and material. Bill James is the father of modern baseball statistical research so be sure to read his early and latest books. *(Anything Bill James has published on this subject warrants study.)* Because you're building a solid foundation for statistical research to be your specialty, do not cut corners. Start with basic information and work your way to the more complex.

After becoming well versed in the basic statistical analysis of professional baseball, become an avid reader of these websites:

Baseball-Reference [http://www.baseball-reference.com]

Baseball Prospectus [http://www.baseballprospectus.com]

Fan Graphs [http://www.fangraphs.com]

Baseball HQ [http://www.baseballhq.com]

Brooks Baseball [http://www.brooksbaseball.net]

Reviewing the SB Nation website [http://www.sbnation.com] for your favorite MLB team is good practice as well. Get to know the players on your favorite team and study them. Learn to recognize players' backgrounds and injury histories as well as ballpark factors.

SB Nation has many loyal contributors who post outstanding sabermetrics articles about their favorite MLB team. You'll understand the articles better by having a solid knowledge of the players studied and researched.

This strategy not only builds an understanding of baseball's language and terms in advanced statistical baseball research; it also shows the diversity of your research. Then you can offer a satisfactory reply to an interviewer when asked, "How have you developed your skills in sabermetrics?" or "What websites or blogs do you like, and why?" *(These are actual interview questions for most clubs.)*

FOR PROSPECTIVE COACH CANDIDATES:

Let's do an exercise to put you on the path of master-level coaching. Think about the coaches and teachers from your past in a *positive* light.

- ☐ Which coaches or teachers taught you the *most?* Why?
- ☐ Which coaches or teachers had the *biggest impact* on your career? How?
- ☐ What characteristics made a *positive* impression on you?
- ☐ List those characteristics. You may want to emulate these traits in your career.

Also reflect on their ability to teach, and then think of ways they were successful as coaches or teachers. Allow them to become your role models.

Now ask yourself those same questions but in a negative light.

- ☐ Which coaches or teachers taught you the *least?* Why?
- ☐ Which coaches or teachers had *no impact* on your career? Why?
- ☐ What characteristics *limited their impression* on you?
- ☐ List those characteristics.
  Your answers tell you the traits you *don't* want to emulate so you won't repeat their mistakes.
- ☐ Honest self-evaluation: In your time coaching or teaching, have you ever exhibited any of these negative traits?

This simple, effective exercise can build the foundation of a coaching style.

> # Be Genuine
>
> Let me be clear. You want to emulate the *traits* of your best teachers/coaches, not them as people. *Your best coaching happens when it's authentically from you.* YOU HAVE TO BE YOU! You're building an individual template of your style and approach to coaching/teaching. Also, you're learning to recognize your personal characteristics as an instructor. After completing this exercise, you can then reply in an informed way when asked, "Who are the former coaches that have impacted your career and why?" or "How would you describe your teaching style?" *(These are actual interview questions.)*

FOR PROSPECTIVE SCOUT CANDIDATES:

This exercise relates to the player evaluation that scouts do. Let's evaluate some Major League players you have seen by answering these questions:

- ☐ Which MLB players/pitchers have the best physical tools?

- ☐ Which MLB players/pitchers have the best mental characteristics?

- ☐ As it pertains to winning a championship, would you rather have superior physical or mental characteristics in your players?

Did you favor physical or mental skills? Either way, you're learning who you are as an evaluator. You're forming an *opinion* about the skills of Major League players/pitchers based on what you believe to be most valuable. For player evaluation, your honest understanding of your own value system will eventually allow you to see where your potential mistakes may lie.

Knowing yourself is fundamental to evaluating players, which means having an idea of your personal "scouting barometer" to adjust with the players and the game. For example, some scouts only recommend players they believe to be "gamers," while other scouts lean toward those with "big tools."

TIP: Identifying how you naturally think when evaluating a player is the first step toward developing a scouting barometer and specialty.

Don't look for right or wrong answers in these coaching/scouting exercises. They're designed to help you know yourself because an interviewer might ask, "Describe yourself as a coach or scout." Completing these questions gives you the framework to provide an excellent description of yourself. *(Most candidates stumble on this one.)*

Also learn to offer a full description of your style and what's important to you as a coach/scout. Give the interviewer a brief summary of your value system as it relates to the job and describe yourself in an orderly way. *Honest evaluation* of your perception and your value system are the most important aspects of these exercises. Knowing yourself is a never-ending journey.

TIP: You might find your description changes over time, so keep your answers for future reference. Knowing yourself sets you on your way to a specialty, but it requires comprehensive study.

Consider the Overlap

Expect an overlap of information in the areas of sabermetrics, coaching, and scouting. For example, a coach's duties include player evaluation because a coach's recommendations can influence player personnel decisions of the front office. Coaches routinely use statistical data to help formulate their evaluation of a player. Sabermetricians use player scouting reports to complete research or study baseball theory and to cross-reference statistical information so they can validate their theories. Scouts must have a good idea of proper baseball "mechanics" for all position players and pitchers. It's their job to make value judgments on a player's future ability while applying statistical data to formulate their opinion of a player. Because of this overlap, you're wise to study all aspects of professional baseball.

In addition, studying relevant information from other sports helps gauge your validity compared with professional baseball. Other professional sports have developed insightful theories related to individual and team performance that might apply to professional baseball.

TIP: Determine if ideas from other sports have a practical application in baseball and fit within your framework.

Form Your Own Opinions

FOR FRONT OFFICE APPLICANTS:

After studying resource material on any aspect of professional baseball, form your own opinions. Think critically regarding the information you've gathered. Do you agree or disagree with what the author wrote? Either way, take a stand!

Follow an author's hypothesis during the upcoming season(s) to discern its accuracy *(or were you more accurate?)*. MLB teams do not hire people in the front office to look up stats and do research. They hire them to help improve their teams. Improvement comes by way of the staff's research/study/conclusion. Eventually, your opinions will reveal your talent and skill level in advanced baseball statistical analysis. And it's why the organization is making an investment in you, even as an intern. All Baseball Operations employees are paid to help *improve* the Major League club. Proper conclusions derived from research and study lead to the proper strategies or advanced processes that eventually improve the team. Therefore, you must believe your research/study/conclusion will influence the club's future success.

When you're hired, your conclusions are what determine your value to the organization. Research/study/conclusion will always be a part of Major League Baseball.

TIP: Stay current with an eye to the future because the next great sabermetrics theory is just around the corner. Why don't you develop it?

FOR COACH AND SCOUT CANDIDATES:

The same conclusion is true for both coaches and scouts. The club wants to know your perspective and opinions. *What does your comprehensive study lead you to believe?* Your conclusions formulate your individual core beliefs *(major tenets)* in your specialty. Your keen understanding of specific aspects of your study, combined with your original thought processing, result in your unique conclusions. For example, some pitching coaches conclude that a pitcher's *balance* is the most important aspect of a professional pitching delivery. Some scouts might conclude that a young player's *athleticism* is the key to detecting future Major League players.

Your conclusions describe your perspective on what's important as you begin to define yourself. That way, the executives who hire you can understand exactly what they're buying.

TIP: Forming conclusions becomes paramount to your growth and development in your specialty. Nothing is more important than your ability to analyze the information and formulate an opinion.

Commit to Your Career

Because you'll gain experience by practicing your craft, find work in a related job of your specialty *at any level*. If you're a prospective intern, find a web-based baseball statistical company that needs assistance. If you're a prospective coach, practice your skills with a local high school or college baseball team. If you're a future scout, go to amateur games and ask an MLB scout to be his or her "bird-dog" *(unpaid part-time scout)* for the area.

Work for free if you can't find a paying job. Talk your way into something that will add to your experience in your field. In these ways, you can commit to your future career. Demonstrating passion for your specialty, especially when you're not paid, will be greatly respected by people who are hiring. They'll see your pursuit of a career in baseball is real and not a passing fancy.

TIP: Show your commitment to the game through practice and volunteering.

Interact with Others

Become a regular contributor on baseball blogs and websites. Respond to articles and posts and debate with the other baseball gurus as you strenuously defend your position. Mix it up with these "trolls."

Research and study are great, but interaction and debate are even better. The competitive nature of the exchange challenges your understanding of the material and tests your conviction. When you defend your beliefs against others with a better understanding of the subject matter, you'll be in a position to learn from their expertise. *(Getting pummeled in a debate on some obscure Internet baseball research blog should not be an issue for a tough individual.)* Defending your opinion against the others' challenges exhibits an advanced level of expertise.

TIP: Improve your debating skills so you can gain the necessary confidence of a baseball specialist.

Create Your Own Blog or Website

Start your own blog or website dedicated to the study of specific aspects of professional baseball. Post articles in your specialty. Invite others to share their research as you build a community of like-minded individuals studying various aspects of professional baseball. Having your own baseball blog or website can be impressive to a potential employer. Invite MLB club officials to critique it. Not only does your website exhibit your level of passion for studying baseball, but it serves as a record of all of your studies, which can be easily accessed by a potential employer.

TIP: Because this information will be available for potential employers to view, ensure all your posts accurately reflect your true beliefs. Include only the material you would want to use in an interview.

Join the Community

Join clubs and associations dedicated to baseball: Society for American Baseball Research (SABR) includes some of the best sabermetrics minds in the world; the American Baseball Coaches Association (ABCA) is a highly regarded amateur baseball association. Its national convention is well attended by professional baseball coaches and scouts.

The Professional Baseball Scouts Association (PBSA) is dedicated to MLB scouts, so attend PBSA events and participate in the community. Present your ideas and engage in face-to-face discussions to test your knowledge and confidence at a higher level. Because you won't have immediate access to your data and research, you will have to know it! Your goal is to quickly respond to arguments made against your theory with relevant evidence.

As you become more comfortable with the other members, practice debating with those who don't believe in your conclusion and attempt to change their minds. You learn a lot about *yourself* in the aftermath of these discussions and how to best perform.

Did I get upset when they didn't agree with me?

Did I truly listen to the points they made, or was I just thinking of stating my next argument?

Did I state all of my information about my theory, or was I too caught up in the argument?

These exchanges will have great benefit in your career. Your future bosses won't always agree with your theories or conclusions either, so you'll have to persuade them—and don't ever say "educate" because bosses don't like that description. Specialists' true measure is not only the validity of their information; it's also what they can get others to understand *(even more difficult when it's your boss you're trying to persuade)*.

TIP: Practice your skills of persuasion. Your conclusion might turn from a theory into a practical application strategy for the club to implement.

Build a Library or Manual

FOR FRONT OFFICE APPLICANTS:

I recommend you build a sabermetrics library (especially if you don't have your own website) that allows you to show your work to a potential employer. Documenting your long hours of research and study, forming your own opinions, and debating others should give you a plethora of outstanding data. Occasionally review, update, and reassess the information in your library for its present-day merit. *What can you add to make a particular study more meaningful? Do you still believe your conclusion of a particular study to be accurate?*

FOR COACH OR SCOUT CANDIDATES:

Write a manual about your specialty. Organize a comprehensive manuscript detailing your thoughts and ideas. Use it to show the dedication, passion, and work ethic you possess for your specialty. Ensure this manual is more than a collection of notes and reflects good organization and professionalism. It will never perfectly represent all of the information you know, but it forces you to organize your beliefs and thus assists in your development. By detailing your thoughts, you start to define yourself as a coach or scout.

TIP: Maintain your library or manual by keeping it up to date and relevant.

Meet with Someone in Your Desired Role

Meet with someone in MLB who holds the position you're attempting to acquire. This is your best source of gaining practical knowledge into the daily aspects of the position. You will also acquire an idea of the type of research and study needed to prepare yourself. Getting advice from former candidates who competed and won spots in MLB is invaluable. They can help you in your attempt. ONLY ask for this meeting after you have prepared yourself with exhaustive research/study/conclusions. Meeting prematurely is dangerous.

Your goal is to make a positive impression on the employee of an MLB club. In fact, treat this meeting as an initial interview. The impression you make with the employee could leave a lasting impression on that club, and in turn, influence other MLB organizations. This employee could become an advocate and a professional reference. *Do your homework first!*

It could be wise to ask if you could "shadow" the employee for a few days. This would offer insight into the issues faced in the position and allow time for all of your questions. However, shadowing would probably require having an existing relationship with an MLB employee.

TIP: Establish a relationship before calling to shadow someone.

Find a Mentor

FOR COACH OR SCOUT CANDIDATES:

Specific information that pertains to statistical research is easily found on the Internet. Aspects of coaching and scouting are not. Baseball intricacies are often passed down through generations by word of mouth, as baseball people tend to commit what they know to memory. They do not like to put their valuable treasures in written form for all to see, so their "tricks of the trade" are held as coveted secrets and discussed sparingly. Coaches and scouts rarely share what they believe to be important with just anybody; it would be like offering the "crown jewels." *Personal interaction* is essential to mine these jewels and puts you in a great position to garner this information. Experienced coaches and scouts love the mentor role.

TIP: A mentor can transfer advanced knowledge on a specific subject and also confer a degree of credibility to the candidate. A mentor can even become a professional reference. Find one!

Covert Action: Cheat a Little

If you have a close friend in professional baseball, ask to review the Baseball Operations' office, field, or scouting manual. This may not be popular with an MLB club *(so be careful who you ask),* but it's a good way to get indoctrinated into a perspective. Manuals document specific aspects of an individual department and detail how staff members are to perform their tasks *(as required by standard operating procedure).*

Prospective front office interns, be aware that some MLB clubs require completing a Baseball Operations questionnaire at the start of the application process. The questions gauge your administrative ability, overall baseball intellect, and creativity. Some also test your baseball knowledge. Attempt to acquire these questionnaires to help you in your preparation before applying for an internship.

TIP: These suggestions can be a little sensitive, so you must have a close personal relationship before asking the employee for manuals or questionnaires. But if you're not cheating, you're not trying!

2. Which Examples Show It's a Specialty?

This question will be answered by successfully completing all of the necessary work discussed in the previous question (What are the formative steps to develop your specialty?). *Allow the organization to view examples of your work to help acquire an interview.* It will be your evidence to show you are a worthy hire for an MLB organization. Have pertinent information available for review by the organization both before and during the interview process.

TIP: Most applicants will send an email or letter with no corresponding evidence. They will have difficulty competing against the applicants that send examples of their study.

FOR FRONT OFFICE APPLICANTS:

☐ Be careful when sending research/study/conclusions regarding the clubs you wish to interview. When selecting candidates to interview, the executive may disagree with your written conclusion and you have no way to defend your argument. Keep in mind they know their club better than anyone.

☐ Compile your current research/study/conclusions on either other teams and/or various aspects of the industry. Send a broad range of material *(e.g., Major League statistical research on players/teams, Player Arbitration case or study, Amateur Draft studies, Minor League, etc.).* You want to be considered a candidate for any need the club may have.

☐ Show your website. *(Have links to your clubs/associations.)*

☐ Allow the organization to access your baseball statistical analytics library.

☐ List references rather than "References on Request." *(Don't make potential interviewers work to know you. They won't!)*

FOR COACH OR SCOUT CANDIDATES:

☐ Detail your pursuit of learning the art of coaching/scouting.

☐ Detail your work experiences to learn your craft.

☐ Detail what you learned from each job.

☐ Offer access to your blog or website.

☐ Show your manual.

☐ List references and mentors.

3. What are the Major Tenets of Your Specialty?

After studying baseball through advanced statistical analytics or countless hours at ballgames, determine your true convictions.

☐ What are the core beliefs you have learned through your study?

☐ What will you defend with all of your heart?

☐ What do you firmly believe should be a foundational piece of the philosophy in an organization?

If you have researched, studied, formed your own opinions—then documented them, challenged them, and had others challenge, review, and update them to be current—specific conclusions you believe to be true will emerge! What are they? *Be prepared to present them.*

TIP: Organize these major tenets in a concise fashion so you can discuss them in an interview. Be ready to defend your conclusions!

Value of Presentation and Networking

Presentation

This chapter will only be helpful in your academic preparation; it's not meant to help you with your *presentation* as a professional. Nobody can help you in the interview room; you are totally exposed. You will most likely not be hired if you come off as cocky, arrogant, egotistical, argumentative, sloppy, ill-mannered, vulgar, or disrespectful. Former Major League Manager Felipe Alou calls it your *presentation*—the image you project to others through your interaction with them. The masses are filled with candidates who have a poor *presentation*; the candidate hired possesses a strong professional *presentation*. A great self-evaluator has the ability to see his own presentation through the eyes of the interviewer. Can you?

Networking

This chapter focuses on developing a specialty, not the specific "how to" of acquiring a job in MLB. Many of the interactions *(on websites or in person)* discussed earlier are great examples of networking.

Honestly, networking will never go out of style. Personal and professional contacts may be important in acquiring an opportunity to interview with a team. It behooves a prospective candidate to have as much positive interaction with professional baseball staff members as possible.

TIP: Do not be a pest; respect them and their time, but inform them of your ambitions.

In my experience, almost all professional baseball employees will try to help an aspiring professional MLB candidate. Many of the prospective candidates you interact with could become among the *hired*. They *can* hold a great deal of influence on who will be the next to be hired. You never know how your next opportunity may present itself. Remember, it's not *who you know*; rather it's *who you know who believes you will be a good employee.*

TIP: Maintain your networking relationships and learn from them.

Summary: The Extra-Ordinary

Review these points of preparation needed to acquire an interview.

☐ Learn the proper language of the specialty through your research and study.

☐ Create your own opinion regarding studies on the specialty.

☐ Actively discuss and debate with others in the area of the specialty.

☐ Join clubs/organizations dedicated to the specialty.

- ☐ Shadow or meet with people who have jobs in the specialty.

- ☐ Have work experience directly related to the specialty. What did you learn?

- ☐ Create a website/blog dedicated to the specialty.

- ☐ Create a library/manual dedicated to the specialty.

- ☐ Create personal major tenets of the specialty.

An applicant who shows this type of work on a specialty is definitely out of the ordinary. It's the extraordinary candidates who separate themselves from the masses with their evidence of a specialty.

Given the strengths and lesser strengths you possess, you'll accomplish some of these items easily while others might be difficult. The competition you face weeds out the average applicants and allows the strongest candidates to emerge. If these items seem too difficult, then remind yourself what Tommy Lasorda screamed at Jon in Chapter 1:

"YOU'RE NOT TOUGH ENOUGH!"

It's time to get tough and decide if or when you will get the job. Those who have been hired relentlessly pursued careers in MLB by not taking "no" for an answer. *It's up to you and only you.* You may not get an interview the first time you blanket MLB with résumés. You may not be hired after you finally experience an interview. You may not get hired after you interview a second time! *You will be humble, though!*

TIP: Never give in, keep battling, stay positive, remain confident in your ability, adjust to the feedback you receive, and continue to develop your specialty! Your path may be longer than others. Delay is not denial!

CHAPTER 5:

AN INTERVIEW GONE SIDEWAYS

An Interview to Learn From

IT'S INCREASINGLY DIFFICULT TO SEPARATE YOURSELF FROM OTHER CAN-
didates and appear as a worthy hire to a Major League Baseball club. You
will need as much *evidence* as possible to show *you* should be hired over
everyone else. Even if your evidence checks all of the boxes and you have
drawn interest from an MLB club, the most important element of the process is yet to come: *the interview.* I won't tell you how to dress or what col-
ors to wear. Nor will I discuss eating a healthy pre-interview meal to settle
your nerves or advise you on how much sleep you need the night before.
I'll only tell you of my experience interviewing for general manager of the
Houston Astros in 2011.

Evaluating My Interview

Let me share my thought process leading up to the interview and
detail my activities for preparation. Admittedly, I missed the mark on a few
counts. In fact, Chapter 4 is made up of lessons learned from mistakes of
others and my own missteps.

Both positive and negative experiences can be the best teachers if
you're an *honest self-evaluator.* Typically, when results are *positive,* poor
self-evaluators don't analyze why; they simply assume the successful outcome came from their extraordinary ability. Also, they may not learn anything from the *negative* experiences in their careers. Many lessons will be

chalked up to an unfortunate set of circumstances or someone else's fault, but most of the time, lessons can be learned with analysis and self-reflection.

In Major League Baseball, successful people "shower off" the negative and attempt to gain something positive from every experience. *What just happened? How did it happen? Why did it happen? What is the strategy to ensure it doesn't happen again?* In the aftermath of my interview with the Houston Astros, I was confused by the executives' decision until I made the conscious choice to *reflect* on the entire experience, evaluate my performance, and view myself *from their perspective.* Taking ownership of my poor performance put me in a position to learn because I chose not to blame anyone but myself. Here's what happened.

What I Didn't Know

The 2011 MLB season had ended and we were going through the paces of improving our team for the 2012 Colorado Rockies' season. In my role as AGM, the 40-man Major League roster was my biggest concern in October and early November. We would identify which players from our Minor League system to add to the Major League roster and not leave them exposed to other clubs in the December Rule V draft. But if we protected all of the draft-eligible prospects we liked by adding them to our Major League 40-man roster, we'd limit our available spots for any free agents we wanted to sign. These difficult roster decisions required dozens of conversations with Minor League staff members and scouts.

I was completing employee evaluation forms with salary recommendations for Rockies Human Resource VP Liz Stecklein and reviewing the 2012 budgets for various departments in Baseball Operations for Michael Kent and Hal Roth, VPs in the Finance Department. Added to these was attending an organizational meeting and completing other administrative tasks (it's not all baseball in the front office). Just when I thought I'd had enough of another day at Coors Field, Rockies GM Dan O'Dowd entered my office. Because it was next to Dan's office, he'd normally yell from his desk or poke his head in the door to talk. This time, he came in and sat down.

The Day Turned Upside Down

Dan had been on the phone with George Postolos, President of the Houston Astros. George had asked Dan for permission to speak to me regarding the Astros' vacant general manager position. I was stunned. Even though I'd worked in all of the departments of Baseball Operations and with both large and small market clubs, I'd never been asked before. Not a self-promoting kind of guy, I felt it was unbecoming to sell myself for jobs with other teams while professing to be loyal to my present organization. In my mind, though, the opportunity to interview for a GM position was long overdue. (In retrospect, I wasn't being humble.)

A million thoughts raced through my head. I loved the Rockies' organization. Owners Dick and Charlie Monfort had always been great to me and my family. I enjoyed my working relationship with Dan and everyone in Business Operations. My wife Bonnie and our children had no interest in moving again; they loved Colorado. I had given up on the thought of a team considering me for a GM position when this call came through. Do I really want to do it? I knew I wanted the experience of a GM interview, but did I sincerely want the Houston job? That was an important question.

Dan asked, "Do you want permission granted? I can tell them no if you want."

"Yes, I want to interview," I replied quickly. I had waited entirely too long for the chance (again, I wasn't very humble). Dan recommended I speak with Dick Monfort to inform him of my desire to interview. I wanted to explain to Dick that I loved the Colorado Rockies but would like the opportunity to talk to the Astros. I hoped he wouldn't view me as disloyal or a traitor, but I also had confidence in how reasonable Dick would be. When I called Dick about this, Dan had already informed him of the request for permission. He was well aware of the situation when he walked into my office.

"So you want to interview, huh?" Dick said.

"I guess I probably should," I replied.

"If they offer it, would you take the job?" he asked.

"At this point, I don't know. I haven't even met them," I replied.

"Good answer," said Dick.

"Are you okay with me interviewing?"

"I guess I probably should be."

I had taken that response to mean Dick felt 50/50. He didn't want to limit my opportunities, but he also didn't like the idea of my leaving. Dick and I sat in my office for some time discussing general aspects of MLB and the Houston market size, in particular, for the business side of baseball. We discussed the Rockies organization and the Major League club as it stood at that time. We reminisced about the rebuilding effort from 2003 to 2006, the Rockies' run to the World Series in 2007, the disappointing year in 2008, the return to the playoffs in 2009, and the untimely death of our beloved Keli McGregor, Rockies president, during the 2010 season. We covered a lot of Rockies history in our conversation. It reminded me of how much we had been through and how much I loved the Colorado Rockies organization.

We shook hands at the end of our conversation and I told Dick I would keep him informed on the process. Shortly after, Dan came in and dropped a slip of paper on my desk. "You need to call George Postolos—I told him you wanted to interview." Dan acted as if it were no big deal, but I knew he was excited for me.

My mind raced again in a surreal daze. What did I need to do to prepare for this interview? What would I do first if I got the offer? I pulled out my folders of front office information and baseball reference material, having no idea where to begin. I suddenly realized what I had better do immediately. Call George Postolos. It was real now!

The Phone Call

I sat and stared at George Postolos' phone number. What type of call is this? Will he ask me baseball questions? Should I study the Astros' organization before I call him? At this point in the process, I went from a cocky know-it-all who wondered why I'd never been asked to interview, to a guy who didn't know the first thing to do now that he had the interview! I looked over the Astros' prospect list and 40-man roster then quickly studied the team's player contracts and future salary commitments. I also looked at the team's present front office structure and familiarized myself with names and titles. Then I took a deep breath— and called George.

George Postolos couldn't have been more engaging. He didn't ask me who their California League Trainer was, but I was ready if he had. Instead of details, he asked me to describe my philosophical ideas about scouting and player development, and enlighten him on what I believed most important to win at the Major League level. His basic questions were easy to answer, and they'd better be. This was the only subject I'd ever studied. In college, baseball was my passion; my economics program was a hobby.

I responded confidently with long answers to his questions for more than an hour. George complimented me on my answers (I'm definitely not feeling humble now). Then he asked me to fly to Houston for a meeting with him and Astros Owner Jim Crane. I quickly accepted. (Okay, I was excited!)

Being in the Rockies' office for the next few days, I felt a sense of guilt. How could I feel comfortable preparing for this interview while completing my work with the Rockies? Keeping my thoughts on my present job was difficult but I managed.

Preparation

To prepare, I studied the Astros' rich history and reviewed past players and teams. I even felt a sense of the pride they must have in their organization. The team recently had a few bad years but experienced success in the not-so-distant past. I studied the financials and expenditures to review how much money they'd been spending in Baseball Operations. I noted what appeared to be heavy spending at the Major League level and a relatively less-than-ordinary financial commitment to acquire amateur talent. In my opinion, this club needed to build a strong core of younger, less expensive talent to have a contending team.

I reviewed the Astros' entire Minor League system and made my own evaluations of their prospects. Surprisingly, they had better talent than I'd been led to believe; our Rockies' scouts liked many of their young players. The Astros' employee personnel I knew were well respected in the industry. I saw the foundation for turning the Astros into a winning club was in place. The Houston market size ranked anywhere from fourth to eighth compared to that of the 30 teams in MLB—definitely the size of market that could support a relatively high team payroll once the club started winning again. Plus, it had enjoyed strong fan support, with attendance being the envy of many clubs. This rebuilding job would not be easy, but it showed signs of a potential winner. My confidence in the Astros' organization was growing. I wanted the job.

The Game Plan

The new owner was also new to the MLB and had no experience in his current position in professional baseball. Jim Crane was a successful self-made Houston businessman who had played college baseball. Astros' president George Postolos had been president of the Houston Rockets and was a Harvard-educated intellectual type, also with no previous MLB experience. I had a sense of the type of general manager the club needed—a baseball veteran who understood the ins and outs of the MLB landscape. The new GM should have existing relationships with people in other MLB clubs to facilitate trades and know a good number of agents for signing desired players. This GM should have professional baseball savvy—a longtime professional who'd worked in the bowels of organizations and would bring an innate "feel" for what was needed.

I felt confident (or delusional) I was the perfect person for the job.

I wanted the challenge because I felt I knew exactly what the club needed (big mistake). Jim Crane, a former college player, would want to be involved in baseball decisions, so I wouldn't attempt to come on too strong or act too rigid from a baseball standpoint. I expected he'd want to have a say on player personnel decisions (wrong). For George, I should be prepared to show I understood the financial aspects of professional baseball, which would be his main perspective (I was correct). I had a game plan!

Dan offered to conduct a "mock interview" with me to help me prepare. Caught up in my arrogant thinking that I knew exactly what the Astros needed, I respectfully declined (another mistake). I did realize I should go into the interview with my thoughts on paper, so I prepared packets of information to bring to Houston. In them, I detailed my thoughts on organizational culture, a hierarchy flow chart of the Baseball Operations Department and its positions, amateur player acquisition costs for each MLB team from 2002 to 2011, prospect rankings for each MLB organization, and various systems for ranking players' characteristics at the Major League level. This was an acceptable way of describing topics of importance to me fairly concisely. I believed there'd also be lively back and forth conversation. I thought I was completely prepared for the interview (delusional again). And I knew from colleagues that nobody had been hired for a GM job based on one interview. From what I'd been told, first interviews would be informative conversations in which I'd provide a sense of my skills but save the rest of my ammunition for the next round of interviews. "Don't use all of your bullets," I told myself. (What a fool!)

I have to stop here for a minute. At this point, I hadn't even been through the first face-to-face interview and already was planning a second one—one that never came. My advice now? Use the interview opportunity as if it's your one and only chance. Prepare to throw the kitchen sink at them with more information about you and your skills than they'd ever imagine. Impress them to the highest level possible.

I still believe no GM has ever been hired following only one interview, but I learned a valuable lesson. The majority of candidates who don't get hired only get one chance.

The Interview

Reporters and television camera crews awaited my arrival at the Houston airport, which only served to heighten my confidence. After answering a few questions from the media, I caught a taxi to the stadium. Eileen Colgin, long-time Astros executive assistant and a great lady, greeted me at the Astros' offices. Waiting for George Postolos, chatting with Eileen made me feel comfortable in that environment. I felt no nervousness as I was shown to the conference room where we would meet. While I was waiting, Astros Public Relations VP Jay Lucas, an old friend, came in to say hello. His brief visit only served to make me feel more comfortable—and confident.

A few minutes later, George entered the room and we greeted each other. George said Jim Crane was flying into Houston and would meet us later. Jackie Traywick, the Astros CFO, joined us. We reviewed the budgets of all of the Astros Baseball Operations departments and discussed detailed aspects of expenditures within each department. I was fully prepared to offer my opinion of total dollar budget numbers required for each of the Baseball Operations departments. Jackie seemed agreeable with my estimations, and the conversation went smoothly. Then George asked a few specific operational questions regarding how I envisioned the setup and costs of various departments to build a championship organization. It seemed I was "nailing" this interview. I had answered their detailed budget questions perfectly (in my mind), and I wanted them to ask more questions. Jackie departed the room to get back to her business of the day, and I relaxed even more because I felt I had aced that part of the exam.

(Nobody would have described me as humble at this point.)

Just then, Jim Crane walked into the room.

Houston, We Definitely Have a Problem

Wearing a beautiful suit (I really like nice suits), Mr. Crane carried the look of a successful "gazillionaire." Despite being an imposing figure, he was friendly and cordial as we began to converse. Mr. Crane had a strong successful presence about him, which instantaneously made me feel nervous. Before he sat down, he removed his suit jacket, so I took off mine as well (seemed like a good idea at the time). Just then, my cuff link got caught in the inside lining of my jacket and tore the material. As the jacket came off, the ripped fabric hung from the open sleeve. (Okay, now I'm really nervous and try to laugh it off.) Then I reached into my satchel and distributed the packets of information I'd prepared. Mr. Crane browsed through the pages quickly and asked only a couple of questions. I tried to discuss each item in the packet, but no meaningful questions followed. Instead, Mr. Crane closed the folder and set it down on the table. He then leaned back in his chair, interlocked his hands behind his head, and said, "Well, what do you want to tell me?"

WHAT DO YOU WANT TO TELL ME? I never prepared for that question! I was ready to answer any and all baseball questions they could have thrown at me. Ask me anything you want to know about professional baseball, and I'll answer it. I possessed a wealth of knowledge in the intricate aspects of professional baseball clubs, and I had performed like a champ answering each detailed question from George and Jackie. There was no way to stump me on professional baseball questions. What do you want to tell me? What kind of a question was that? Well, the kind that threw me off my game. I didn't know where to start, and I sure as hell didn't know where to finish. I had no presentation, no "pitch."

Every working day of Mr. Crane's life as a big-time business owner, someone pitched him on "buying" an idea—from within the organization and from without. That was his world, and I had (mistakenly) focused on information to answer questions, not to provide a presentation. I knew it was downhill from there. (I was humbled.)

Later, as George drove me to the airport, he talked about meeting again, likely at the Winter Meetings in Dallas the following week. Yes, there would be a second round of interviews. That meant I could make up for my mistakes and prepare a proper presentation. On the flight home, I wrote a brief "interview recap" to document the experience.

The Winter Meetings and the Verdict

My name made the rumor mill on the lobby floor of the Winter Meetings, hinting I'd be offered the GM position with the Astros, although other candidates were still to be interviewed. To my knowledge, Jeff Luhnow and I were the only candidates who had interviewed in Houston so I believed we were the frontrunners. I was sure George would call me to discuss our next interview, but I didn't want to appear pushy or desperate so I never called him.

Then the night before the Rule V Draft, the "lobby grapevine" spread the FACT (not a rumor) that Luhnow was named the new GM of the Astros. George called me soon after I'd heard the news. He told me I didn't make it and, in fairness, also apologized for how I'd learned the news. I never got more rounds of interviews, but I guess Jeff Luhnow did.

I sat quietly alone in the Rockies' suite of the Hilton Anatole hotel in Dallas (okay, now I'm as humble as ever possible) and collected my thoughts on my interview performance. Jim Tracy, the Rockies manager at the time, and Danny Montgomery, the Rockies assistant scouting director, attempted to console me until the early hours. I tried to make them understand I wasn't upset or feeling robbed. I understood all of my mistakes, and I owned them. I needed to perform well in the interview and I didn't, plain and simple.

Dick couldn't have been nicer in our conversation afterward. He seemed genuinely happy that I was staying in Colorado, and it made me feel great to be wanted in an organization by a man I admired so much. I was very fortunate to be working with the Colorado Rockies, and I loved it there.

Want to know the irony of my poor interview performance? Mr. Crane conducted his phase of my interview in the same way I interviewed prospective employees. My motto was to let the interviewee talk as much as possible to learn about them. Mr. Crane took the strategy to another level by simply asking, "What do you want to tell me?" Simple, but brilliant.

Here's my advice: The written reference material you bring into an interview should primarily detail your presentation as outlined in Chapter 4. Be sure to document the *major tenets* of your philosophies with the corresponding research evidence in the material for the interviewer to review. Doing this gives you the ability to discuss the topics you believe to be important without relying only on questions asked of you.

TIP: Prepare a presentation as if you won't be asked any questions. Build a presentation for your future dream job and organize it in a way you can clearly convey it to others. Your prepared pitch allows you to be in command of the interview.

Summary

It's not easy to relive one of the worst performances of my career, but I wanted the story of my flawed decision-making exposed for your benefit. At the expense of my own humiliation, these points summarize what to do in your quest to obtain a career in MLB.

- ☐ Study the subject matter to answer any and all questions you may be asked.

- ☐ Accept any assistance others offer in the form of mock interviews *(which I declined)* and feedback *(which I didn't seek)*.

- ☐ Organize your beliefs in presentation form in addition to being prepared for questions. Follow the outline in Chapter 4 to craft a persuasive presentation.

- ☐ Your presentation should include what you learned from each employment experience.

- ☐ Be fully prepared to pitch your presentation.

- ☐ Own up to your mistakes so you can perform better in future interviews.

- ☐ Don't wear cuff links!

CHAPTER 6:

YOU'VE BEEN HIRED—NOW WHAT?

Make a Great First Impression

REGARD YOUR FIRST JOB IN BASEBALL OPERATIONS AS A WONDERFUL learning opportunity. Remember, you're on scholarship. Your career has started! And then what happens? You'll accumulate knowledge to complete the day-to-day tasks of your position and gain a better understanding of how to improve them. You'll also learn the organizational philosophies and application processes of an entire department.

Know that you'll be judged and scrutinized as soon you accept a position in Major League Baseball. Because you can only make a first impression once, your initial job can set the tone for your entire career. Momentum you gain at the start of your career can help your future employment opportunities. Less prepared employees might commit costly mistakes that diminish their careers before they have a chance. So plan your actions and thought processes well as you survey the landscape of professional baseball. Potentially, this is the most important position in your career.

Your Mindset Matters

In your first job, always maintain your focus on your primary goal: a career in MLB. That means consider any future ramifications as you make decisions today. Think before you act! Word about missteps travels quickly in an organization; expect no one to keep a secret. *(Tommy Lasorda used to say, "I can keep a secret, it's the people I tell who can't keep a secret.")*

This is when others in the organization begin to identify your "ceiling" or categorize as your potential related to the club's future. They may not have a public succession strategy for all to see, but the duty of those at the highest administrative levels is to protect and plan the organization's future. Be part of it!

Be a Prospect for the Future

What are the 10 characteristics of a prospect seeking a career in Baseball Operations?

Complete the list in Figure 6.1. By doing so, you are developing a personal contract with yourself, knowing your future will be defined by your decisions. Make these your personal 10 Commandments and use them to guide your professional career.

Figure 6.1

My Personal 10 Commandments	
1. Be honest	6.
2. Help others	7.
3.	8.
4.	9.
5	10.

Assume the Posture of a Student

Chapter 4 discussed how a *defined strength* would help you acquire an interview and aid in your quest for a job in Baseball Operations. *I lied.* But here, I'm totally honest with you. You have no defined strength! You have only laid the groundwork for a future specialty.

If you were to build a house, would you hire a contractor who had never built a house or one that had built many houses? Veteran employees with practical experience in the field—those who have worked in jobs you hope to have someday—won't regard you as a specialist yet. You're a rookie in their eyes, so accept this fact and know you are a *student* who's limited by a lack of practical knowledge. In the posture of a student, learn as much as possible in your future area of expertise.

Those who are experienced hope you have the desire to be guided so they can mentor you in the intricate aspects of the job. *(Typically, they've been told by their boss to spend time with you.)* Aim to gain from experience. They'll respect your willingness to learn, but they'll lose interest in trying to mentor someone who doesn't believe help is needed. And don't tell them what you think or argue with them, especially if your view contradicts their information. Instead, ask why they think the way they do. This respectfully shows you value their opinions.

By asking questions, you're taking a student posture. Seeing that, experienced employees will accept that you're being realistic about your present experience. It's possible these employees have the power and close relationships—within the club and even outside it—to solidify your initial reputation. The good student becomes known as an employee who's willing to learn.

Conversely, it won't bode well if experienced employees refer to you as "that snot-nosed know-it-all." *(I've actually heard that one.)* Being receptive to and exhibiting more knowledge gives you the benefit of the doubt. Whom do you think your boss will ask about your potential and future ability: you or the experienced employees?

TIP: Give experienced employees the respect they deserve and learn from their valuable information. Ask questions!

Put the Organization First

Train your thought processes to place the organization in the forefront of your decision-making. That means *put the organization first.*

You'll be involved in many decisions that affect the club's health and vitality. By helping protect it from harm, you can also help maintain a strong future for the club and for your "teammates". If others see your judgment focused on what's best for the organization, they'll hold you in high esteem. And an "organization first" mentality keeps you from acting in a way that limits your potential or doing something detrimental to your goal.

TIP: Put the organization ahead of your ambition, your salary, your title, your duties, and certainly your ego in all of your actions.

Time?

Years ago while I was working with the Colorado Rockies, my old friend Tommy Lasorda called and said he was traveling to Denver to watch our series against the Dodgers. My co-workers—and especially Billy Witter, a tremendous baseball fan—were excited to meet Tommy. Billy had been working in Sales and Marketing for a short time. He was a great kid with a wonderful sense of humor who had already built up a lot of respect within the organization. Billy wanted to meet Tommy and take a photo with the legendary manager. As Tommy's visit neared, Billy excitedly checked with me every day as if it were the biggest event in his life.

When Tommy arrived at the stadium, he called me and asked for my eight-year-old son Sam to escort him to the offices. From our time working together with the Dodgers, Tommy always wanted Sam at his side. After greeting Tommy in my office, I told Sam to beat it, and we headed over to see Owners Dick and Charlie Monfort along with President Keli McGregor. They loved getting a dose of Tommy whenever he was around. A little secret: The Montforts grew up as Dodger fans, so Tommy would tell them stories of the old Dodger players in a way that only a coach or manager could.

After paying our respects to the top brass, we made our way back toward my office. As I looked down the hallway, I could see the figure of a young man standing next to my door—Billy. Honestly, I was having such a good time with Tommy I had completely forgotten to call him as promised. But he couldn't wait.

Billy smiled from ear to ear when he saw Tommy. I knew this young man liked to joke around, so as Tommy and I got close to him, I whispered to Tommy, "Get on this guy." He knew exactly what I meant. Like a tiger eagerly awaiting his prey, Tommy was ready to pounce.

When I introduced Billy to Tommy, I could see the excitement in Billy's face. I snapped a photo of the two of them and we chatted, following Tommy's lead.

"Billy, what do you do for the organization?" Billy seemed a little nervous but answered his question.

"Billy, do you enjoy the organization?" He replied that it was a dream come true. Tommy then went into a long dissertation about all of the good things the Los Angeles Dodgers had done for him and his family. He stopped and asked, "Billy, have the Colorado Rockies been good to you?"

"Yes, very good," Billy responded.

"Well, that's great. What do you give the Colorado Rockies in return?" At that point, Billy struggled to offer any response.

Tommy asked again—loudly, "What do you give the Colorado Rockies in return?"

After a lengthy awkward pause, searching for the correct response, Billy finally replied, "My time?"

Then Tommy went crazy, screaming so everyone nearby could hear.

"TIME? YOUR TIME? THAT'S ALL YOU GIVE BACK, YOUR TIME? THIS ORGANIZATION DOES SO MUCH FOR YOU AND ALL YOU HAVE TO OFFER IS YOUR TIME? HOW ABOUT YOUR PASSION? HOW ABOUT YOUR LOYALTY? HOW ABOUT YOUR LOVE?

"TIME? YOU OWE THE ORGANIZATION MORE THAN YOUR TIME. YOU OWE THE COLORADO ROCKIES YOUR UNDYING COMMITMENT AND LIFELONG GRATITUDE!

"TIME? MY ASS! YOU OWE THE ROCKIES YOUR HEART!"

We walked away and left Billy alone. The young man had the biggest smile on his face. He loved getting blasted by Tommy. It gave him a memorable story to tell forever. Once we'd walked a distance from Billy, Tommy leaned over and asked,

"Did I get him good?"

"Yes, Tommy, you're really good at yelling at people."

I don't understand how Tommy can scream so passionately at people and still relay the appropriate lessons for the occasion. Tommy knew a young employee like Billy had likely not yet developed a sense of loyalty or love for his organization. He wanted Billy to admit to the good things the Rockies had done for him and then understand he had more to give. He also wanted Billy to reflect on what type of commitment he was making to the organization.

Tommy offered Billy a lesson that takes years to fully comprehend—that you *owe* the organization. You owe gratitude, you owe passion, you owe loyalty, you owe love, and you owe your undying commitment. That's how Tommy has spent 60-plus years with the Los Angeles Dodgers.

TIP: "Give the organization your heart!" No one ever said it better.

Organizational Hierarchy

The simple act of *existing* in an MLB organization at the start of your career can be difficult because you're in unfamiliar territory. Although departments and employees attempt to work toward a common goal, there can be divergent opinions or agendas among them. You may be called upon to express your views of a particular situation, and your opinion may differ from some of your colleagues' opinions. You must also coordinate between departments, as duties will intersect from time to time. Knowing how to act or respond to situations constructively may depend on your understanding of the "organizational hierarchy."

The Flow Chart

An organization's *flow chart* illustrates its lines of authority and communication. From top to bottom, these lines of authority should guide you when dealing with employees in your department and all other departments. The chart in Figure 6.2 diagrams the communication channels necessary to keep concerned personnel informed of important issues.

Figure 6.2

Baseball Operations Flow Chart

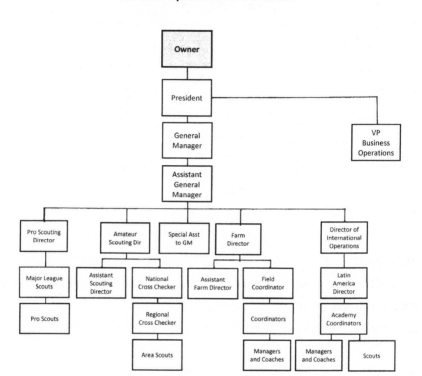

Organizations will vary as some Scouting or Farm Directors will be titled as Assistant General Managers, or Vice Presidents

Effective Communication from the Bottom

In an entry-level position, if you were any lower on the flow chart, you wouldn't even be in the organization! This fact should enlighten you to respect others and effectively communicate with anyone involved in what you are doing. I say this because I have witnessed many employees and even high-level executives create negative issues by failing to adhere to this "chain of command." Missteps occur when employees skip over authority levels. Lines of authority and communication should be easily understood both for positions at the top and at the bottom of the chart.

For example, if the GM communicates a plan of action to a department director but doesn't alert the VP overseeing that department, what happens? That VP may feel as if he/she lacked the proper authority to affect change in the organization. The VP should learn about the GM's plan for the department under his/her watch firsthand, not secondhand or the VP might believe his/her opinion is not valued.

The same applies throughout the organization. When a pitching coach doesn't inform the Minor League pitching coordinator of a strategy to develop a pitcher, the coordinator may feel frustrated, believing he had no input into the strategy. More than that, the coordinator may feel disrespected by the lack of communication and an opportunity to impart his perspective.

TIP: Make everyone in the direct line of authority aware of your activities. You'll benefit from the opinions of others and that can limit the probability of missteps and save you from creating a negative situation.

Effective Communication with Your Boss

A first-year employee may feel intimidated at times. If that's you, the normal tendency is to keep your head down, keep your mouth shut, and do your work *(if you're smart).* As such, this situation may lead to a lack of interaction with your boss if you're not careful.

Be aware of *your* need to effectively communicate and make it a point to update your boss on a regular basis. Don't wait for the boss to ask about your work assignments; take the lead. Some bosses feel they are imposing if they ask about your assignments too often. They might even hesitate to inquire, even though they are curious. What should you do? Ask the boss regularly if he/she wants updates on your work assignments.

TIP: Do not let three days pass without some type of update on your work-related activities with your immediate supervisor.

Keep department employees informed of your whereabouts at all times. You never know when someone will look for you, so tell your boss your schedule *in advance.* It's easy for people to jump to negative conclusions when they have no idea of your physical location. The last question you want to answer is, "Where were you?"

E-mails are the best way to document your schedule. Do *not* rely on word of mouth! *(Okay, you don't have to e-mail that you are going to lunch, but make sure you tell your boss you are getting something to eat and offer to bring back a sandwich—a classic brown-nose move.)*

Almost all issues or misunderstandings involving first-year staff seem to result from poor communication. Achieving perfect communication would be like batting 1.000; it will never happen. However, striving for perfect communication is realistic. Communicate with your boss for guidance. That person is your safety net.

TIP: As your first order of business, for every aspect of your new job, make a detailed plan for effective communication in your department and beyond.

Baseball Operations and Business Operations

If your first position is in Baseball Operations and you are interacting with someone in Business Operations, adhere to the flow chart and respect position levels. Respect these lines of authority (Director, VP, etc.) across the entire organization. On occasion, when you are involved in activities of another department, you will be required to perform duties for the benefit of the organization. Complete these tasks with the same diligence you would display in your normal duties.

Many Baseball Operations employees have been looked on negatively because they lacked enthusiasm for duties outside of their normal realm of activity. All duties should be completed in the best interest of the club, with an "organization first" mentality.

TIP: If you're ever approached by a club official other than your immediate supervisor and given an assignment, tell your boss immediately to keep him/her informed. If you set up a standard practice of keeping your boss in the loop, you should rarely be involved in any issues that cast you in a negative light.

Practical Guidelines in Your First Job

Stay under the Radar

When you step into an organization, you will be introduced to many people in various aspects as the new employee—a rookie. Every MLB club has the common goal of success. They call a professional baseball club a "club" for a reason *(definition: an association of two or more people with a common interest or goal).*

Therefore, existing employees want to make sure the rookies are people the club can rely on to attain success. Soon after you arrive as a new member of the club, everyone will be curious about you and your background. They'll also want to make sure you fit in, and they act like dogs in the park sniffing out the tails of the newcomers (or another part of their anatomy).

☐ Does he/she seem like a good person?

☐ Do you like him/her?

☐ Can he/she do the job?

Meeting all of the club's employees takes time, especially if you've taken a field job in Scouting or Player Development. The worst-case scenario is when employees you haven't yet met learn your name after hearing something negative about you or your job performance. You want all employee discussions concerning you and your ability to be complimentary so you can build a good reputation and create positive momentum for your career. Believe it or not, the reputation established at the start of your career can follow you throughout your working life. Positive or negative; it's up to you.

I suggest you stay under the radar so no drama gets attached to your name. If it feels like you're being slighted, let it go. You have too much at risk if you worry about trivial issues early on. Take what they give you and don't ask for anything more.

Sometimes, a new employee runs the risk of being labeled "entitled" *(a common word "old folks" use to characterize millennials)*. Don't think you're entitled to what the club offers to employees with multiple years of service. Wait your turn.

How to Stay Under the Radar

Here are a few helpful hints to stay under the radar:

1. Maintain a positive approach and don't draw negative attention to yourself.

2. Avoid confrontations with anyone at any time. Your first goal is to build a positive reputation within the organization, not win an argument. (Keep your cool.)

3. Show up early and stay late. Beat your boss to work and leave later than he/she does.

4. Don't finish your assignments *on time*; complete them *early*.

5. Keep your mouth shut—unless someone asks you a question or you ask one.

6. Don't inject yourself into situations that don't involve you.

7. Keep your use of alcohol to a minimum. *(I have seen many negative employee issues associated with the use of alcohol at team functions.)*

8. Similar to other "high-profile" businesses, you are always a representative of the organization. Whether you're at work or not, act appropriately.

9. Dating another employee within the organization is frowned upon. No fishing off the company pier. *(Okay, but be discreet.)*

In your first year, establish yourself as a reliable, respected employee. Act humbly. Conduct your business professionally with a quiet confidence. Attend all of the "optional" *(in your first year, "optional" means "mandatory")* functions, and show you feel proud to be part of the team. Volunteer to help organize team events. Consider yourself a "pledge" as if a club is like a fraternity or sorority *(even Major League players experience good-natured rookie initiation rituals).* Be a "low-maintenance employee." Remember to look for opportunities to pay your dues. Show your respect for tenured employees; your actions toward them reflect how much you admire their years in the game.

Make Life Easier for Your Boss

In your first MLB job, you must recognize if you are making life easier for your boss or if you're making it more difficult.

Middle management and directors of departments contend with a great many issues. In my opinion, middle management is the most difficult position in an organization's hierarchy. Middle managers have to answer to their bosses (maybe the owner) and must know the most detailed aspects of their department and their employees. In Baseball Operations, most staff members are out in the field, so middle managers have little direct contact with them. They may oversee many remote staff members yet spend their time putting out fires and endlessly problem solving. It's very difficult. Understand this: *You are working in your position to help your boss do his/her job.* So in support of your boss, dedicate yourself to finding ways to assist him/her.

These questions can help you gauge your progress as an employee:

- ☐ Do my actions cause my boss to work *more or less?*
- ☐ Do my actions make my boss's job *easier* or *more difficult?*
- ☐ Do my actions cause my boss to *look good* to his bosses, *or bad?*

Let me emphasize the concept behind these questions—*making life easier for your boss!*

Ask these questions of yourself and every one of your co-workers.

- ☐ Do I help my co-workers do their jobs?

☐　Do I make life easier for my co-workers?

☐　Do I help my co-workers look good to the boss?

TIP: Be supportive of everyone around you, especially the BOSS!

My Boss in My First Director Job

Felipe Alou was the Manager of the Montreal Expos when I started there as Farm Director in 1994—my first front office position. An outstanding mentor to me, Felipe was a man I admired greatly. Stoic in demeanor, Felipe never appeared too upset or overly happy, and he spoke only when he deemed it necessary. There was no idle chatter with him. I believe Felipe Alou to be one of the most intelligent men I've ever met in professional baseball. He taught me lessons that have lasted my entire career. I took his answers to my questions as gospel because of the respect I had for his intellect.

When I started working with him regularly, I'd go into his office and discuss the business of the day. I'd update him on the Minor League players and the happenings in the department. He mostly listened. Every day when I departed from his office, I'd ask him if he needed anything. He typically didn't, but I asked him every time.

Working with Felipe, I was never sure what he thought about my decision-making. He was tough to read. After a couple of months, I was in need of assurance that he liked how I was performing my job. Did he trust my judgment and, more important, did he trust me in my first director-level position in MLB? I wished he'd tell me something—anything!

As if he were reading my mind, one day Felipe asked to speak to me. He had never before asked for me; I'd go to his office on my own. What could it be?

I entered Felipe's office, sat down, and had a not-so-typical personal conversation. It took me by surprise. Felipe spoke of his love for fishing, his brothers, and his childhood in Haina, Dominican Republic. I spoke of my wife Bonnie and how our first child would be born soon, my daughter Rachel. We had a pleasant, friendly conversation.

"Mr. Geivett, we have worked together for a couple of months now," Felipe began.

"Yes sir," I responded, wondering where this was going.

"Do you know exactly when I knew I could rely on you?" asked Felipe.

"No," I responded while thinking, did he just say he could rely on me?

"When you left my office the very first day we worked together, and you asked me if I needed anything. That was when I knew you were here to help me.

I learned how that simple question carried great meaning for Felipe. I was only making sure he had everything he needed to do his job. In return, he recognized my desire to help him and trusted me as a person to be there when he needed assistance. It was the biggest compliment I could ever receive—that he trusted me to help him.

I'm positive Felipe took an interest in mentoring me because of the interest I'd shown in helping him. In the same way, one of your responsibilities as a member of the "club" is to help others do their jobs. The people who say "that's not my job" won't become valued, respected teammates.

TIP: Do not attempt to hide behind a job description. If an employee needs help, it means the organization needs help. Do what you can to assist! When you establish the reputation of somebody who helps others, you set the foundation for a long career in MLB.

Summary

☐ Create positive momentum for a career.

☐ Assume the posture of a student.

☐ Act like a prospect.

☐ Put the organization first.

☐ TIME?

☐ Always communicate effectively.

☐ Perform duties outside of your normal scope to benefit the organization.

☐ Stay under the radar.

☐ Make life easier for all employees.

CHAPTER 7:

A FRAMEWORK OF PROGRESSIVE THOUGHT

A New Age of Professional Baseball

The Game that Never Changes?

GIVEN ITS LONG-HELD, WELL-EARNED REPUTATION OF RESISTING CHANGE, professional baseball has preserved many traditional aspects of the game. Similar elements from different eras can be compared. Because few new ideas have penetrated our seemingly stubborn "grand old game," even necessary advents take longer than they should.

Lately, though, I've noticed something peculiar happening in professional baseball. And though it may not be popular with the game's traditionalists, I believe a new age of Major League Baseball may be upon us. For example, MLB appears to be more willing to adopt uncharacteristically progressive ideas to improve the game. With the agreement of the MLB Players Association, the following practices have been recently enacted:

- ☐ performance-enhancing drug testing

- ☐ regulations to decrease game times

- ☐ video replay to assist umpires

- ☐ use of technology in the dugout

- ☐ regulations in expenditures on amateur player signings

In addition, MLB organizations are embracing a more "data-centric" approach to solving their day-to-day club issues. They're also putting progressive-thinking leadership in place. The digital age of technology is gaining solid footing. All of this makes baseball more receptive to change.

New Theories and Applications

With passing time, some of the lessons we've learned have become archaic in today's evolving environment. The progress of modern technology and advanced study of the game have complicated the landscape. Astute baseball aficionados are developing advanced theories. How can past lessons and new discoveries be combined in the present? If they're applied appropriately, they can help make all aspects of Baseball Operations more efficient. Some may even revolutionize the game of baseball (as depicted in the book and movie *Moneyball*). Advanced technology can have a tremendous impact as club employees transform these theories into practical applications. But how? You need a plan to apply any progressive ideas. And it starts with a collective mindset and dedication to finding a better way.

Blueprint for Guiding Actions

Before turning your attention to the challenging pursuits of Scouting and Player Development in Chapters 8 - 18, let me introduce a basic thought process—a pattern of thinking that provides a blueprint to guide your actions. It's an *executive-level* approach that aims to examine issues while designing solutions and properly executing a plan. To identify, design, and alter strategies in line with a stated mission, ask these questions:

☐ What is truly important?

☐ What are the strategies designed to achieve what is important?

☐ How can we solve issues and repeat successes?

Each duty required in Scouting and Player Development can make a positive or negative impact on the Major League club's future performance. That means identifying each critical responsibility and then developing all of them. This work must be consistent with and designed to achieve what's important to the Major League club at the executive level—*a view from the top!*

An Executive-Level Perspective

Horizontal Recall

People tend to learn aspects of professional baseball "horizontally," remembering the detailed aspects of their job at their particular level. If the staff member is a Minor League pitching coach in Rookie-Ball, he will assiduously study the art of coaching pitchers in Rookie-Ball. Often, following a promotion to a higher level, he looks to those lessons learned in Rookie-Ball, but they may not apply at the higher levels where pitchers are more experienced and emotionally mature. They have also likely developed better skills and proper fundamentals. A change of perspective is required. Pitching coaches have to alter their thinking and employ different strategies to account for the change in circumstances.

Vertical Understanding

Relying solely on lessons from the past or what someone has told you at lower levels makes your transition into new roles more difficult than need be. Understanding the entire plan for the department puts you in a good position to make the appropriate adjustments. More than that, employing the correct strategies for whatever position you hold comes by truly understanding the organizational philosophy.

TIP: Know the plan for the entire organization from top to bottom. It allows you to know what's important at each level and each department.

The Concept of a Basic Construct

Do you understand the concept of a "basic construct"? (*Definition: to form by assembling or combining parts/elements*) Here's how it works.

The Architect

Chapter 3 pointed out that every action begins with a thought. House construction isn't initiated by pouring the cement for the foundation. A plan comes first. It starts with the architect's drawings of the finished product. YOU are the architect!

A Baseball Operations Department is charged with assembling a championship team. Its combining elements are the collection of players on the Major League roster. You also apply this concept to individual players, so when you "assemble" a championship Major League player, the combining elements are the championship player's individual skills. (*If it sounds as if we are manufacturing a product, it's true.*) The questions to ask are:

☐ What are we trying to build?

☐ Who is involved with the process?

☐ What are the strategies to build it?

This is a straightforward strategy for producing a desired end result.

An Eye on the Future

Future success calls for designing a basic construct assembled to produce the desired result. It must be one that can handle progressive thought and changing situations—not be beholden to the past. Future employees of professional baseball clubs will be forward thinkers—men and women unbound by past constraints and traditions. That requires scrutinizing all aspects of the realm for improved results and possessing the will to improve the product.

TIP: Use your basic construct as the architect's blueprint of how to assemble the desired product. Maintain an eye on the future and look to improve the construct itself.

Combining Elements

In planning the basic construct and then developing it, you must ensure the individual elements work efficiently when combined. For example, various aspects of a Baseball Operations Department must work in unison to achieve the best product. Scouting must be in concert with Player Development, and these two departments must fit the overall agenda of the Major League club and its organizational philosophy. Then, beyond Baseball Operations, the entire organization must work together and allow all departments to influence the development of the basic construct when applicable. The best construct works within the scope of an entire organization.

TIP: Channel your ideas into a specific area of attention and then coordinate a comprehensive strategy to apply within the organization. Remember, you're forming your own construct for a desired result with no inhibitions. Your pre-conceived ideas of what you have learned in the past may or may not fit. That is up to you.

Media Relations Example

Let's use one responsibility of Major League players as an example of the desired product. Players are representatives of the entire organization and often have interactions with different departments within the club. Therefore, the construct must include perspectives from all of the departments. For the players to be the best possible media representatives for the organization, what is your basic construct for player media-relations development? Consider these possibilities:

☐ Should the amateur scouts be concerned with how high school or college prospects deal with the media? Should the professional scouts?

☐ What are the overall media development strategies in Player Development?

☐ What is the media development strategy for the Latin American Academy?

☐ What is the media development strategy in A-Ball?

☐ What is the media development strategy in AA or AAA?

☐ What involvement does the Public Relations Department have with the Minor Leagues?

☐ Should you involve the club's broadcast partners in the media development plan?

☐ Who manages media issues with MLB players? Front office or manager?

☐ Should player guidelines for social media posts be imposed?

You started in the Major Leagues with an issue, examined the Scouting Department, worked your way through Player Development, considered other departments in the organization, and then returned to the Major Leagues. This series of questions was designed so you could apply an "executive-level" perspective and create the best possible strategy for the finished product. You can also use this approach to find a solution that fixes a problem. With a specific goal in mind, you examined the entire organization to find the best course of action for preparing your players to be the best media representatives for your club. The questions didn't allow you to think from the perspective of a limited role. Instead, you would have to complete a comprehensive plan involving a vertical organization. You considered these questions:

- [ ] What are we trying to build? *(A media darling at the Major League level)*

- [ ] Who is involved with the process? *(Members of the entire organization)*

- [ ] What are the strategies to build it? *(You have to answer this.)*

To review, you begin with knowing the *end product* in the Major Leagues. Then you *form a construct* throughout the entire organization for the desired result. With this *vertical* perspective, you understand the importance of your individual duties related to the *end product,* no matter what position you occupy in the organization. Every duty will be an integral part of developing that championship team or player. This means no matter what job you hold, you're in a good position to arrive at resolutions that will accomplish things better than in the past and are consistent with the *organizational philosophy.*

TIP: Do not rely only on what you have learned or your own experiences. Rather, create and execute a plan that fits into the framework and goals of the organization.

Example of Increased Need for Base Stealing

Here's another example scenario. The recent decline of hitting and offense in MLB has made some organizations believe in an increased need for *base stealing.* The goal, therefore, is to steal more bases. You'd ask these questions:

- [ ] Do your scouts value speed appropriately when they evaluate amateur players?

- [ ] Do your scouts differentiate between a player's speed versus ability to steal bases?

- [ ] Does your statistical analysis account for this base stealing goal?

- [ ] Does your statistical analysis properly value stolen bases?

☐ What is your speed program in the Strength and Conditioning Department?

☐ What is your organizational philosophy of base stealing?

☐ How do you teach base stealing throughout the Player Development Department?

☐ How much time do you devote to base stealing in Spring Training? During the season?

☐ Do you emphasize the delay steal for your slower runners?

☐ How much should you use video to teach base stealing?

☐ Does each Minor League team have a staff member responsible for base stealing?

☐ Does your Major League advance scout study opposing pitchers for keys to base stealing?

☐ Do your Major League players study video of opposing pitchers for keys to stealing bases?

☐ Do you have count tendencies for pick-off attempts of each opposing pitcher?

☐ Do your base runners "look in" to see opposing catcher's signs for off-speed pitches or pick-off attempts?

☐ Do you have the opposing manager's count tendencies for pitchouts?

☐ Do you review count tendencies of your manager for when his players attempt to steal?

☐ Is the opposition stealing your signs?

☐ Have you highlighted base stealing as an organizational characteristic?

☐ Should you examine a virtual reality device to help train base stealers?

You get the picture *(this could go on forever)*. Answering these questions helps you to see how an organization works to solve problems or gain the desired end product.

TIP: Use your executive-level perspective to discern the best course of action and execute the strategies that create the desired result. Don't attempt to be an expert at all different levels of baseball. Instead, focus on implementing the strategies that align with the organizational objectives. Also focus on the specific aspects of your specialty. The more you direct your attention to studying specific aspects of baseball, the more problem-solving strategies you will amass.

The concept of a basic construct helps you dissect a particular aspect *(player media skills or need for base stealing)* and form the best possible practical application framework. In a similar way, you can examine any particular issue at the Major League level and plan a construct throughout the entire organization, vertical understanding.

Plan the Work and Work the Plan

My First Personal Guarantee: I try to never make guarantees! In this unpredictable game of baseball, it would directly contradict my instincts to make a guarantee. However, I feel so confident on one subject that I will make an exception. I will guarantee that if you ever acquire the position of department director (or higher), one of your bosses will ask you one day, "What is our organizational strategy for _____?" By thinking in terms of a vertical basic construct, you can have a complete and thorough answer for the boss. *(As my old friend Joe Kerrigan, former Major League manager and pitching coach, used to say, "Plan the work, and then work the plan.")*

Create Documentation for Review

A key strategy for assisting club executives in leadership of successful departments is providing documentation for their review. Especially in an ever-changing environment, you must have the ability to analyze your department's activities and recognize where problems exist. How can you have a specific remedy for a problem when you don't have a record of what you've done? How can you effectively fix the issue when you have not documented and reviewed all of the activities in place? If you don't, you have no way of ascertaining what needs to be done to solve problems.

Forming a basic construct allows you to detail important strategies while you are planning. You will know exactly what you are creating and make decisions to create a comprehensive strategy. Then, as you monitor the results, you're in a better position to decipher what has had a positive impact as well as what is lacking. The construct can be evaluated and modified at any time.

TIP: *Plan the work, work the plan, and then review the results.* These easy steps require discipline but will help you to solve the issues in the department and evaluate how effective strategies have been.

From Thoughts to Action

I suggest building a construct of special interest to you. If you are a statistical guru, select an important sabermetric statistic and form a construct to help the entire organization. For example, On Base Percentage (OB%) is an important statistic to me personally because I believe the more base runners we can create will result in more runs scored. How do you get there? You plan strategies through Scouting and Player Development. You involve other departments as well. For practice, you can choose any aspect of professional baseball, but I suggest selecting a simple construct first. If you select "creating a championship club," you may never have time to finish reading this book!

Summary

Know exactly what you're attempting to attain at the Major League level as you form a way to apply these lessons from this chapter:

☐ Acknowledge that advanced study has changed the game of baseball.

☐ Maintain an executive-level perspective.

☐ Form a construct to plan your work.

☐ Maintain a focus on improving your product.

☐ Look at solving issues with a vertical perspective.

☐ Include the entire organization in your construct.

☐ Plan the work and work the plan.

☐ Document for review.

This chapter has provided an executive-level perspective so you can form specific constructs related to your specialty that work throughout the organization. See yourself as the executive and the architect. Think for yourself; don't merely recall past strategies. At the same time, add your unique talents, and be mindful of this ever-changing game.

First, understand the executive-level goals and then imagine how you can make it better than it has ever been. Next, develop a conceptual understanding of what you'd like to build, form the basic construct to plan, and implement your goal.

You now have a framework of how to think about solving issues. Any company's best employees understand the thought-processes of the executives and formulate their work to attain the goals of leadership. Their innovations align with the stated executive direction.

So no matter what position you hold in an organization, consider the perspective of an executive and act accordingly. You may be one someday.

CHAPTER 8:

SCOUTING—SUCCESS STARTS HERE

Unsung Laborers

IN MY OPINION, PROFESSIONAL BASEBALL HAS NEVER SHOWN THE APPRO-
priate recognition for a group of people who play an extremely important
role developing championship teams. They are the unsung laborers of the
game and the backbone of any successful organization. They spend half of
the year traveling for their jobs, with most of them knowing the slightest
nuances of every hotel chain in existence. They have to skip special family events because of their job responsibilities, experiencing memorable
occasions through photos or videos instead of firsthand. They sacrifice as
much *(or more)* than any other set of employees in a professional baseball organization. They routinely work away from their club's home city,
yet remain dedicated and loyal to their organization. None of them get
handsomely compensated, but they work for the love of the game. It seems
Tracy Ringolsby, the Hall of Fame baseball writer, has taken the lead as the
media person who goes out of his way to support and celebrate them. Most
baseball writers and broadcasters fail to recognize this group of employees.

Even to the most ardent baseball fans, they are anonymous. They
receive little reward *(not proportionate to their contributions)* and they usually seek only one desire from their ball club—an employee contract for
the next season.

They are the scouts!

Don Lindeberg (1915-2006)

Don Lindeberg had more than 50 years in baseball scouting, mostly with the Yankees but also the Dodgers, White Sox, Royals, Indians, and Devil Rays. He started as a personal assistant to Branch Rickey following his Minor League playing career after World War II. His baseball playing career was broken up by his military service as a Navy fighter pilot.

To this day, I have never seen a better one-look scout than Lindy. He could watch a hitter take a couple of swings and tell if he was a future big-leaguer or not—an uncanny ability. As he got up in years, Lindy might have dozed off occasionally during the game, especially while scouting all-day tournaments. Still, I thought he could see through his eyelids!

He knew the players and had a keen sense of their abilities. Possibly scouting was just too darn easy for Lindy. I couldn't believe his accuracy, and I would pay special attention to the players he liked, hoping to catch him with an incorrect assessment of a player. I used to think, "Nobody can be that good of a scout to see a player for one game and have that guy figured out."

A few years after our NY Yankee days together and just before the Amateur June Draft, I bumped into Lindy at a game at Cal State Fullerton. He'd tell stories about Mr. Rickey and others from a time of professional baseball long since passed. I loved Lindy's stories. He'd also "break down" the player we were scouting, and we'd discuss his future potential.

Now, every scout in Southern California was in attendance to watch this Fullerton college game. Plus, scouting directors and national cross-checkers representing nearly every Major League club had flown into town specifically for it. That night, Lindy seemed particularly critical of the college player we were scouting, but he loved the high school kid at Long Beach Poly

High School he'd scouted for the first time the day before. Why hadn't the others flown in one day earlier to see Lindy's high school player?

Then Lindy said he'd give this high school kid anything he wanted to sign a contract. Anything? I'd never heard him say that before! He boldly added, "He's an All-Star." That got me excited. In essence, he was saying the player was one of the best players he'd ever scouted and would be an All-Star in MLB.

Still, I thought, "Give me a break! Lindy is getting pretty old. He only saw the kid one time. Maybe his one-look skills have deteriorated."

I'm ashamed to admit my desire to use this opportunity to prove Lindy wrong. I recall thinking, "I'm going to get Lindy this time! His remarkable run of one-look scouting is about to come to an end."

After spotting other scouts at the Fullerton game, I excused myself from conversing with Lindy to ask them about the kid at Long Beach Poly High. The scouts working Southern California would know him better than anyone. From them, I learned the kid was a well-known prospect and a good hitter. Some scouts questioned his defensive skills, while others were worried about his power potential. "Good hitter and good worker" was the general consensus sprinkled with a few concerns about his Major League ability. Not one scout called him a future All-Star.

After that, I made up my mind to keep track of this kid from Poly High and try to prove Lindy wrong. I told him his All-Star comment was recorded and duly noted. This veteran scout didn't seem bothered by my challenge; he just laughed it off (false confidence, I thought). So I followed the careers of both the kid and the college prospect for the next few years. The college player (I'm not naming him on purpose) eventually signed a contract with an MLB club. He played well in the Minors but was never promoted to the Majors. The kid from Poly High was drafted that year and chose not to sign a professional contract. Instead, he accepted a scholarship to UCLA.

Lindy kept scouting until his health gave out, and he died at age 91 in 2006. That same year, the kid from Long Beach Poly High—Chase Utley—played in his first MLB All-Star Game. Somehow I know Lindy is looking down and laughing at me.

The Art and Study of Scouting

Scouting is the art and study of comparing baseball players. The "art" represents the *subjective* element reflecting personal taste and opinion. It requires human perception to ascertain the future value of a baseball player in MLB. The "study" represents an *objective* element with statistical analysis and/or reference information. Opinions are formed by studying relevant historical data to discern a player's value. The art and study combine to provide an assessment of a particular prospect based on the value in MLB.

The Eyes of True Artists

Historically, scouts have been credited for applying the element of art in their job as if they have a magic crystal ball to foresee the future. Over time, they gain a "gut feel" and an "eye" for predicting who can play in the Major Leagues successfully. Remember the romantic depiction of an old scout relying on nothing but his instinct to find the undiscovered "diamond in the rough"? They're true artists.

Scouts are perceived to push aside objective methods including statistical information and historical reference. Many people think they won't use any measures beyond their own human sensory perception. They trust *only their eyes* when they evaluate players.

Not true. Scouts today use all measures available to discern the best players for their organization. Information on a player's history has become increasingly available in this digital era—and more detailed than in years past. Study has become commonplace *and* required by every MLB organization to assess prospective players accurately. Time-tested predictions they employ come by judging with a blend of art and study.

What some consider "art" I believe is actually "study" that's verbally passed down through the years from scouts of yesteryear to present-day evaluators. Naturally, some scouts rely on statistical analytical data more than others, and all scouts take historical reference into consideration. Individual discretion plays a big role; so does using a framework for evaluating players.

A Framework for Player Evaluation

An Organized Progression

No matter how you believe scouts *should* arrive at their player assessments, this chapter examines the art and study of baseball scouting. Advanced statistical analytical baseball research has improved and will continue to progress. It's up to you to determine the amount of credence it deserves.

As a scout, your ability to judge baseball talent with your eyes will also improve with experience. It will be at your discretion how much credence your eyes deserve. Either way, to hold a position in Baseball Operations requires the ability to evaluate players, which is why I offer a "framework" for making player evaluation decisions.

Bigger, Faster, Stronger

If you have played in Little League, you likely have nightmare stories about the best player in the league: the kid who was bigger and stronger than everyone else; threw harder than any other pitcher in the league; hit the ball farther than any other player in Little League history; struck tremendous fear in the opposition; had to shave between innings; and brought his birth certificate to the games to prove he wasn't too old! *(My best player nightmare was Reid Rousseau. I still have a bruise on my leg from when he drilled me with a fastball at age 10.)*

From Little League to the Major Leagues

The game of baseball turns full circle from Little League to the Major Leagues. In Little League, the best players are supremely advanced physically compared to their teammates and competitors, and they dominate the game. In terms of physical prowess, they have no peers.

In high school and college baseball, though, the more intellectual players become the better players as they use strategy and technique to gain an advantage over the physically gifted. The biggest and strongest can get outfoxed by these "students of the game."

Then in professional baseball, the circle turns back toward the biggest and strongest because all competitors have close to an equal amount of physical ability. The biggest and strongest must now look to strategy and technique for their competitive advantage. They must develop intellectually, devising ways to nullify the effects of the strategies that had given them trouble in the past. By making the necessary adjustments, they can realize their baseball potential.

Experienced MLB players accustomed to various strategies can adjust to the tactics of the opposition. They're difficult to outfox because they've seen all the tricks over the years. Again, in the Major Leagues, physical characteristics determine the best players. For example, a relief pitcher with an outstanding fastball may not have to use his other pitches in a strategic way if he can power past hitters with the devastating velocity of his fastball. Why throw the other pitches when he knows they can't catch up to the heat? However, countering this one-dimensional approach is the hitter who can hit high-velocity fastballs. The pitch execution may be great, but it could still result in a home run and a souvenir for a lucky fan. Much like they did in Little League, physical characteristics have the edge at the Major League level.

Players Still Need Strategy and Techniques

Don't assume I undervalue strategy and technique as it relates to this concept. Major League players have to possess a certain level of proficiency in strategy and technique to remain in the league. Players who aren't proficient in these exist in every sport. Examples are the college football player and first-round draft pick who never lived up to his expectations in the National Football League and the talented college basketball player and high draft pick who could not survive in the National Basketball Association.

These players had all of the physical gifts necessary to be successful *(those leagues have scouts, too),* but they couldn't make the strategy or technique adjustment in a league where similar physical gifts are common. When they do make the required adjustments in strategy or technique, they can be among the best players again.

Learning Scouting from One of the Greats

Bill Livesey

I began scouting with the New York Yankees in 1991, and my boss at that time was VP of Player Development and Scouting Bill Livesey.

Between 1996 and 2000, the NY Yankees won four out of five World Series Championships with a core group of players drafted and developed under Bill Livesey's direction. I believe Bill Livesey (NY Yankees) and Paul Snyder (ATL Braves) were the best in Scouting and Player Development in modern MLB history. Bill Livesey credits: Derek Jeter, Bernie Williams, Andy Pettitte, Mariano Rivera, Jorge Posada, among many others. Mr. Livesey set my foundation for scouting and player development, and I could not have had a better mentor. He spent countless hours helping me. Conceptually, he believed in the power of the team and player profile. I know good decisions I made later in my career directly resulted from lessons learned under his tutelage. I cannot thank him enough.

Choosing the Right Car

Think of choosing a car that goes on long journeys covering thousands of miles and lasting many years. It must be a sturdy car that *sustains accidents* and yet continues to move toward the destination. *(It's in fantastic mechanical condition.)* Your car will be required to work hard climbing hills so it must have the necessary power. *(It's strong and powerful.)* The trip covers *uneven* terrain, so the car will have to steer clear of trouble. *(It's nimble with an ability to maneuver and avoid the issues ahead.)*

That also describes the type of body needed by a Major League player who faces a long, tough, and rocky road during a lengthy playing career in MLB. *(This body is durable, strong, and athletic.)*

My Scouting Education Begins

By the start of the 1992 college baseball season, I had fully prepared myself as an area scout for the NY Yankees (or so I thought). To make a good first impression, I arrived at the LAX Airport Marriott about an hour and a half before I was to meet with my boss Bill Livesey. I used the hotel lobby phone (dating myself) to call to his room and say I was ready for whenever he wanted to depart for the upcoming game. To my surprise, he replied he'd come down to the lobby immediately. We drove north on the Pacific Coast Highway toward Pepperdine University in Malibu. The Pepperdine Waves were hosting the University of Southern California (USC) Trojans that day. Pepperdine had an outstanding pitcher named Derek Wallace we wanted to scout.

Instead of arriving extremely early at the ballpark, Mr. Livesey suggested we stop at a "diner" to have coffee. (I didn't think it was appropriate to tell this East Coast guy, and my boss, that Malibu doesn't have diners.) I stopped at a local coffee/herbal teahouse, and we sat down.

At this time, I'd been a NY Yankees scout for only a few months, but I already believed I'd mastered the activity of scouting (delusional). I anticipated showing this big shot from the East how much baseball we knew on the West Coast. (There was no way to stop my California cockiness from coming out.)

But I'd hardly gotten started when one thing became instantly obvious to me. Mr. Livesey had not come to California to listen to me brag about my knowledge of baseball; he had come to teach me how to scout. He showed no interest in my opinion, nor did he ask for it. As he talked, I listened.

He began by describing a car. (Were we working for a baseball club or a car dealership?) But two minutes into the lecture, I understood I was in the presence of a "master teacher." This became a special day—the day my scouting education began.

As he lectured, he wrote down lessons for me on thin white coffee/herbal teahouse napkins. I was gathering them and stuffing them in my pockets as if they were gold. In fact, they were more valuable than gold! Completely enthralled in every detail he offered, I hadn't noticed 90 minutes fly by. Suddenly, I looked at my watch. We had to get to the ballpark. (My pockets were full anyway.)

Once in the car, I faced reality. I really hadn't known much about scouting before meeting Mr. Livesey. I was a mere student and I was fortunate to be mentored by a man who had a unique perspective and detailed insight into scouting. Not only that, he could teach it in simple ways.

I thanked Mr. Livesey for his time and the detailed lesson. As we drove to Pepperdine, he told me about his former NY Yankee boss, Jack Butterfield, who had died in an automobile accident. Jack had handed down these same lessons to Bill Livesey. Now, they had been passed down to me.

Both mentors had been offering the "car story" for years as a way to present a foundation in player evaluation. A player's long-term future success is largely determined by the vehicle in which he makes the journey—his body. The body will or won't allow the opportunity for the player to achieve a high level of performance and sustain it. The career will go only as far as the body will take it.

A Whole New Way of Thinking

That day, I scouted the game between Pepperdine and USC equipped with my newfound knowledge. I liked the Pepperdine pitcher Wallace for his wiry strong athletic body (adds strength) and his well-above-average fastball velocity. I also spotted another kid who played for USC. I liked him for his athletic body and potential for future strength, combined with his fluid baseball skills. This skinny freshman—future Major Leaguer Aaron Boone—wasn't eligible to draft yet. But with his athletic ability and future strength, I deemed he could make the journey. Would I have thought the same way about Boone before the "car" lecture? Probably not. I would have liked freshman Aaron Boone for his advanced baseball skills, but I wouldn't have known the strategy to compare his athletic ability to Major League players. And I wouldn't have been as focused on his body to predict his future strength as required at the Major League level. Previously, if he had performed well that particular game, I would have liked him. If he had not performed well, I would not have seen beyond that poor performance. I had been scouting only what was happening in the present and offering a general level of improvement to all players.

At that Malibu coffee/herbal teahouse, Mr. Livesey had been teaching me to see into the future as evidenced by the thin white napkins that had filled my pockets. He taught me the foundation of player evaluation: projection (definition: an estimate or forecast of a future situation or trend based on a study of present ones).

My job was to predict the future. (Is that art or study?)

A Practical Analysis of Physical Characteristics

What "Plays" at the Major League Level?

As a scout, you must have an understanding of what "plays" at the Major League level. How can you successfully evaluate future players without having a firm grasp of the physical characteristics of the players who participate at that level? First and foremost, to know what type of body is generally common, study the Major Leagues.

Determine What's "Average"

Many veteran scouts have adages handed down from the past for characteristics you don't often see in Major League players: redheads, square shoulders, no ass, and so on. *(We won't go there! But remember them anyway; you never know!)* What exactly determines the common physical characteristics of players in the Major Leagues? Scouts start by giving them the "eye test," which doesn't mean judging the "player's vision." Use "your eyes" to gauge the size, strength, and athletic ability of Major League players. *(Art or study?)*

The "Eye Test"

While attending a Major League game, examine the players to judge their size, physique, and strength. Watch them move around the field to sense their level of athleticism. Acquire a sense for what's common among Major League players. To draw comparisons of their physical characteristics, separate them into the positions they play. Then draw comparisons to gain a sense of common or "average" physical traits. You'll gain valuable insight into the type of physical characteristics that are consistently prevalent at different positions on the field.

☐ What is the common size/strength/athleticism of Major League position players?

☐ What is the common size/strength/athleticism of Major League pitchers?

As you compare them, find some consistencies in their physical characteristics. You must gain this sense of "normal" at the Major League level to properly judge prospective players against it. Does the young player have the body type and athleticism consistent with what you believe to be common in a Major League player? Does he possess the potential for strength as he physically matures? *(Art or study?)*

Consider Size, Not Height

When I refer to *size*, I don't mean *height.* I understand that tall pitchers may enjoy an advantage over short ones, but height is an irrelevant predictor of future Major League performance. Two players who have enjoyed success in the Major Leagues are Mike Trout and José Altuve. *Nobody would mistake them for being tall.* Randy Johnson was a tall pitcher, but Pedro Martinez and Greg Maddux were not.

TIP: As you look to what's common, don't attempt to quantify specific guidelines for height. Instead, look for a general sense of the "average" size, strength, and athleticism.

Building a Scale

"Average" is the Equilibrium

"Average" at the Major League level must be ingrained in your mind as a gauge to evaluate the physical attributes of prospects. "Average" becomes the equilibrium of the scale by which a player's physical characteristics are judged. So set the concept of "average" in your mind when assessing the characteristics of a player's body that make up the foundation for developing advanced baseball skills.

When making projections, a player's physical characteristics help you set a foundation for your opinion of his eventual ceiling as a Major League player. If a player possesses average physical attributes of athleticism and strength, it may be safe to say he'd have normal or average development of his skills into the future. The characteristics of the body define your view of the player's future. *(The player's physicality is only part of the equation, but in the mind of many scouts, it's the most important aspect in assessing a player's future potential. I didn't say performance; I said POTENTIAL!)*

What is "Above or Below Average"?

Gaining a sense of what is "most common" allows you to sense what's "most probable." *(Ah, probabilities, a statistical analytical term.)* Scouts routinely judge players based on what's average at the Major League level to decide how probable it would be for a player to succeed in the Major Leagues *(art or study?)*. But what is above average or below average? Once you have a feel for what you deem "average Major League strength" or "average Major League athleticism," you then have the ability to grade "above or below average." If a player possessed above-average athleticism and above-average strength, it may be safe to say that player has an above-average chance to develop his baseball skills in the future. Assuming all else is equal, the player with above-average athleticism and strength is more likely to develop into a Major League player than one of "below-average" athleticism and strength.

I liked Aaron Boone as a prospect because I had graded him as "above average" athletically compared to Major League-level standards. I sensed his "car" would allow him to have only "average" future strength at the Major League level. Still, an above-average athlete with average strength, fluid baseball skills, a great work ethic, no discernible negatives, and a supportive baseball family made Aaron a strong prospect.

"Above Average" Leads to "Exceptional"

Major League Baseball is a league of the "exceptional." Only the most physically gifted and talented will participate at the pinnacle of the sport. The players in MLB today are the best baseball players on the planet. The study of the body and physical characteristics of these players is critical to understanding what is "exceptional." Using "above average" as a guide helps you identify what's truly outstanding.

Outstanding physical ability is reminiscent of the traits of the biggest and strongest players in Little League. They dominated the game with their more advanced physical characteristics compared to their competition. In the same way, physically gifted Major League players can dominate with their physical characteristics when competing against "average" or "below average" players. Defining outstanding means learning to identify which prospect could become one of the best of the best.

Adjustments Require Athleticism—the Common Denominator

Baseball is often described as a game of adjustments. A pitcher must adjust to the hitters because hitters learn to recognize any tendencies the pitcher employs. The hitters must adjust to the pitchers because pitchers learn to exploit any weakness they recognize in hitters. Players also must adjust to higher levels of play and skill. High school baseball players who advance to college baseball face an advanced level of play. They are required to make physical and mental adjustments as they compete against players with a higher skill level than they've ever experienced. More adjustments are needed as they continue their playing careers into professional baseball.

As advanced technology and scouting reports make it easier to detect deficiencies in players, career demands are filled with required adjustments. They also have to adjust to playing injured regularly as the grind of the long season exacts its toll with nagging aches and pains. And veteran players must make adjustments as they attempt to compete with the diminishing skills of an aging body.

Clearly, a player's career is nothing more than a series of adjustments, so a certain level of athleticism is required to execute these adjustments through the years. Only the best athletes make the grade. Athleticism *(definition: physical prowess consisting variously of coordination, dexterity, vigor, stamina, etc.)* is the common denominator regarding the players' physical characteristics *(height and weight, not so much!)*.

Fluidity of movement and body control combined with the strength to maintain it prevail in the players at the highest level of baseball. Good athletes develop their skills quicker than others. They can play hurt and better adjust their game as they age. Among scouts, you'll hear talk of size, strength, and athleticism. If one of these characteristics had to stand alone as the driving force of a player's career, having a high degree of athleticism offers the best chance to succeed.

TIP: As a scout, strive to gain a subjective feel for gauging athleticism. It's an art!

Pitchers ARE Athletes!

The 1985 California Angels' Arizona Instructional League program was nearing completion. We nicknamed this physically demanding camp "De-structional League" because we were physically exhausted by the intense daily workload. Joe Maddon and Bruce Hines made us work hard, but they were "pussy cats" compared to Player Development Coordinators Joe Coleman and Rick Down. These staff members almost killed us with their enthusiasm for work. We constantly complained about them, but we loved them. We wouldn't have traded them for any other coaches in professional baseball.

On Sundays, our only day off, we often enjoyed a rafting trip on the Salt River. One particular Sunday, because of exhaustion, we decided to watch NFL football games on television instead. They sparked a fire in us, inspiring us to go outside to throw a football around. Our young minds had forgotten how physically tired we felt, but this was football, not baseball. After running a few plays against an imaginary defense, we got bored scoring defenseless touchdowns. Against better judgment and team rules (they prohibited basketball, skydiving, football, or anything else that could have been construed as fun), we decided to play a two-on-two variation of football. Chuck Finley and Bryan Harvey versus Willie Fraser and me.

Being the fastest of our group and a position player, I thought I could run circles around these three pitchers. Position players had to hit, run the bases, play defense—we did it all. Of course, I thought that, like all position players, we were better athletes than the pitchers. (In our minds, pitchers were like bowlers. It doesn't take much athletic ability to bowl.) The running joke between pitchers and position players at morning workouts was "athletes meet over here and pitchers over there!"

As our touch football game started, I noticed Chuck was difficult to defend because of his height. He was also quicker than I'd anticipated, and he ran sharp routes. Harv, who had great hands for a big guy, was also quicker than I thought. Chuck and Harv were both difficult to cover because they were strong and could push me away at the line of scrimmage. My teammate Willie made a great receiver with his extra-long arms and big hands. He ran with long strides and could have caught any ball I threw in his vicinity.

As the game progressed, one thing was certain: Our teams were evenly matched and this would be a dogfight!

We battled that day until we remembered how sore and tired we were from our baseball workouts. Willie and I won on the last play of sudden-death overtime. As I walked back into our apartment, I remember thinking how physically impressive those pitchers had been—quick and agile for big guys. They were tough to cover and difficult to block because of their size and strength. I had to give them credit. Their athleticism and strength paved the way for excellent Major League careers. They could make the necessary adjustments with their pitching deliveries to succeed against the best hitters in the world. Because I was completely shocked by their athletic ability, that day has stuck in my mind.

Later in my front office career, I was watching the first day of our 1994 Montreal Expos Florida Instructional League. There were several young players in the Instructional League program I hadn't seen yet. I started by watching the pitchers. Our coaching staff was directing Pitchers Fielding Practice (PFP), and I was eager to see the kids so I could put a face to a name. One kid who had a slender athletic body caught my eye as he was running to cover first base. He sprinted to the bag with the grace and speed of a superior athlete. Watching him reminded me of that day long ago playing football with those three athletic future Major League pitchers.

So I asked Assistant Director of Player Development Neal Huntington, "Who's that kid?"

Neal responded, "The kid we drafted in the fifth round—a high school kid from Puerto Rico. Javier Vasquez."

I watched Javy Vasquez struggle early in his Minor League career, but his athleticism and intelligence allowed him to make adjustments in his delivery. As he improved his strength, he graduated to being a tremendous Major League pitcher. Making his Major

League debut at the age of 21, Javy pitched for 14 years in the Major Leagues.

Even at 18 years old, Javy passed the eye test. The Major League pitcher is an athlete!

Impact and Longevity

Role of Strength and Athleticism

You can tangibly identify the explosive strength or quickness Major League players possess by watching them perform. You can see the raw power of a hitter when he drives the ball out of the ballpark and the tremendous raw speed of a pitcher's fastball as he fires it past hitters. The physical attributes of a player can show us the degree in which his physical characteristics could potentially "impact" the game at the Major League level. Home runs definitely affect games, and power hitters are often recognized for their ability to hit a baseball great distances. Strikeouts definitely affect the game, and strikeout artists are often recognized for their ability to throw the ball with great velocity. In both cases, a high degree of strength (either bat or arm) is required to be considered outstanding. A player's impact, you'd assume, is directly correlated to the degree of strength related to that particular aspect. However, the physical demands of a Major League season exact a toll on every player. The stronger the player, the more strength he may lose and still remain impactful. The players with "well above average" strength may lose some during the season but will still be rated "above average" in strength. The player with "average" strength cannot afford to lose much or will be "below average" in strength toward the end of the season.

In addition, players lose strength and stamina as they get older. To continue to have impact, they must have the necessary athleticism to support their strength while aging.

TIP: While evaluating the strength and athleticism of an individual prospect, be mindful of how the prospect's traits correlate to impact and longevity. Remember that:

- ☐ Strength directly relates to impact (when combined with the necessary athleticism).

- ☐ Athleticism directly relates to longevity (when combined with the necessary physical strength).

The most valuable players in the game at the Major League level have a high degree of impact and longevity. They possess the strength to impact the game and the athleticism to last a long time. Every player inducted into the Major League Baseball Hall of Fame (HOF) has enjoyed a career that can be defined by both impact and longevity. Hall of Famers had significant impact in their era, amassing the career bulk statistics to rank among the best in the history of the game. Examining the strength and athleticism of a prospect leads to a reasonably accurate picture of your opinion of his future potential. It will also define the degree of improvement you believe he can make. The higher the degrees of strength and athleticism, the more confidence you'll have in the player's ability to develops skills and have a future in MLB.

I think it's not possible for a well-below-average athlete with well-below-average strength to play in the Major Leagues. My contention would be, if there's a deficiency in one of these aspects—athleticism or strength—it would have to be made up by the other. To have a career of any longevity at the Major League level, a player is at least "average" in both athleticism and strength. If he is "below average" in one area, then the other must be "above average."

This graph in Figure 8.1 depicts my beliefs about strength and athleticism as they pertain to Major League players. The grade for strength and athleticism must be at least 10.

Figure 8.1

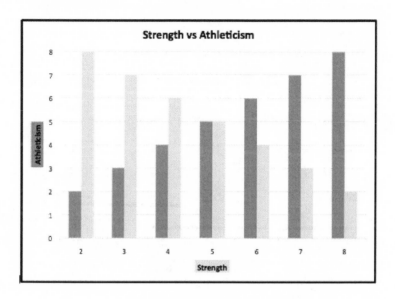

Food for Thought

What current Major League players would you consider to be "below average" in athleticism? Do they make up for it in strength?

Maturity Issues

Players' bodies mature at different ages, with some maturing earlier than others. *(Remember the Little League dominator who was shaving at age 12?)* The human body doesn't follow a strict timeline of athletic ability or maximum strength potential. Youthful, athletic 18-year-old players can still be maturing physically and have yet to develop their peak "man-strength."

These athletic players have difficulty when fatigued. Their youthful bodies do not have the physical strength to maintain proper mechanics or body control when they're physically taxed. Therefore, you can expect the consistency of their performance to improve as they get stronger and their bodies naturally mature.

Conversely, some mature 18-year-old players might have already reached their maximum ability. They might exhibit the strength of fully grown men but can't improve their performance as they get older. Even though they're relatively young chronologically, they have realized their potential. As scouts like to say, they are maxed out.

Assessing the physical maturity of an 18-year-old player is extremely difficult, especially when the best player at a young age can look like "a man among boys." *This is truly an art.* Think back to your own player references and compare the bodies. Trust your instincts and knowledge of an individual's age and normal *(common or average)* physical development. Stick with characteristics you believe to be youthful and those you deem to be mature. Ask these questions:

- ☐ Does he have a baby face?
- ☐ Does he appear young for his age?
- ☐ Does he have well-developed musculature for his age?
- ☐ Does he have a thick body?
- ☐ Is he shaving between innings?

TIP: Give the youthful athletic players full credit to progress with time and normal development.

Scouting as a Science

What is science? *(Definition: knowledge from the careful study of the structure and behavior of the physical world, especially gained by watching, measuring, and doing experiments, and the development of theories to describe the results of these experiments.)*

Given this Cambridge dictionary definition, scouting is a science that encompasses elements of art and study. The complexity lies in the "human" aspect of this science. For your subjects, you aren't using chemicals that, when combined, form a compound resulting in a consistent predictable outcome. Instead, human beings are the subjects, studied by other human beings, and they may react differently to similar situations with no consistently predictable outcome. For example, you don't know how a particular 18-year-old kid will react after giving him a multimillion-dollar signing bonus. Will he still have the drive and passion to become a great Major League Player after becoming rich at this young age?

In addition, the subjective nature of a study can lead to inconsistencies in the results. Testing using human perception can only result in theory, not fact. Objective testing using empirical data can also only result in theory, not fact. Either way, theories will prove to be less than 100 percent accurate.

TIP: Accept scouting is a never-ending study of the science of predicting the future of baseball players. Scouts are scientists! *(My scouting friends will like that one!)*

Summary

This chapter offers the foundation of scouting and introduces you to the art and study of "projecting"—forecasting a player's future ability in the Major Leagues. *(Sorry, you don't get to use a magic crystal ball.)*

Here's the starting point:

☐ Identify the type of "cars" already in the Major Leagues.

☐ Gauge what you consider to be *average* physical traits of Major League players.

- ☐ Build a scale to include "above average" or "below average," and then go one step further to include "well above average" or "well below average."

- ☐ Understand the correlation between strength and impact and between athleticism and longevity.

- ☐ Be mindful of physically mature players.

- ☐ "See" the future.

These activities put you in position to make a "projection" or "educated guess" of a prospect's potential. The projection sets your barometer for that player's potential in MLB. If he seems to possess "above average" athleticism with "above average" strength potential, you'll think highly of his future development. If he has "below average" athleticism and "below average" strength, then he might not be a Major League prospect at all.

Either way, you use this barometer to assess how you feel about a player's future as the first step. Then you take this physical projection and combine it with the next set of variables—tools.

CHAPTER 9:

SCOUTING—TOOLS TO JUDGE PLAYERS

Barometer of Future Strength and Athleticism

WHILE INITIALLY EVALUATING A YOUNG PLAYER, YOU HAVE LEARNED TO
first evaluate the player in regard to his future strength and natural athleticism projected to the Major League level. Your barometer for the player
will then be set. As such, you have formed the foundation for your opinion
of the player's overall future potential. If you grade the player "above average" in strength and athleticism, your barometer will be set high and you'll
have confidence in his *potential*. Still, not all players with a high level of
strength and athleticism possess satisfactory baseball skills. A player may
at present be a strong, gifted athlete but cannot hit or throw well enough to
play at a professional level.

Conversely, some players who grade low in future strength or athleticism may have surprisingly good baseball skills. They may appear to lack
natural athleticism or have weak-looking bodies but be as good a hitter as
you've ever seen.

The next phase evaluates the tools and playing ability of the player
you're scouting. It gets a little more complicated from here.

An Organized Progression of Evaluation

A Consistent Framework

This takes you through a comprehensive, organized progression of player evaluation that serves you in two distinct ways.

1) A framework that's designed in a comprehensive fashion ensures you are considering all critical factors while scouting a young player. It becomes a complete study of the player's projected future performance and value at the Major League level.

2) If you evaluate prospects in a consistent organized manner, you'll be able to properly review your decision-making process in the future. *I cannot overstate the importance of having an organized, consistent plan for player evaluation.* Through consistency and review, you will be able to study yourself, your strengths, and your lesser-strengths related to scouting. After identifying your faults, you have the ability to make the necessary adjustments to improve your player evaluation performance.

TIP: The more consistent your scouting process, the greater your chances for personal development in player evaluation. You are building a consistent, organized framework to be executed and reviewed.

The Tools

Breaking Down the Player's Skills

You first examine a player by separating specific aspects *(tools)* of the player's ability and evaluating them individually. Next, you break down the player into a set of tools. This allows you to fully examine the player's most important traits for success as a Major League player. The present characteristics of each tool must be scrutinized to determine the tool's potential. It's a clinical examination of a particular physical tool separate from all other factors. Independently studying each tool will help you not be influenced by other factors *(positive or negative)* related to the player. You can systematically judge the individual tools without prejudice.

Occasionally, you have a good feeling about a player at first sight and deem him a Major League prospect. However, you can't allow your opinion to sway your grades on the tools, nor should you attempt to align your projection of tools to match your overall opinion of the player.

TIP: Allow for the accurate estimation of the tools. They will show a reasonable depiction of the future Major League player.

Figure 9.1

TOOLS	
POSITION PLAYERS	**PITCHERS**
1. HIT- ability to hit for batting average	1. FASTBALL VELOCITY (FB)- raw arm strength
2. POWER- homerun frequency	2. CURVE BALL (CB)- action of pitch
3. RUN- raw running speed	3. SLIDER (SL)- action of pitch
4. ARM - raw arm strength	4. CHANGE-UP (CH)- action of pitch
5. FIELD- defensive ability	5. OTHER PITCH (OT)- action of pitch
	6. CONTROL (CON)- strike-throwing ability

Our progression thus far:

☐ Barometer of future strength and athleticism

☐ Tools

The Present and Future Tools

Scouts are required to complete an assessment of a player's present level of ability in each tool as a starting point. To predict his future requires knowing the player's "now tools." *What are the player's tools at present compared to the Major League level?*

MLB organizations' scouting departments use a process to "grade out" and rate the player's individual "now tools," which helps the scout project the player's future performance. Similar to evaluating *the car*, you must evaluate the player on *present attributes* and then estimate how each tool will respond in a long journey. When you have the younger player's *present tools* ascertained appropriately, you will be in position to make a reasonable projection of his future performance. You must learn:

- ☐ What are the now tools *(present)*?

- ☐ What are the future tools *(projection)*?

Grading Major League Tools

The Major League Grading Scale

Most MLB clubs employ a 2–8 or a 20–80 grading scale. *(I use 20–80 in the examples.)* These grades pertain to the Major League level, with a score of 80 assigned to the highest attainable score and 20 representing the lowest score. Major League *average* tools would be graded as a 50, the median of the scale. Next is determining a present and future grade for each individual tool.

Figure 9.2

MAJOR LEAGUE GRADING SCALE	
OUTSTANDING	80
VERY GOOD	70
ABOVE AVERAGE (PLUS)	60
AVERAGE	50
BELOW AVERAGE	40
WELL BELOW AVERAGE	30
POOR	20

Through the use of the 20–80 scale, you assign grades of 25, 35, 45, 55, 65, and 75 when in between grades.

The Objective Grades

You have to study the Major Leagues to have a reasonable chance at appropriately grading-out a young player's tools. The tools *(present and future)* will be assigned based on the Major League level, and you must become an expert in these various grading levels. Most players will be judged *subjectively*—that is, you rely on your eyes and your knowledge of tools at the Major League level. In only these two tools can an amateur player be judged *objectively*:

1) In position players, only the RUN GRADE may be evaluated objectively using a stopwatch.

2) In pitchers, only the FASTBALL VELOCITY grade may be evaluated objectively using a radar gun.

Let's examine these present tools using a grading scale to rate these two tools in an objective manner. We'll start with the RUN grade.

Position Player Tools: HIT/POWER/*RUN*/ARM/FIELD

Figure 9.3

GRADE	RUN GRADE	
	HOME TO FIRST BASE (SEC)**	60 YARD DASH (SEC)
80	4.0	6.3
70	4.1	6.5
60	4.2	6.7
50	4.3	6.9
40	4.4	7.1
30	4.5	7.3
20	4.6	7.5

**Nearly all Major League organizations will distinguish between right- and left-hand hitters (RHH and LHH) when timing runners from home to first base. LHHs are required to be $1/10^{th}$ of a second faster in their times to be considered of the same grade as a RHH (80–3.9 sec., 70–4.0 sec., etc.). For these purposes, I use only one RUN scale for both RHHs and LHHs.

HOME TO FIRST BASE: The generally accepted rule is to start the stopwatch exactly when the batter makes contact with the ball and then stop the watch when the batter-runner touches first base. On a ground ball in the infield, you want to see the batter run hard out of the batter's box, giving his full effort to reach first base. *If you don't think the player ran at maximum effort, don't use that time to determine the grade.*

You quickly learn to anticipate when the batter will make contact with the ball, which is precisely when the stopwatch should start. Scouts have to anticipate contact and start the watch when the ball enters the contact area in front of home plate.

As a scout, if you don't anticipate contact, your reaction time influences the time you record. The manner in which hitters leave the batter's box is inconsistent because it depends on the pitch or pitch location *(jammed or out on front foot)*. This in turn influences the time recorded. You will want to make sure the batter departs the batter's box in a reasonable manner. It's best to record as many times as possible to determine the grade that is truly accurate and reflects the player's raw running speed.

TIP: By using your index finger instead of your thumb on the stopwatch, you can time runners more accurately.

60-YARD DASH: The accepted practice calls for starting the stopwatch when the player makes his initial movement to run, not on the sound of someone shouting "go" nor a coach's arm movement. You stop the watch as he breaks the finish line.

It's standard to run players of a similar speed two at a time. The competition encourages them to give their maximum effort. In fact, they should run twice to confirm the findings. Typically, the 60 yards will be measured on the smooth surface of the outfield grass. Make sure it's not a "bad track," which means uneven terrain or soft turf. Don't let wind be a factor that helps or hinders the runner.

TIP: Timing a runner is not as easy as it seems. It takes practice for your anticipation skills to become natural to you. Check with other scouts who are timing the runners to make sure it's reasonably accurate. The most veteran scouts check with other scouts on a running time they have recorded. You have no reason to feel shy or unwilling to confirm times with other scouts.

Pitcher Tools: *FASTBALL VELOCITY*/CB/SL/CH/OTH/CON

Figure 9.4

FASTBALL VELOCITY*	
VELOCITY (MPH)	**GRADE**
96+	80
94-95	70
92-93	60
89-91	50
87-88	40
84-86	30
<84	20

*The pitcher will be evaluated in raw arm strength in accordance with the chart in Figure 9.4. The scout records the average four-seam fastball velocity as the grade. (A two-seam fastball, or sinker, is typically not used to determine raw arm strength.) Most pitchers show their best fastball velocity with a *four-seam* fastball (or across the seams) from a full wind-up delivery. A pitcher may throw fastballs with a velocity range of 90–95 mph, and the scout decides on what grade to record: 50; 55; 60; 65; or 70; depending on "the velocity of the pitches." You may hear a scout say, "That kid *carried* a plus fastball for five innings." That means the average velocity the scout recorded for five innings was 92–93 mph. The pitcher may have pitched in a range of 90–95, but the scout records his present fastball velocity grade as a 60 or 65. The scout may grade him as a present 65 depending on the number of 95 mph fastballs thrown.

TIP: I was taught that the highest mph a young pitcher (16–18 years old) could touch on the radar gun was the number you could reasonably project he'd pitch at that velocity in the future. Taking into account his age and natural development of strength, you'd give him credit for increased future velocity. However, this general rule won't apply to every pitcher. Your physical barometer only begins the process of whether you predict that pitcher will improve or stay the same. Arm speed, arm action, pitches, and delivery will also be factors in the decision.

You'll need a radar gun to accurately record the speed of a pitcher's fastball. In my experience, no other measure *(stopwatch or eyes)* have proven reliable. Position yourself in the stands behind home plate, ensuring the catcher is directly between your radar gun and the pitcher. Point the radar gun directly at the pitcher's head.

TIP: Your readings may be inaccurate if you are too high in the stands. Always position yourself directly behind the catcher and level with the pitcher.

Run Grade and Fastball Velocity

I separated the objective grades of RUN and FB VELOCITY from the remaining tools because of their ease to quantify at the Major League level. These "raw tools" can be accurately compared to current Major League players. The stopwatch does not alter the readings because of any difference in talent between high school and Major League levels; it only records the actual time it took the runner to reach first base. Similarly, the radar gun can't distinguish the ability level of the hitters the pitcher is facing; it can only record the speed of the pitches.

In scouting young position players or pitchers, I find running speed to be a good indicator of athleticism. Although it's not the absolute and only test of athleticism *(many good athletes have below-average running speeds),* it can be an excellent indicator of acceptable athleticism. To run fast, the body must possess the natural athletic coordination to propel itself against the resistance of the ground. *An extremely slow runner should be carefully scrutinized and assumed to be of suspect athleticism.*

In pitchers, FB velocity is a good indicator of potential *impact* at the Major League level. The higher the speed of the fastball, the less time the hitter has to make a decision on whether to swing and the more difficult the ball becomes to hit. This is no surprise to anyone who has faced a hard-throwing pitcher.

TIP: Rely on these two tools to grade objectively. They provide tangible evidence to lead you to your overall opinion on a player. Because these are objective grades, not opinions, they cannot be argued. Scouting young players is a comparison combined with projection—the scout's opinion of how the player will perform as a Major League player. RUN and FASTBALL VELOCITY, when combined with our physical barometer for the player, help assess individual futures.

A young player's remaining tools are judged by *subjective* examination, a matter of opinion. *Subjective* grades will prove more difficult to gauge.

The Benny Story

Jim Benedict (Benny) has been called a pitching guru for the Pittsburgh Pirates and Miami Marlins for developing and refining many of their pitchers. Nicknamed the "Mechanic," he has been successful at his craft, especially helping pitchers struggling with their pitching delivery.

Benny and I started scouting Southern California about the same time in the fall of 1991—me with the NY Yankees and Benny with the Texas Rangers. We were both area scouts so we'd see each other regularly at amateur games. Both former college coaches learning the intricate details of scouting amateur players, we talked about player evaluation and gaining confidence in the art of scouting. It wasn't easy. We were studying players' bodies, learning the grading system, and applying what we were being taught as best we could. This was an overwhelming time.

One day, we were both scouting a junior college game at Griffith Park in Los Angeles. Benny's boss and regional cross-checker Len Strelitz was with him. They were standing together as I walked into the ballpark. The game hadn't started, so I approached them to generate a stimulating conversation that would teach me something about scouting. Anything I could learn would be helpful!

Len was tight-lipped. This veteran was my only link to the unknown world of scouting that day, and I felt as if he didn't want to give me any secrets because I was with the competition. He probably reserved his opinions for only Texas Ranger scouts. Understandable.

But Benny acted as if he'd become a scouting expert and had this scouting stuff nailed. He was preaching his views on amateur scouting in a forceful fashion and clear vibrato in his voice. Benny's newfound confidence amazed me. We had just discussed how difficult scouting was to learn! I felt happy for Benny and the knowledge he'd gained that put scouting in order for him—as if he'd seen the light. As for me, I was still living in the deep darkness of a newly hired scout.

Later during the game that day, a relief pitcher came in from the bullpen. He warmed up with good fastball velocity and had a strong athletic-looking body. He showed a "plus" fastball and a "near-average" slider. (Above-average fastball pitchers are rare in amateur scouting.) I used the radar gun from behind home plate to get accurate velocity readings and see how his pitches *looked to the hitter. I then made my way down to the third-base area to see this right-hander from the side. I wanted a better viewing angle to see his pitching delivery and arm action. Benny came down near me with the same intention in mind.*

I studied how the pitcher's body and arm worked together to throw the ball and made my assessment. All this time, Benny and I never said a word to each other. Then Len walked over for a couple pitches and returned to his spot behind the plate.

I liked the kid's compact simple delivery and how his arm action appeared smooth to deliver his pitches. I thought the pitcher was a Major League prospect, but I was a little unsure how much I should like him. I looked to my right and saw Benny furiously writing notes in his little black scouting book. He was obviously putting his newfound knowledge confidently to work. But I still lacked that confidence. I wanted another opinion to solidify my findings, so I moved closer to Benny.

"Hey Benny, do you like this guy?" I asked.

"He's got a strong body, plus arm, and okay slider," he replied.

"Yes, but do you think he's a prospect?" I asked.

"He's got a pretty good delivery and arm action," he replied.

I repeated, "Yes, but do you think he's a prospect?"

After a long, awkward pause, Benny gave me a quizzical look and responded, "Hell, I don't know."

Len was walking over in our direction from behind the backstop. Benny saw him coming over and yelled, "Hey Len. Do I like this guy?"

Shaking his head from side to side, Len said, "Yes, you do Benny. Yes, you do."

All three of us started laughing. Len knew exactly where both Benny and I were in our progression as scouts. He must have had the same experience starting out having no confidence or commitment. Until Benny and I understood the system, we didn't know right from wrong. Once we became more comfortable with it, we both ultimately became more confident in our scouting opinions.

Don't worry if it seems difficult to put player evaluations in order at the beginning. Simply focus on learning the organized progression to evaluate players. It will all come together after you become more at ease with the system.

If all else fails, just ask a veteran scout, "Hey, do I like this guy?"

The Subjective Grades: Position Players

To be realistic, it's not reasonable to give any high school or college baseball position player a *present grade* of higher than 40 in HIT/ POWER/ FIELD based on Major League standards. Pitching in amateur baseball isn't comparable to the Major League level. To suggest that a high school or college hitter can step into the Major League level and hit .255 is improbable. The intricate adjustments and speed of the game on defense at the Major League level would make any good amateur defender struggle.

The best system I have seen is to rate an amateur position player in Present HIT or FIELD grade according to the scale but focus on the present level to better describe the hitter or defender. Instead of realistically grading all high school hitters as 20 Present HIT or FIELD grade, make use of another scale to describe what type of development will be necessary for him to be a Major League hitter or defender. Consider these estimates:

☐ A very crude amateur hitter or defender would be a 20 Present HIT or FIELD.

☐ A very accomplished, skilled high school hitter or defender would be a 30 Present HIT or FIELD.

☐ A crude college hitter or defender would be a 30 Present HIT or FIELD grade.

☐ A very accomplished, well-skilled college hitter or defender would be a 40 HIT or FIELD.

All others would fall into the in-between grades of 25 for high school or 35 for college players. This allows the scout to accurately describe the type of hitter the club is investing in. It may also offer a clue about the development time. (See Figure 9.5 for details.)

Figure 9.5

HIGH SCHOOL			COLLEGE	
RANK	GRADE		RANK	GRADE
BEST HITTER	30		BEST HITTER	40
GOOD HITTER	25		GOOD HITTER	35
CRUDE HITTER	20		CRUDE HITTER	30

TIP: I would carefully review the prospect status of any position player you classify as a crude hitter. Is he ready for professional play if he's a crude hitter?

After you understand this concept, then focus your attention on the *individual characteristics* of Major League players to reasonably grade a younger player's "now tools."

☐ What are the characteristics of a Major League hitter?

☐ What are the characteristics of a Major League power hitter?

☐ What are the characteristics of a quality defender at each position in the Major Leagues?

Always study players in the Major Leagues to accurately assess potential Major League talent. The better you understand what characteristics are necessary to be successful, the more accurately you can determine which young players have the potential to play in the Major Leagues.

Beauty is in the eye of the beholder in the subjective exercise that follows. I will not offer my beliefs on which characteristics I consider most important. That you can decide for yourself. I'll offer examples of what many veteran scouts examine to form their assessment. They include:

☐ Hitting Characteristics

☐ Offensive Grading Scales

☐ Grading Defense

☐ Arm Grade

Major League Hitting Characteristics

The following characteristics are important aspects to study in Major League hitters. Your ability to spot certain aspects of hitting may be key in determining which young players will be the future Major League hitters. Look to prioritize this list or make additions and subtractions as you see fit. (*Caution: Some of these characteristics are physical and may be difficult for a player to make vast improvements. Others are mental or technique-oriented, which may be altered with proper professional instruction.*)

Figure 9.6

HITTING CHARACTERISTICS		
Approach	GB/FB %	Rhythm
Awareness	Hand action	Running speed
Backspin	Launch angle	Separation/load
Balance	Loft	Skill offense
Bat speed	Plate coverage	Stance
Base hit bunting	Plate discipline	Stride length
Contact rate	Pitch recognition	Stride direction
Exit velocity	Posture	Swing path
Finish	Raw power	Timing

Offensive Grading Scales

The offensive scales you use will be appropriate only for a certain point in time. They're like a survey of the current landscape of MLB. The corresponding numbers to a particular grade may change with the changes in the game. Home runs in MLB were not as prevalent in the 1980s as they are today, and the grading scale would have to reflect the change in power of Major League players. *(For example, when I began my scouting career in 1991 with the NY Yankees, 28+ home runs were considered 80 POWER in a hitter. In the early 2000s, some clubs used as high as 40+ home runs to grade 80 POWER.)* The numbers and corresponding grades may fluctuate from year to year depending on MLB player trends.

TIP: Stay current with your statistical data to ensure you're accurately grading for the most recent player performance in MLB.

Figure 9.7

HIT SCALE	
BATTING AVERAGE	**GRADE**
.315+	80
.295-.314	70
.275-.294	60
.252-.274	50
.238-.251	40
.220-.237	30
<.220	20

Figure 9.8

POWER SCALE	
HOMERUNS	GRADE
36+	80
29-35	70
22-28	60
15-21	50
10-14	40
5-9	30
0-4	20

A common scouting practice is to identify the RAW POWER of a young hitter to use as an indicator of future Major League power. You're required to recognize the varying degrees of RAW POWER at the Major League level and gauge the amateur hitter in PRESENT RAW POWER based on Major League standards. Then you project the RAW POWER into the future and grade according to the scale noted in Figure 9.8.

Many organizations use distance charts to gauge the RAW POWER of a young hitter. The farther he can hit the ball, the higher the grade. Because of varying climate, wind, and weather conditions, I suggest learning to recognize the degrees of RAW POWER in players at the Major League level. Then compare that to a young hitter. This will take practice.

TIP: An old saying in MLB is "POWER comes late for a young hitter." Research various Major League players by reviewing their offensive statistics as an amateur or in the Minor Leagues. See if you agree with that statement. Also look at the number of doubles amassed. Some scouts believe a high number of doubles in a young hitter predicts future Major League POWER and homerun potential.

Established Major League position players have developed a track record of performance to grade hitting and power. You can locate their career statistics to rate how they fit into these scales of HIT and POWER grades. You can only estimate what a young hitter may accomplish at the

Major League level by comparing his individual characteristics to present or former Major League hitters.

RAW POWER may be the best indicator for future home runs. As a scout, you cannot whole-heartedly rely on a high school player's statistical information when attempting to predict the future of a hitter because their offensive numbers are attained against high school pitching. The statistics may become more useful in college level players as the ability level of the competition is more advanced.

TIP: The lower the level of play, the more difficult it is to rely on statistics as valid evidence of a future Major League player.

Grading Defense

DEFENSE may be a very difficult grade to assign when evaluating young players. These grades are position specific, but many amateur players do not play the position in high school or college that would fit them best for professional baseball.

Often, the scout must attempt to evaluate the player's DEFENSE while envisioning him at another position. Some characteristics might be more impactful at another position than the one position they currently play. Again, the study of Major League players and the characteristics of each individual position are extremely important.

You must know "what plays" at the Major League level at each position. Different from HIT and POWER grades, there's no standard defensive statistic to grade DEFENSE. Statisticians and sabermetrics gurus alike debate the effectiveness of the present-day measures of DEFENSE.

Errors have been a key standard when evaluating defense, but the total number of errors doesn't take into account those players with exceptional range. They may make errors on plays that other players with lesser range may never have a chance to make.

Other measures such as UZR (Ultimate Zone Rating) and DRS (Defensive Runs Saved) are studied, but no one particular DEFENSE statistic has been widely adopted by Major League clubs to gauge position players. Your eyes will be critically important to evaluating the characteristics of younger players in DEFENSE.

Figure 9.9

MAJOR LEAGUE DEFENSIVE CHARACTERISTICS		
Aggressiveness	Decision making	Range
Angles/routes	Effort	Reactions
Anticipation	Fluidity	Reading hops
Awareness	Foot quickness	Rhythm
Body control	Hands	Route efficiency
Concentration	Mechanics	Running speed

Arm Grade

The arm strength of a player can be highly influential in determining the future position of a young player at the professional level. Many young shortstops have been converted to second basemen because of their lack of arm strength. Other players have been converted to catcher because of their strong arm and game awareness. You're required to gain a sense for the varying degrees of ARM grades at the Major League level at each position. This makes up a "raw grade." Throwing accuracy will be dismissed for now.

> *Larry Corrigan offered the best advice that helped me acquire equilibrium for grading arm strength. He believed that if the player's arm strength was of no concern for an average Major League play at the position, the player had an AVERAGE ARM. Positioned in a normal spot with nobody on base, a shortstop should be able to make regular plays to his right or left and throw to first base to retire an average runner with no issue. That would constitute AVERAGE. A 50 ARM should cover all of the standard throws in a Major League Baseball game. A 50*

ARM is not impactful at the Major League level. However, it's not a detriment to the player's effectiveness as a defender.

Use Your Words

Have you heard a mother say to a child throwing a temper-tantrum, "Use your words!"? It's easy to get caught up in the minutia of scouting terminology and the grading system to evaluate players. So while discerning the proper ARM grade or any particular grade, USE YOUR WORDS. Try not to focus on the number value. Instead, put your attention to the words you use to describe the grade.

While scouting a Major League game, try using these words to describe your opinion:

- ☐ That's an OUTSTANDING (80) ARM.

- ☐ He is a BELOW-AVERAGE (40) defender.

- ☐ He is a VERY GOOD (70) Major League hitter.

- ☐ He is a POOR (20) runner.

Compare that with scout language:

- ☐ He has a SOLID (55) ARM.

- ☐ He is a FRINGY (45) runner.

- ☐ He has a RIGHT-FIELD ARM (70).

- ☐ He has a LEFT-FIELD ARM (40-45).

- ☐ He is a BASE-CLOGGER (20 RUN).

Using the words that describe the grade make the evaluation process easier than remembering what a 60 ARM looks like. Gain a sense for the scale by using words to describe your rating from the beginning. When you do, grading tools will be easier. This is more effective than trying to remember the characteristics of a certain number value.

It's difficult to describe a 70 ARM, but you will know what a VERY GOOD Major League ARM looks like. And you know it when you see an OUTSTANDING ARM or a BELOW-AVERAGE ARM. Your overall opinion should derive the accurate grade.

TIP: Ignore the numbers and focus on your words to describe the tools at the Major League level. Use words to reflect your true opinion of the player's tools, and you'll be surprised how accurate you will become.

The Subjective Grades: Pitchers

Fastball

As discussed, grading the FASTBALL VELOCITY can be easily rated by using a radar gun but there are other aspects of the FASTBALL in command, movement, sink, and late action (life) to be judged. These characteristics give you an idea of a pitcher's future effectiveness at the Major League level. Some scouts would argue that the development of a professional delivery, more use of a sinker *(two-seamer)*, and advanced grips on the ball help create the late action that a young pitcher may not possess. This may all be developed with professional instruction. The added characteristic of *very good fastball movement* is a bonus for a young pitcher who has developed a moving fastball at a young age.

Curveball

Most scouts use the term CURVEBALL to describe a down-action off-speed breaking pitch. It is typically the pitcher's slowest breaking pitch, and at the Major League level an AVERAGE CURVEBALL usually varies from 72–76 mph. The CURVEBALL is an off-speed pitch designed to fool the batter with a slower speed and a downward break. Scouts will look to see a late breaking CURVEBALL that appears to the hitter to be a FASTBALL, and then breaks sharply downward making it difficult for the hitter to adjust to the slower speed and downward action. Scouts will look for a tight spinning CURVEBALL that has a consistent shape and spin to help gauge its reliability and effectiveness. In watching Major League games, you will gain a sense of the type of curveballs that are thrown at that level. The size, shape, velocity, and spin of the curveballs thrown at that level will give you a good idea of what they look like. *Use your words to grade the curveball.*

Slider

The SLIDER is a breaking pitch thrown harder than a CURVEBALL and will move across the plate and downward. The AVERAGE SLIDER at the Major League level is typically in the 82–84 mph range. It can be slower or faster, but its hallmark is moving across the plate from the pitcher's arm side to his glove side. The pitch is designed to appear as a FASTBALL in velocity, but at the last moment it breaks sharply away or into a hitter with downward action.

Scouts look for the appearance of a fastball with a tight-spinning late break. Consistent shape and spin always indicate the pitcher's feel for the pitch. In fact, some of the best SLIDERS can appear to go straight down. The *depth* of the SLIDER is critically important to its effectiveness on the hitter. Flat horizontal spinning sliders have a tendency to be hit great distances. That's why it's imperative that the SLIDER breaks downward.

TIP: "Spin rate" is a pitching evaluation method that's popular in MLB. Advanced technology allows measuring the spin rate of a pitcher's various pitches. The faster a pitcher can make the ball rotate, the later action or movement he can put on a breaking pitch to deceive the hitter. Although studies have shown high spin rates are good in four-seam fastballs, the same studies have shown slow spin rates are effective for ground-ball pitchers.

TIP: Research spin-rate after you've evaluated with your eyes to determine the effectiveness of a certain pitch. See if you can detect a high-spin rate, late-action breaking pitch.

Change-Up

This is an off-speed pitch designed to deceive the hitter into thinking it's a fastball. It may have some movement downward and toward the arm side of the plate, but its hallmark is slower velocity. It should mirror the fastball and be difficult for the hitter to detect until it arrives into the hitting zone. A pitch of deception in speed, it appears to be the pitcher's best fastball but is actually 10–12 mph slower. Most Major League change-ups will be from 80–85 mph, but the speed will be relatively slower than the pitcher's fastball. The best change-ups will have sinking actions to ensure their effectiveness. There's nothing easier to hit than a high, straight change-up, and the downward action will make it more difficult for the batter to hit even when the hitter is anticipating the pitch.

Other Pitch

This is a catchall category for other pitches used in baseball. A CUTTER, SPLIT-FINGER FASTBALL, FORKBALL, SCREWBALL, KNUCKLEBALL, or any other pitch is graded in this category. Much like the pitches described above, deception in speed and action are how you are to judge their effectiveness. Can the hitter detect the pitch? Does the velocity of the pitch disrupt the hitter's timing? Can the hitter adjust to the late movement?

TIP: Scouts should know the standard professional grips of all pitches. Asking a young pitcher to show you his grips on his different pitches allows for the scout to make projections on his potential improvement of movement or late action. It's easier to project how a player's pitches will develop when you know the proper grips of each pitch.

Control

There's a well-known story about former Boston Braves Manager George "Tweedy" Stallings. Nicknamed the Miracle Man, he led the Boston Braves from last place in July 1914 to a World Series Championship. Bill James has called Stallings the first MLB manager to make use of platooning players in the lineup depending on the starting pitcher the team was facing.

As the story goes, in 1929, the longtime baseball manager was lying on his deathbed. As his health was failing, a close friend came to see him before he died. The friend asked Stallings, "What's killing you, George?"

In a soft whispery voice, he replied, "Bases on balls."

Food for Thought

Regarding bases on balls (walks) per innings (BB/9) and earned run average (ERA), complete a study of Major League pitchers. Can you find a correlation between the ability to limit walks and Major League success? Is there a point when the pitcher's "stuff" has no consequence because of his inability to keep runners off base?

Effectiveness for all pitchers is enhanced by having the ability to throw the ball in the strike zone. Managers won't have confidence in pitchers who give free passes to hitters. Pitching success is attained by limiting the number of runners on base.

CONTROL at the Major League level is defined in an objective manner (see Figure 9.10).

Figure 9.10

CONTROL SCALE	
BB/9 (Bases on balls per 9 innings)	GRADE
<1.5	80
2.0	70
2.5	60
3	50
3.5	40
4	30
4.5+	20

Figure 9.10 is a simple standard chart for grading CONTROL. It's difficult to discern future CONTROL of a high school pitcher; it directly coincides with your view of his overall athleticism, present command and control, delivery, and arm action, combined with his repertoire of pitches or future pitches.

Major League Pitching Characteristics

From this list of pitching characteristics, determine which are the most important to you as an evaluator. Then decide which can be developed further.

Figure 9.11

MAJOR LEAGUE PITCHING CHARACTERISTICS		
Aggressiveness	Feel	Movement
Arm action	Fielding	Out-pitch
Arm angle	Finish	Plane
Awareness	Fluidity	Rhythm
Balance	Grips	Separation
Can he pitch?	Hand action	Spin rate
Change speeds	Hand speed	Stride direction
Concentration	Hides ball	Stride length
Contrast	Holding runners	Strikes
Deception	Late action	Timing
Delivery	Load	Uncomfortable AB
Emotional control	Mechanics	

Summary

This chapter introduced the basics of professional baseball scouting and the grading of tools used by scouts. Your subjective analysis will require much study and practice.

Here's a scouting progression:

- ☐ A comprehensive study of Major League players.

- ☐ Learn the 20-80 grading scale.

- ☐ Use your words to describe what you see.

- ☐ Prioritize hitting, pitching, and defensive characteristics.

- ☐ Set your barometer for the younger player.

- ☐ Grade the present tools.

- ☐ Use objective tools to help you form a foundation for Overall Future Potential.

- ☐ Project subjective tools by using your physical barometer combined with the tool characteristics.

CHAPTER 10:

SCOUTING—OVERALL FUTURE POTENTIAL

Body, Athleticism, and Tools

CHAPTERS 8 AND 9 EXPLAINED THE STUDY OF SCOUTING AMATEUR BASEball players. The construct of your player evaluation system begins with *foundational* pieces (athleticism and future strength). These important elements serve as the building blocks for the art of *projecting* the future performance of each specific tool of a baseball player. Having an organized progression maintains a consistent order that simplifies each successive analysis. As such, the *order and structure* of your player evaluation process is important, and it should be your main focus. You will be the architect and caretaker of your personal player evaluation system. Only *you* will understand the intricate details of your process, and only *you* will be able to review and refine your system. FOCUS ON THE PROCESS!

Your Scouting Process

Make sure you're reasonably proficient in these four areas before moving forward in the process.

1. Know the common physical characteristics of present Major League players.

2. Know "what plays" at all positions in the Major Leagues.

3. Have a sense of priority in the characteristics of Major League position players or pitchers.

4.   Have the ability to decide if a younger player possesses the "now" or "future" characteristics consistent with Major League players.

Your goal is to rate the present ability or "now tools" in a young player in accordance with a Major League scale. To project into the future, you need to know the "baseline or starting point" of each tool. Once you've projected each tool into the future, you're in position to derive an opinion about the player.

From there, you'll transition from grading a set of tools to grading the complete player and his overall projected value in MLB—what's called the player's Overall Future Potential (OFP).

Projection of Tools

The Master Scout

Projecting a young player's baseball tools at the Major League level is difficult. By nature of their superior comparison history and vast access to player analysis, master scouts may make scouting appear easy. It is not. Their evaluation skills have been honed by comparing many successful Major League players, from former to present-day Major League players. Master scouts have scouted amateur players before they signed a professional contract and then studied these players' entire professional careers and applied the lessons learned. All the while, they test and review their hypotheses to advance their process.

As historians and scientists, master scouts understand every position and the individual characteristic priorities necessary to have Major League success. They project the level of Major League impact on certain body types, strength, athleticism, swings, pitching deliveries, and arm action in younger players.

The 20–80 Game

Larry Corrigan was instrumental in teaching me basic lessons in scouting. One day we were sitting waiting for a game to begin and started discussing players in MLB. He asked if I felt comfortable using the grading scale and putting numbers on players for their tools or OFP. I told him I was getting more comfortable but didn't feel 100 percent confident. Larry told me I should rate everything I saw and put a grade on it from 20-80. Then he gave me this example:

Larry said, "I like this mechanical pencil I use to write my notes.

The 0.55mm lead is the perfect size for my scouting cards.

The clip is great to fasten to my shirt when I'm not using it.

The smooth plastic feels good, and the etched part at the end makes it easy to grab.

I don't like the blue color all that much, but it's okay.

My only complaint is I wish it had a better eraser.

I'm putting a 70 on this pencil."

Ha! He graded out a mechanical pencil. To this day, I still grade out rental cars to cell phones to hamburgers. I truly believe it has helped me in my player evaluation skills. It requires me to make a final decision on whatever I'm grading and have a reason for doing so. I have only one recommendation: Do not use this exercise to grade out your spouse. It doesn't go over well!

Position Player Example

It's time to put our player evaluation knowledge to work in a practical situation. We will derive a FINAL OFP grade for a hypothetical player. We will examine this player in a simplified manner, but we will use a professional baseball approach to scouting. Let's examine a high school outfielder named Rocky. Study the simple description of Rocky's tools and characteristics carefully. The descriptions should lead to an opinion of his future ability.

BAROMETER:

Rocky exhibits 50 athleticism when graded at the Major League level and below AVERAGE (40) strength at present. He has a good solid body and should acquire future strength consistent with AVERAGE at the Major League level. There should be no reason Rocky cannot handle the physical demands of professional baseball and should progress satisfactorily. Rocky is AVERAGE in athleticism and has future strength for a Major League Player.

BAROMETER: 50

HIT:

Aggressive hitter; competes in box; looks to hit

Possesses a fluid swing, balanced, all-field approach

Good idea of the strike zone; rarely chases bad pitches

Good hand action to start the bat; shorter path into the contact zone

Solid hand-eye coordination; makes contact on all pitches

Near AVERAGE bat speed

Skilled high school hitter with a track record of success

HIT: 30 PRESENT (20–30 Scale for High School)

POWER:

Can occasionally drive the ball when he gets his pitch

More of a line-drive/contact-type swing

POWER: 30 PRESENT (Raw Power)

RUN:

Quick out of the box; good running form; always runs hard through the bag

Aggressive on bases; looks to steal; gets good jumps to steal

Timed to first base (4.3) and 60-yard dash (6.9)

RUN: 50 PRESENT

ARM:

Okay arm strength when feet are under him; good arm action; ball has tailing action; aggressive to throw

ARM: 40 PRESENT

FIELD:

Played CF; aggressive outfielder and appears to like playing defense; fearless defender; solid jumps and routes to the ball; always in the right spot backing up bases

FIELD: 30 PRESENT (20–30 Scale for High School)

With this short synopsis, you have likely developed an opinion on how to project Rocky's future tools. It's a feeling of his offensive and defensive abilities and a sense of his potential impact at the Major League level. It's difficult to derive a full opinion on such limited information, but you've gained some. It should be enough for a projection of the future player.

The "How"

Barometer, Tools, and Projection

We have set our barometer at 50 for Rocky, and we have rated his present tools. We're now in position to project his grades into the future at the Major League level. We project by examining the individual present characteristics of each tool and then determine Rocky's *potential* for development. How will it happen? We use the assigned present grades and the tool descriptions as our guide. Let's examine the tools carefully to decide on a future grade.

Athleticism and Strength

BAROMETER:

AVERAGE athlete" at the Major League Level. This allows for the necessary adjustments to be made in proper mechanics and technique as the competition becomes more advanced moving up through the Minor Leagues and into the Major Leagues. "AVERAGE future strength" should allow for the projection of future strength gains in this player. Strength that should improve his development and *impact* in his game overall. This means Rocky is a good athlete with okay strength, but he is not a superior athlete at the Major League level.

BAROMETER: 50

HIT:

Very skilled high school hitter with a track record of success

Aggressive hitter; competes in box; looks to hit

Good fluid swing; balanced, all-field approach

Good idea of strike zone; rarely chases bad pitches

Good hand action to start the bat; short path to contact zone

Solid hand-eye coordination; makes contact on all pitches

Near AVERAGE bat speed

Almost every hitting characteristic appears consistent with a good hitter for a high batting average. There are no major concerns with his characteristics as a hitter. The only blemish is that we cannot rate his bat speed as AVERAGE. We believe he will get stronger and should project for increased bat speed in the future to AVERAGE bat speed. We can reasonably assume his characteristics warrant a projection of at least a SOLID-AVERAGE Major League hitter (.270–.280).

HIT: 30 PRESENT/55 FUTURE

POWER:

Can drive ball when gets his pitch

More of line-drive-type swings

Doubles type

Shows occasional raw power

It doesn't appear that POWER is a positive characteristic of his game. At 30 present RAW POWER, it is WELL-BELOW AVERAGE. With the barometer set at 50, we believe he will gain strength, so we can project him higher. But we cannot envision future AVERAGE RAW POWER. BELOW-AVERAGE RAW POWER with solid hitting skills in the future leads us to project him with 35 POWER (7–8 homeruns) *potential* in the future.

POWER: 30 PRESENT RAW POWER/35 FUTURE POWER

RUN:

Quick out of the box

Good running form; no flaws

Always runs hard through bag

Aggressive on the bases

Looks to steal bases; gets good jumps to steal

Timed to first base (4.3 sec), and 60-yard dash (6.9 sec)

AVERAGE present RUN. We can project his speed to improve as his strength improves to SOLID AVERAGE or 55 in the future. His characteristics indicate he's a good aggressive base runner who has the potential for stolen bases, but probably not a high number.

RUN: 50/55

ARM:

Okay arm strength when feet are under him

Ball has tailing action

Aggressive to throw

Rocky doesn't possess a strong arm. However, this may be an area where improvement is possible. *Okay arm strength when feet are under him* suggests he may not have consistently proper footwork. *Tailing action* may be helped with proper mechanics, improved grip, or long-toss program. These characteristics may be altered for potential gains in his throwing. One full grade is probably the most we can project on an ARM grade, even for a high school player.

ARM: 40/50

FIELD:

Played CF

Aggressive outfielder

Appears to like playing defense

Fearless defender

SOLID AVERAGE jumps and routes to ball

Always in the right spot backing up bases

The defensive characteristics suggest a good future defensive outfielder in the Major Leagues with no obvious weakness on defense. He appears to be a natural defender. We have rated him the highest we can on our scale for high school players at present (30). His characteristics suggest a future SOLID AVERAGE defender in centerfield in the Major Leagues. If he were a better runner, it would be safe to project Rocky as a 60 or 70 defender, but he doesn't appear to possess the quickness and top-end speed of an impact defensive centerfielder.

FIELD: 30/55

PHYSICAL REVIEW

We have now examined the present tools of this high school outfielder and projected these physical baseball tools into the future at the Major League level. We started with a barometer set high enough (50), making improvement of these tools a possibility. We made assumptions of "how" these physical tools may improve into the future at the Major League level and to what degree. Here is our finished potential product:

TOOLS

Present and future projected tools:

Figure 10.1

TOOL	PRESENT	FUTURE
HIT	30	55
POWER	30 RAW	35
RUN	50	55
ARM	40	50
FIELD	30	55

Our potential Major League player:

.275 BA, 8 HR'S, 14 SB's. SOLID-AVERAGE DEFENSE in centerfield with an AVERAGE ARM

Remember, this is Rocky's *potential* based on what we believe his tools to be. We are taking a fairly positive posture because our barometer is set at 50. Thus, Rocky should progress in a normal fashion with no true hindrance to his development. If all goes according to plan, Rocky can *potentially* achieve these numbers. If anything goes wrong (injury, illness, work habits, personal issues), he'll most likely fall short.

Make-Up

One of the most influential factors to a player's success is his make-up, which encompasses personal aspects of his mentality that influence his potential achievement. Key questions:

- ☐ Does the player work hard?

- ☐ Does the player have the desire to achieve?

- ☐ Is the player a gamer?

- ☐ Does the player like to compete?

- ☐ Does the player have emotional issues that may limit his potential?

- ☐ How does the player respond to authority?

- ☐ Is the player coachable?

- ☐ Is the player a good teammate?

- ☐ Is the player a positive leader?

- ☐ Does the player have an issue with drugs or alcohol?

Many players with the physical ability to star in the Major Leagues will never rise above the Minor League level because of their make-up. Their personal deficiencies won't allow for skill development when faced with the rigors of professional baseball. The tools will be meaningless if the player has major issues with his make-up that prove detrimental to his progress toward the Major Leagues.

Conversely, players with great make-up may have a better probability of realizing their potential. Their make-up offers them the best chance to maximize their talent or overachieve their tool potential. They may also be positive leaders in the organization and affect other players to help them develop their skills as well.

MLB organizations have varying opinions on make-up. Some believe young players can be taught a more mature professional approach; therefore, make-up in a young player is inconsequential. They assume young players are "acting their age" by committing youthful mistakes and need only to be taught how to be a professional. Other clubs take the position that "leopards don't change their spots," and the issues young players have today will always be present. What do you think?

Food for Thought

The players in an organization are representatives of their MLB club. As the most visible employees in an organization, they're a reflection of the entire company. When a scout signs a player, the scout is essentially hiring a new employee and representative for the organization. Scouts are judged by the players they sign, and the players become a reflection of their work. Scouts put their names and reputations, as well as the company's name and reputation, on the line. As a scout:

☐ What type of make-up would you like to represent you?

☐ Are you too tough on make-up for young players when they have not fully matured emotionally or intellectually?

☐ Did you ever make a mistake as a younger person that you regret?

☐ What characteristics of make-up would make you pass on a young player with future Major League ability?

Make-Up in Rocky, Our Hypothetical Outfielder

Let's review Rocky's tools and gain valuable insight into his make-up by examining these words chosen to describe his tools.

"Aggressive hitter; competes in box; very skilled high school hitter; track record of success"

We can construe these words as positive remarks toward Rocky's make-up as potentially an aggressive competitor. Some may think *very skilled* and *track record* speak to Rocky's baseball talent, but others may believe he's always prepared to achieve, that he must have a good work ethic.

"Always runs hard through the bag; aggressive on bases; ready to take the extra base; looks to steal"

Again, this indicates an aggressive competitor—a "team player," a "gamer." Many staff members in professional baseball believe you can see make-up in base running more than in any other activity. The aggressive base runner who always runs hard wants to help his team by scoring a run. (Base running is commonly viewed as an act to benefit the team; it is not for the benefit of the individual player.)

"Aggressive outfielder; appears to like playing defense; fearless defender; always in the right spot backing up bases; aggressive to throw"

You've got to love this kid! Rocky looks to be aggressive in every phase of the game. I imagine Rocky's teammates and coaches must respect how he prepares for and plays the game. Let's assume no key off-field personal issues exist and everyone has positive comments regarding this kid. After discussing Rocky's tendencies and character traits with his coaches, rival coaches, scorekeeper, snack-bar lady, guidance counselor, teachers, neighbors, and mailman, we can put Rocky at 60 (plus) make-up. This leads us to feel confident in Rocky achieving his physical talent potential.

We have set the physical barometer at 50, graded the present/future baseball physical tools, and rated his make-up at 60.

Overall Future Potential

The Raw Overall Future Potential (OFP)

Next, we'll grade the RAW SCORE or Raw Overall Future Potential of our hypothetical high school outfielder. The RAW OFP reflects our belief in the Major League *potential* of Rocky's tools. Let's complete a simple mathematics exercise to arrive at the RAW OFP using the future grades as our guide to predicting Rocky's future value at the Major League level. See Figure 10.2.

Figure 10.2

TOOLS	PRESENT/FUTURE
HIT	30/55
POWER	30/35
RUN	50/55
FIELD	30/55
ARM	40/50

We'll add the values of the future grades and then divide by 5 *(the number of tools).*

55 + 35 + 55 + 55 + 50 = 250 ÷ 5 = 50 RAW OFP SCORE

This RAW OFP SCORE should indicate where Rocky would fit into a Major League value scale. We use a 20–80 scale to categorize Major League position players and pitchers by their OFP and relative value in the game. See Figure 10.3.

Figure 10.3

MAJOR LEAGUE OFP VALUE CHART	
OFP	**MAJOR LEAGUE ROLE**
80	Perennial All-Star Player; #1 Starter Pitcher; Premium Closer
70	Occasional All-Star Player; #2 Starter, Average Closer; Premium Set-Up
60	Above Average Everyday Player; #3 or #4 Starter; Solid Set-Up
50	Average Everyday Player; #5 Starter; Swing Starter; Solid Middle Reliever
40	Platoon or Extra Player; Long or Situational Reliever
30	AAA Player, Emergency Major League Player
20	Minor League Player Potential

Rocky rates as a RAW OFP of 50—at the bottom of the AVERAGE everyday Major League position players. The majority of the work has been completed to assign a FINAL OFP grade to our high school outfielder. Yet one important step still has to be completed to make our final determination on his value as a future Major League player.

The Scouting Instincts Factor

Most professional systems reflect the scout's true opinion of the player's OFP by allowing for wiggle room at the end of the process. A scout's instincts are taken into consideration to adjust the FINAL OFP by five points in either direction. As such, if the RAW OFP is 50, the FINAL OFP may be adjusted up or down by typically one to five points at the scout's discretion. That means the scout could place Rocky anywhere from 45 to 55 as a FINAL OFP grade.

Scouting Instincts allows the scout to record the player's tools as accurately as possible, knowing he/she can adjust the RAW OFP at the end of the process to reflect a true opinion of the player. The scout must be in position to grade the player's tools accurately. If a scouting system didn't allow for Scouting Instincts, the scout would then align the grading value of each tool to ensure the FINAL OFP matched his/her overall opinion of the player. In essence, the scout would be creating a final determination of the player's value at the Major League level and then making sure the tool grades fit that role. Instead, the tools should be graded independently of any preconceived ideas.

Some scouts would focus on Rocky's 60 make-up and the number of AVERAGE future tools (four of five). They'd see Rocky has no major weakness, and his make-up will help him to achieve his future potential. Therefore, these scouts may grade Rocky *up* from the RAW OFP (from 50 to 51-55) as a FINAL OFP. They believe his baseball strengths and make-up will outweigh his lack of "top-end" tools, and he'll become an everyday Major League centerfielder.

Conversely, other scouts would focus on the lack of a 60+ tool and believe Rocky has no true impact as an everyday player on a Major League team, lacking one big tool as strength to carry his career. They'd view his set of tools as AVERAGE with no CARRY TOOL, preferring a better defender in centerfield or more POWER or RUN to guarantee impact in an everyday role. Therefore, they'd adjust this player *down* from a RAW OFP of 50 to 45–49 as a FINAL OFP. These scouts may indicate Rocky would be a platoon or extra player at the Major League level.

The FINAL OFP should be consistent with the corresponding projected role in the MAJOR LEAGUE OFP VALUE CHART (Figure 10.3).

Food for Thought

Although scouts have the same information, they may all grade differently for a FINAL OFP. You must recognize your natural posture and be able to understand yourself as a talent evaluator. Where do you sit in this debate?

☐ Do you favor gamers?

☐ Do you favor big tools?

☐ Would you favor Rocky or a player with big tools but poor make-up?

☐ KNOW YOURSELF!

Pitcher Example

Let's complete a FINAL OFP grade for a college pitcher named Hank following the same process of evaluation as for Rocky. This example provides a basic description of Hank's physical attributes, tools, and make-up without offering a recommendation for tool grades. It's your job to derive present and future grades for his tools as well as a FINAL OFP. At the end of the process, you can compare your results to mine.

Remember, there are no right or wrong answers in this hypothetical situation; it's about being subjective and a matter of personal taste.

Hank: *College junior; right-handed; starting pitcher; 21 years old*

BODY:

6'2"; 230 lbs.

Strong solid thick build; good now strength; fair athleticism; okay fluidity and body control

Ran a 7.3 60-yard dash on Scout Day.

Appears to have a mature body for his age.

BAROMETER: _____

DELIVERY: (USE TO PROJECT)

Simple full wind-up delivery; lacks separation; ball is late getting out of glove; arm swing is off-line behind body so hitter gets a good look at the ball in his hand; stride foot lands across body; arm slot lower than preferred; near average arm speed; some recoil to arm and upright finish; stride leg direction better from stretch delivery; effort-type guy with quick tempo approach and delivery

FASTBALL:

91–96 mph, mostly 93–94 for first three innings

Aggressive, attacks hitter with FB; some flat tailing action (moves toward the arm side of the pitcher); trackable; hitters seem to get good swings on high velocity FB especially when up in zone.

Can cut (moves to glove side of pitcher) occasionally when throws to glove side; fair command; some feel for in/out but misses arm-side; no big misses; follows catcher okay

FB: P _____ / F _____

SLIDER:

82–85 mph

Consistent shape and spin; sweepy, flatter action; medium length. Decent angle to right-handed hitters (RHH); has good effectiveness to them; left-handed hitters (LHH) see it well when in zone; not as effective to LHHs; lacks depth and true late action necessary for success versus LHHs

SL: P _____ / F _____

CHANGE-UP (CH):

80–82 mph; rarely used; doesn't look comfortable using pitch; some sink and depth; makings of a decent pitch but needs to throw it; slows delivery and arm to throw CH

CH: P _____ / F _____

CONTROL:

Works behind in the count mostly but doesn't have a lot of walks in his history; appears to overthrow FB and get himself behind in the count; can get the ball into the strike zone when he has to

CON: P _____ / F _____

RAW OFP: _____

MAKE-UP:

Aggressive pitcher and appears to like competition; his coaches confirm he's highly competitive, sometimes to a fault; a pretty good kid but undisciplined in work habits; okay overall but not a leader; no off-field concerns or issues

MAKE-UP: _____

SCOUT INSTINCTS: *(+ or – 5 maximum)* _____

The beauty of scouting is that the identical descriptive information can be viewed in many different ways. Your unique personal Scouting Instincts help form your FINAL OFP on Hank.

In this example, some scouts see the higher-end FB velocity on a strong body and discount the imperfections. These scouts believe that FB velocity will carry Hank's Major League success. Other scouts will recognize Hank has a big arm, but they will downgrade him because he has no secondary pitch close to AVERAGE. These scouts believe everything must go perfectly for the pitcher to have AVERAGE secondary pitches. That will still not give him an "out pitch" besides the FB.

What do you believe?

Is it rare for college pitchers to throw 96 mph?

HANK'S FINAL OFP: _____

MY ESTIMATIONS: HANK

BAROMETER:

> *Strong solid thick build; good now strength*
>
> *Fair athleticism; okay fluidity and body control*
>
> *Appears like a mature body for age*
>
> *Ran a 7.3 60-yard dash*

I envision Hank as a mature-bodied, strength-oriented, BELOW-AVERAGE athlete. He has a chronological age of 21, so I'd give him credit for physical improvement, but the descriptions lead me to believe his body is close to being "maxed out." Putting more credence on the language in the description than the age, I'd set my barometer at 40 for Hank. If scouts were to put more credence on the chronological age, they might set the barometer at 50.

BAROMETER: 40

DELIVERY:

Fairly simple full wind-up delivery

Lacks separation; ball is late getting out of glove

Arm swing is off-line behind body

Stride foot a little across body; arm slot lower than preferred

Some recoil to arm, upright finish

Near AVERAGE arm speed

Effort-type guy with quick-tempo approach and delivery

This description of flaws- *"lacks separation"* and *"ball is late getting out of glove"*— reflects almost every college pitcher. No descriptive terminology is used to depict Hank's arm action as a detriment to future pitch development. Near AVERAGE arm speed, while not great, leads me to believe progress is possible. It's not a slow arm. We assume adjustments to the delivery will lead to future development and an increase in effectiveness of pitches. *Study the delivery to gain a sense of potential improvement of his pitches with adjustments to his pitching mechanics.*

DELIVERY: P: 40/ F: 45 (RATING IS FOR PROJECTION USE ONLY)

FASTBALL:

91–96 mph; mostly 93–94 for three innings

Aggressive; attacks hitter with FB

Some flat tailing action; trackable; hitters get good swings on high velocity FB.

Can cut occasionally when throws to glove side

Fair command; misses arm-side

No big misses; follows catcher okay

At 21 years old, Hank averaged 93–94 mph in his first three innings. His FB is grading as a 65 or 70 now, but he is maxing out his FB with few strikes early in the count. His age may hint to the potential of improvement in velocity, but he already throws with good arm strength. Potential adjustments to his delivery will help FB velocity and command. Hank doesn't miss big and follows the catcher okay (*TIP:* A prospective Major League pitcher at 21 years old should be reasonably able to get the ball into the strike zone on a regular basis and not routinely miss big).

FB: P: 65/ F: 70

SLIDER:

82–85 mph

Consistent shape and spin; sweepy flatter action

Decent angle and effectiveness to right-handed hitters

Left-handed hitters see it well when in the zone; not as effective to LHHs

Lacks depth and true late action for success versus LHHs

Hank sounds like he has a BELOW-AVERAGE SLIDER (SL). The slider has more sideways action than depth at present. I like the velocity, consistent shape, and effectiveness to RHHs. Hank must have a feel for this pitch. Delivery improvements allow the SL to have better depth and late action. Better depth will lead to increased effectiveness of the pitch, especially versus LHHs. I believe it could develop to AVERAGE at best.

SL: 40/50

CHANGE-UP (CH):

80–82 mph

Rarely used; doesn't look comfortable using pitch

Makings of a decent pitch, but needs to throw it

The "makings of a decent pitch" statement offers hope. Hank doesn't use the CH as a weapon now, and there is no evidence to believe it can't improve. The delivery improvements combined with his "near AVERAGE arm speed" should allow for an AVERAGE CH. Typically, a *"guesstimate" is required by the scout to determine the potential of an amateur pitcher developing a CH. Most amateur right-handed pitchers either don't use a CH or have an underused one.*

CH: 35/50

OTHER:

Hank has no other pitches at present, but I'll use my imagination based on information collected. His FB description stated "can cut occasionally when throws to glove side." This leads to assuming that Hank may eventually have a CUTTER. When combined with his arm strength, it should be a high-velocity CUTTER.

TIP: Most MLB clubs don't allow for the grading of pitches the pitcher doesn't presently use. If you have solid evidence the pitcher can develop another pitch, add it to the overall picture.

CONTROL:

In the area of CONTROL, it's stated *"works behind in count, but doesn't have a lot of walks in his history; seems to be able to get the ball in the zone when he has to."* These positive statements lead me to believe Hank could have AVERAGE CONTROL in the future. As a college pitcher, a track record of statistics exists.

CON: 35/50

TOOLS:

Present and future projected tools.

Figure 10.4

PITCHING TOOLS	PRESENT/FUTURE
FB	65/70
SL	40/50
CH	35/50
CON	35/50

We'll add the values of the future grades and then divide by 4 *(the number of tools).*

70 + 50 + 50 + 50 = 220 ÷ 4 = 55 RAW OFP SCORE

SCOUTING INSTINCTS:

Let's review the information.

21-year-old college pitcher; mature body; may be maxed-out physically

Appears to be a BELOW-AVERAGE athlete

Simple delivery; some flaws that are correctable; near AVERAGE arm speed

Big arm, 91–96 mph; hitters get good swings; throws strikes

SL and CH need development to get to AVERAGE

Projecting a CUTTER in future; doesn't throw it now

Works behind in the count, but projecting AVERAGE CONTROL

Borderline MAKE-UP; competitive, but not a hard worker at present

RAW OFP: 55

In my opinion, the descriptive information sways our Scouting Instincts negatively regarding Hank. Specifically, his lack of AVERAGE athleticism and AVERAGE make-up would both be viewed negatively. Hank's mature-looking thick body at his young age also causes concern. If Hank were to make the adjustments necessary to improve his delivery and secondary pitches to the degree consistent with AVERAGE at the Major League level, he would need to be a good athlete. Also, he must be a conscientious worker to improve his skills to an acceptable level. As my personal process requires, I use my Scouting Instincts to grade Hank lower than the RAW OFP of 55.

How is all of this development to transpire with just fair athleticism and questionable make-up? His high-end FB velocity would have to carry Hank's Major League career. It's presently ABOVE-AVERAGE on a Major League scale. That is why I consider him a prospect. At 21 years old and with his present arm strength, I hope he occasionally throws a secondary pitch that I could rate as AVERAGE. That would be reasonable evidence to project him to have another future weapon versus Major League hitters and to feel positive about Hank's future. I like what he presently shows for FB velocity, but Hank needs vast improvements in secondary pitches and command to become a Major League pitcher.

Besides the FB, what is Hank's other out pitch? (Am I imagining a CUTTER because I'm looking for an acceptable secondary pitch to add to his repertoire?)

Let me make the FINAL OFP 52 minus three points from the RAW OFP of 55. I can envision Hank in a middle relief role, 6th or 7th inning, but not an impactful set-up man for winning games, especially facing left-handed hitters. None of his secondary pitches will develop to the degree needed.

RAW OFP: 55

SCOUTING INSTINCTS: -3

FINAL OFP: 52

Hank's lack of AVERAGE athleticism worries me about his future progress and role. I want a better athlete for a starting pitcher or, to be a quality late-inning reliever, he needs an impactful secondary pitch. Hank has neither. Additionally, the lack of late action of his pitches lead me to believe he has a low spin rate. A lower spin rate on his FASTBALL would make it more beneficial to use a 2-seam fastball instead of a high velocity 4-seam fastball. Potentially limiting his high end velocity.

Refer to the MAJOR LEAGUE OFP VALUE CHART in Figure 10.2 to check if *your* opinion of Hank's FINAL OFP is consistent with your projection of Hank's future role. There's no right or wrong answer. Remember, Hank touched 96 mph as a starting pitcher. How hard could he throw if he only had to pitch one inning in the future? 100 mph? We are projecting a pitcher's tools with limited information, having never seen this hypothetical player. Instead, we're practicing the art of projection—predicting the future—to hone our ability to identify the present nuances of a player and correlate them into a future Major League assessment of him. It's not easy!

MY PROCESS:

Athleticism is the common denominator of high-level performance and longevity. I'm willing to "dream big" on a young player when I sense he has ABOVE-AVERAGE athleticism. Conversely, I have little belief in an un-athletic player developing to compete against the toughest competitors on the planet. Also, make-up plays a tremendous role in professional baseball achievement. Athleticism and make-up are foundational pieces of my player evaluation construct, sometimes to a fault.

While cross-checking, my first question to an area scout regarding a player we're about to watch is "What type of athlete is this kid?" My second question is "What kind of make-up does he have?" I know my inner belief system well enough to know I *cannot* overestimate athleticism (I will project too high) or underestimate make-up (I will not project high enough). Otherwise, I will make mistakes.

I know where I make my mistakes. Do you?

Summary

Flawed Players

The Hall of Fame players or the "best of the best" are special and extremely rare. The majority of Major League players will have some flaw in their athleticism, strength, make-up, or tools. It is up to the scout to determine which flawed players will succeed at the Major League level. The scout is required to see the beauty and potential of the flawed players, knowing which characteristics are priorities and which flaws have lesser consequence. Your characteristic priorities are important to your future success as an evaluator.

Rocky and Hank were flawed. I could have had you grade out a high school outfielder with a tremendous body and great athleticism that had 70 or 80 tools across the board. We could have put an OFP of 75 on the player and called him a future Hall of Famer. Sorry. That's not reality. The vast majority of prospects are bunched between an OFP of 48 and 52 with both positives and negatives. The scout discerns which flaw is of little or no consequence to each particular player. He also exhibits his value to the organization by understanding which flawed player to appreciate over all of the others. Never expect perfect players!

The Physical Ability and the Tools

Your proficiency in projecting depends on your ability to discern if the natural physicality of a player will help or limit his future baseball ability. Then you factor in his present tools and make-up to project if they will improve, stay the same, or decrease as time goes by. You will face many flawed players and be required to determine which ones could be Major Leaguers. Some players will "look like Tarzan, but swing like Jane." (I've always liked this saying.)

Each player will present a different set of circumstances. This is the subjective aspect of scouting. It's an art. Whichever you lean toward—athleticism, strength, make-up, or tools—is at your discretion. Every scout leans slightly one way or another when judging young players, but some will lean heavily one way. Some believe strength and athleticism are necessary components for a Major League career and won't like young players who appear weak or nonathletic. Others like any pitcher who can throw 95 MPH no matter what they think of his body. You bring your unique background and perspective to determine which way to lean. Here's a standard rule I've found to be fundamentally appropriate: The lesser the physical ability (barometer), the bigger the "now tools" should be.

I call this fundamental principle of scouting the Car Theory. Compromising on the "car" (body, strength, and athleticism) requires the player to have "good now tools" or solid present baseball skills. Conversely, a player with a high degree of athleticism and strength may be given the benefit of the doubt in projection. *Your* characteristic priorities for each spot on a Major League diamond helps you determine when the tools are good enough in a questionable athlete or when the tools are lacking in a great athlete.

The essence of scouting is the study and projection of a young player's physical characteristics, make-up, and present tools. Keep these principles in mind:

- ☐ Accept that you will scout flawed players.

- ☐ Assess "now tools" as the baseline for projection.

- ☐ Note that the barometer and characteristics are the keys to "how."

- ☐ Keep in mind that make-up may determine success.

- ☐ Have a reason for your Scouting Instincts adjustment.

- ☐ Match your FINAL OFP to a corresponding Major League role.

- ☐ KNOW YOURSELF!

CHAPTER 11:

SCOUTING—THE FINAL ANALYSIS

Building a Championship Profile

THIS CHAPTER DEFINES THE SCOUTING PROCESS EVEN FURTHER AND attempts to distinguish the best players for a championship club.

Chapter 7 introduced the idea of a *basic construct*—to study the desired result and then construct a plan to produce that result. Our intended result is a World Series championship. As such, we examine the common characteristics of a championship Major League club and then build a corresponding profile of positions that will raise our player evaluation standards to a championship level.

This championship profile technique systematically scrutinizes the positional priorities and impact each player should bring to a championship club. This enables the organization to identify the type of player desired at each position. In the end, the result should be a process designed to distinguish between ordinary Major League players and championship Major League players. We are not only scouting for players who can participate satisfactorily at the Major League level. We're acquiring players who will have a higher impact on a championship club.

Characteristics of a Championship Club

Our scouting process intends to acquire the talent necessary to produce a championship club—an impactful team that's well balanced with no true weakness in any one area. The construct should reflect team and player characteristics necessary for the club to achieve impact and balance. The manager needs a complete arsenal of baseball weaponry to win against the best teams in MLB.

As scouts, we formulate a set of basic characteristics of a championship club:

☐ It must be able to prevent opponents from scoring runs through excellent pitching and defense.

☐ It should have a potent offense, allowing the manager to construct a batting order with position players who can get on base and others who can drive in runners.

The player personnel of a championship club can vary, but our mission is to determine the common characteristics that exist among them.

PITCHERS:

The clubs that qualify for the MLB playoffs in October are among the most talented pitching teams in all of Major League Baseball. Championship clubs have at least three starting pitchers who can dominate an ABOVE AVERAGE Major League lineup. Their starting pitchers throw relatively deep into the game, giving the offense an opportunity to score enough runs to take the lead. If they can pitch at least into the 6th or 7th inning, it helps rest the relief pitchers, usually comprised of dominant late-inning relievers. Not only do these bullpens consist of high-velocity arms, they also feature relievers who specialize in match-ups with either right-handed or left-handed hitters. The manager must possess the weapons to match his relievers against the opposing lineup in critical situations during the game.

> Offense wins individual awards, but great pitching and defense wins championships.

SIMPLE CHAMPIONSHIP PITCHING PROFILE:

☐ Three impactful starting pitchers

☐ Dominant late-inning relievers

☐ Impactful match-up relievers for both RHHs and LHHs

Food for Thought

If the top three starting pitchers must be impactful for a championship club, what do you believe their OFPs should be, at minimum, to be considered for this grouping? Which of these would you select: 55, 60, 65, 70, 75, 80?

POSITION PLAYERS:

The position player personnel on a championship club are typically well balanced in terms of solid defense and a productive lineup. Defense is critical for players in the middle of the field (SS, CF, C, 2B), often referred to as premium positions. Players in these positions field the majority of batted balls and have the most difficult defensive challenges on the team. To win a championship, these players must have excellent defensive impact to limit the opponents' base runners and scoring opportunities. *Defense up the middle* is viewed as a primary characteristic. They are premium position players due to a relative scarcity of players who can have impact in both halves of the inning (bat and glove) at the Major League level. These premium position players are viewed as defense-first players but also (at minimum) AVERAGE performers on offense, with a combination of batting average, speed, or power to be EVERYDAY players. If a premium position player is capable of ABOVE AVERAGE offensive impact and also has defensive prowess, he's among the most elite players within the championship profile.

The corner players (3B, 1B, LF, RF) are typically the *run producers* on a championship club. As corner players, they have fewer demands for defense, but they must provide offense with their bats as their primary characteristic. They provide power in the lineup and drive in base runners. Also, the corner players must be (at minimum) AVERAGE performers on defense to be EVERYDAY players. The corner player with ABOVE AVERAGE defensive impact plus offensive prowess is among the most highly regarded players in a championship profile.

If you stand on the corner, you must lean on the pole.

SIMPLE CHAMPIONSHIP POSITION PLAYER PROFILE:

☐ Premium position players must provide impactful defense.

☐ Corner players must provide impactful offense.

The players of past championship clubs may not fit our simplistic model perfectly, given that no strict standards exist. For reasons such as injury, performance issues, or lack of talent, we can point to past championship clubs that didn't have the impactful pitchers and position players who fit neatly into this profile. We're not concerned with the exceptions; we're looking for common characteristics of championship clubs. Let's focus on acquiring players who offer the best chance to build an impactful, well-balanced team that's the most likely to win a championship.

Figure 11.1

POSITION PROFILE

(Diagram of a position's PRIMARY IMPORTANCE to a championship club)

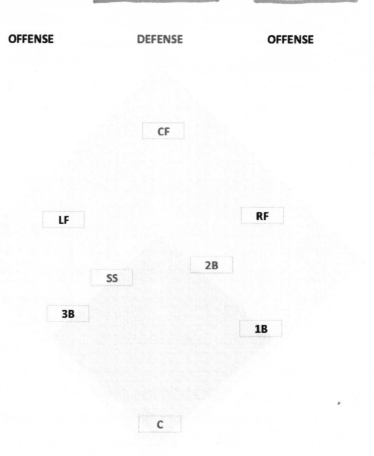

The Rule of 110 and 160 Applied to Position Players

Let's construct a simple profile for prospective players—one designed to recognize a player's individual characteristics that best fit into this championship basic construct. It starts with setting minimum criteria for each individual position on the team. This includes specific tools necessary for players to be of impact in the area of their corresponding PRIMARY

IMPORTANCE. The PRIMARY IMPORTANCE CHART in Figure 11.1 begins to develop a simple profile in offense or defense.

Chapter 8 featured a story about me stuffing napkins into my pocket in a coffee/herbal teahouse in Malibu. The napkins were covered with handwritten lessons from Bill Livesey, my mentor in scouting and player development. That's when I first learned a *profile of positions* and the differences between corner players and premium position players. Mr. Livesey graciously offered me this valuable scouting guideline: use of the numbers 110 and 160 (110 and 160 relative to the 20–80 grading scale).

In Mr. Livesey's estimation, these were two important numbers for determining if a player was of championship caliber. He contended that corner players must have a minimum total grade of 110 in their PRIMARY IMPORTANCE tools of HIT + POWER to be considered a championship Major League prospect. He also said the FIELD grade must be at least AVERAGE or 50 to be considered an EVERYDAY corner player. *110 + 50 = 160*

Mr. Livesey offered the minimum criteria for a corner player's PRIMARY IMPORTANCE tools and followed with the minimum criteria for the SECONDARY IMPORTANCE tools for an EVERYDAY corner player. After further reflection, I think Mr. Livesey's guideline of 110 was used to teach inexperienced scouts such as me the importance of *impact*.

By nature of his position on a championship club, each player has a role, and a corresponding PRIMARY IMPORTANCE. At minimum, the player's PRIMARY IMPORTANCE should be better than AVERAGE to be considered. *Nothing less will be acceptable.* Acquiring players with PRIMARY IMPORTANCE tools graded above 110 and 160 make it increasingly more *probable* the club will win a championship.

To summarize:

☐ Minimum for HIT + POWER (110)

☐ Minimum for HIT + POWER + FIELD (160)

☐ *Maximum* for HIT + POWER (80 + 80 = 160)

☐ *Maximum* for HIT + POWER + FIELD (80 + 80 + 80 = 240)

Subscribing to Mr. Livesey's theory of the PRIMARY IMPORTANCE tools of HIT + POWER for championship corner players means believing a player's overall offensive impact should be better than AVERAGE. As such, the *minimum criteria* for offense in a championship corner player would be 110 HIT + POWER (50 HIT + 60 POWER or 40 HIT + 70 POWER or other variations). The combination must be equal to or greater than 110, with no prescribed individual requirement for either HIT or POWER. When scouting corner players, we evaluate *offensive impact* in whatever fashion the player provides it. Any combination of HIT + POWER that adds up to 110 or better will suffice. The higher above 110 in the combination of HIT and POWER, the more *impactful* the corner player will be in producing runs for the team.

This formula doesn't attempt to paint a picture of the type of hitter desired. As Mr. Livesey wrote on one of my napkins, "It's a profile, not a portrait."

"It's a profile, not a portrait." – Bill Livesey

Figure 11.2

EXAMPLES OF 110 FOR CORNER PLAYERS

HIT	POWER	AVG	HR'S
30	80	.230	40
40	70	.245	34
50	60	.264	25
60	50	.285	19
70	40	.305	12
80	30	.320	7

Food for Thought

As a scout, consider these questions:

☐ Should the RUN grade factor into this equation for offense in corner players?

☐ If you upgrade a corner player because of his speed, do you downgrade a poor runner?

☐ How would you factor RUN with HIT and POWER to appropriately reflect offensive impact?

PREMIUM POSITION PLAYERS:

In a classic profile, the premium position players of SS, C, CF, and 2B are to provide defensive impact for the club as their PRIMARY IMPORTANCE. These positions have distinct differences in the particular characteristics that would be valuable in performing defensively at an impactful level. It can be advantageous for the centerfielder to possess outstanding running speed to cover his position, but is the catcher required to have good speed to play impactful defense? Also, it can be advantageous for the catcher to have great arm strength, but does the second baseman require a strong arm to play impactful defense? This means designing a standard measurement for each individual position, describing the physical qualities needed to perform defensively at an impactful level.

Let's use Mr. Livesey's guideline of 110 to judge defensive impact in premium position players in Figure 11.3

Figure 11.3

SECOND BASE:

Second base is a difficult position to profile. A championship second baseman must have *defensive impact,* but this may not be reflected by our standard position player tool grades. An *impactful defensive* second baseman can have quick lateral movement and good range but rate BELOW AVERAGE in RUN grade. He can also possess quick hands and a great transfer to throw but be BELOW AVERAGE in ARM grade. He can make all of the plays with his skill but not RAW TOOLS.

In my opinion, the defensive impact of a second baseman should not be viewed as the sum of particular tools used defensively but through overall performance. Often, scouts have to "use their eyes" to assess the defensive impact of a second baseman. The grading of RAW TOOLS in a second baseman doesn't always accurately depict his ability, especially with the ARM because of the short throw to first base he's frequently required to make.

Many MLB clubs in today's game appear willing to sacrifice impactful defense for offensive production at the second base position. These clubs use a profile of a second baseman that's more complex than what we've discussed. They combine the tools of offense and defense to formulate a profile that has offense as an equal priority to defense. Thus, they look for offensive impact from the position and discount needing a great defender at second base. They may employ a profile that examines the top three tools noted in Figure 11.4.

Figure 11.4

SECOND BASE

FIELD + HIT	MUST TOTAL AT LEAST 110
FIELD+HIT+POWER OR RUN	MUST TOTAL AT LEAST 160
THROW	
POWER OR RUN	

Some clubs might want a FIELD/HIT/RUN second baseman or a FIELD/HIT/POWER second baseman so they have a more detailed profile to fit their beliefs of what's required for a championship club. They allow for the different styles of offensive impact. By doing so, these clubs are ensuring they acquire *offensive impact* and only require sound defensive play at the second base position.

Food for Thought

Are you in agreement with clubs that sacrifice up-the-middle defense at second base for offense? Is second base the only premium position in which it's comfortable enough to sacrifice defense for offense?

The Rule of 160 Applied to Pitching

Our goal is to design a pitching profile using Mr. Livesey's guideline. We use 110 and 160 (the sum of the three priority tools) to represent the minimum criteria for *pitching impact* at the Major League level. But first, let me share a story.

Felipe Alou

In my time with the Montreal Expos, I learned a great deal from Major League Manager Felipe Alou. We had long philosophical discussions about all aspects of professional baseball, and I feel blessed to have learned from such an accomplished professional.

Sometimes he would ask me baseball questions, and we'd debate a certain topic at length, almost never arriving at any conclusion satisfactory to both of us. That was okay—he would consistently allow me to speak my opinion in this free exchange of baseball analysis. Other times, it was quite different. I could always detect when Felipe was stating what he believed to be fact.

One such discussion addressed the importance of having dominant pitching for a championship club. That's when Felipe asked me, "What is the most important pitch in baseball?"

At this point, I had spent a great deal of time studying pro-fessional pitching. I studied as a player, spending many hours in Rookie Ball listening to Howie Gershberg (former St. Johns University pitching coach and California Angels instructor) or in Single-A with Chuck Hernandez (pitching coach for California Angels, Tampa Bay, Detroit, Miami) and former Major League pitcher Pete Richert. In my front office career, I was fortunate to work with Joe Kerrigan, a highly esteemed mind who shared his pitching beliefs with me. When I asked them a myriad of pitch-ing questions, they offered greater-than-brilliant responses. They had asked me Felipe's trick question—what's the most important pitch in baseball?—so I knew the answer.

Felipe had egged me on to answer with a certain pitch type such as a change-up or fastball, but the correct answer is a situation, not a pitch. So I'd confidently respond, "A first-pitch strike."

In my mind, I had answered the question correctly. Felipe nodded his head in what appeared to be agreement and then paused. I'd learned to read this stoic man well at this point in our relationship, so his hesitation unsettled me. After a long, deliberate pause, I knew what was coming—he was preparing to lecture me. Felipe started with "I believe . . ." Now, anyone who has spent time with Felipe has heard those words and know they're always followed by FACT (not his opinion or something about which he had no conviction). He'd present the answer as a hard-earned, self-taught FACT—the type of knowledge that can only be learned through extensive years of experience and study.

"I believe—it is the FASTBALL," Felipe said.

Then he lectured me on the supreme importance of the fastball. The pitcher should be able to pitch inside for balls and strikes with a good fastball to hitters, setting up off-speed pitches. The pitcher should command all quadrants of the strike zone with a fastball to exploit areas of a particular weakness to the hitter. He described pitching around hitters to walk them with a fastball when there was an open base, which wouldn't allow a wild pitch with a bounced breaking ball to happen. He talked of the intimidation factor and fear applied to a hitter when a pitcher has a high-velocity fastball in his arsenal. He spoke about a pitcher who has the type of fastball to back up his King of the Hill demeanor and mound presence.

Then he ended with this: "That's why they call the fastball number one."

The Fastball

As we develop the priority tools for a championship club pitching staff, we can agree with Felipe and start with the FASTBALL. The FASTBALL is the most used pitch by almost every Major League pitcher. Here's what Vinny Castilla says about it.

Vinny Castilla played in all or part of 16 Major League seasons with the Atlanta Braves, Colorado Rockies, Tampa Bay Devil Rays, Houston Astros, Washington Nationals, and San Diego Padres. Although a slick-fielding third baseman, Vinny was known mostly for his bat and being one of the best FASTBALL hitters in Major League Baseball during those years.

Vinny amassed 320 Major League home runs and was a three-time Silver Slugger Award winner. This two-time All-Star hit 40 home runs in both 1996 and 1997, then 46 home runs in 1998.

Vinny Castilla

While working together with the Colorado Rockies, Vinny and I were on a trip to Modesto, California, to watch our Single-A Modesto Nuts of the California League. We scouted all of the players on the roster for five days and discussed each of them with the Nut's coaching staff. Vinny tended to focus on the position players closely, but he'd also evaluate the pitchers on the roster. One of the pitchers was athletic, had good size and strength, and had a very good FASTBALL. The Nuts coaches were positive about the pitcher's ability and liked his future potential as a Major League prospect.

Following our meeting with the Nuts coaching staff, Vinny and I had a private discussion. Vinny said he wasn't as excited about the potential of the young pitcher as everyone else and didn't like him as a Major League prospect. When I asked why, he said the pitcher didn't throw enough strikes and didn't have a good breaking ball. Vinny stated the kid had nothing for a Major

*League hitter to worry about other than a good FASTBALL.
Only having a good FASTBALL isn't enough to compete against
the best hitters in the world. As Vinny and I ended our conversation, we parted ways and then he looked back at me and said,
"A Major League hitter can learn to time a bullet."*

*Vinny had stood in a batter's box competing against the best
FASTBALLS of his era. In the Major Leagues, he knew a successful pitcher needed more than a FASTBALL because a quality hitter learns to "time" even the best FASTBALL. We can
agree with Vinny that a Major League pitcher must have a solid
SECONDARY PITCH of some consequence to the very best hitters on the planet. Vinny also alluded to the young pitcher not
throwing enough strikes. This would make the FASTBALL even
more vulnerable with the pitcher who's behind in the count often
and would be forced to throw more FASTBALLS.*

This story leads us to the subject of CONTROL. The championship pitcher must limit the scoring opportunities for the opposition, and
"walks" are in no way a deterrent to scoring. A pitcher could have the best
FASTBALL and SECONDARY PITCH in MLB, but if he can't throw them
over the plate, they'll have little value to a championship club.

CHAMPIONSHIP PRIORITY TOOLS PITCHING PROFILE:

☐ Fastball

☐ Best secondary pitch *(breaking pitch, change-up, or other)*

☐ Control

The sum of these three priority tools should be a minimum of 160.

At least one of the three priority pitching tools must be ABOVE
AVERAGE to believe the pitcher will have impact for a championship club.
Many different styles of pitchers and combinations of priority tools will fit

our profile. Our minimum requirement is that the three priority tools are equal to or greater than 160. Obviously, any combination higher than 160 should provide increased pitching impact for the team.

I believe a championship pitcher must have at minimum 40 CONTROL. The pitcher's ABOVE-AVERAGE FASTBALL and SECONDARY PITCH are irrelevant if he allows an out-of-the-ordinary number of batters to reach via a base on balls.

In the Major Leagues there are exceptions to this rule, but the use of "exceptions as evidence" should not determine what's more probable for a team to win a championship.

Figure 11.5

EXAMPLES OF 160 FOR PITCHERS

FB	SECONDARY PITCH	CONTROL	TOOLS TOTAL
40	80	40	160
50	50	60	160
60	50	50	160
70	50	40	160
80	40	40	160

Example Players Rocky and Hank

Let's review our examples from Chapter 10 and further examine hypothetical players Rocky and Hank.

Figure 11.6

THE HIGH SCHOOL OUTFIELDER: *ROCKY*

TOOLS	PRESENT/FUTURE GRADE
HIT	30/50
POWER	40/35
RUN	50/55
ARM	40/55
FIELD	30/55

PREMIUM-POSITION PROFILE: CF	
DEFENSIVE IMPACT	
FIELD	55
RUN	55
ARM	55
TOTAL	165 – DEFENSIVE IMPACT GRADE
OFFENSIVE IMPACT	
HIT	55
POWER	35
TOTAL	90 – OFFENSIVE IMPACT GRADE

☐ Does Rocky profile for a championship club?

☐ Did you factor speed into his offensive impact?

☐ Is he an EVERYDAY player on a championship club?

☐ Did your opinion of Rocky change after you applied a championship profile?

Figure 11.7

THE COLLEGE PITCHER: *HANK*

TOOLS	PRESENT/FUTURE GRADE
FB	65/70
SL	40/50
CH	35/50
CON	35/50

PITCHING PROFILE	
FB	70
SL	50
CON	50
TOTAL	170 – PITCHING PROFILE GRADE

In what role do you envision this college pitcher on a championship club?

Does the lack of a true secondary "out pitch" concern you for the role?

Did your opinion of this pitcher change after you applied a championship profile?

The Recognition of Impact

The championship profile concept helps scouts recognize impact. Prioritizing the tools according to their importance in a given role gives you a better sense of which players might be impactful for a championship club. Players appearing at a similar skill level can be difficult to prioritize, but using a championship profile of positions provides the ability to distinguish which player may be of higher value to a championship club. The ability of a scout to evaluate a team of young players and determine which one will play in the Major Leagues is a tremendous skill. BUT IT'S NOT ENOUGH! Recognizing impact on a championship club tests the advanced skill level of a scout and is one of the common characteristics of a Master Scout.

A MORE COMPLEX PROFILE:

This chapter has built the foundation of a profile of positions on a championship club. This simple foundation comes from a collection of common characteristics and models our construct to best replicate a championship Major League club. Minimum criteria for the most significant tools have been established for each role so each player will provide impact in their PRIMARY IMPORTANCE to a championship club.

In a quest to profile championship club positions, it's time to get more detailed in developing the basic construct. See Figure 11.8.

Figure 11.8

A COMPLEX POSITION PLAYER PROFILE

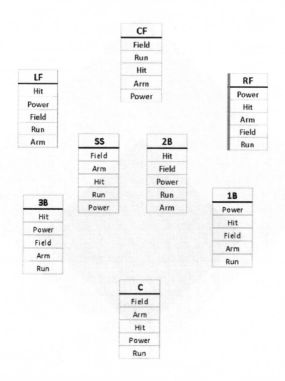

*This is an actual profile of positions used by a Major League club. It's not presented to initiate an argument about which tool should be designated fourth or fifth in priority of the profile. Rather, it demonstrates the practice of position profiling in modern MLB. Some clubs have used this profile system for decades; I was taught this process working with the New York Yankees in 1992.

Food for Thought for Statistical Gurus

Objective: To devise a formula that considers a player's impact on a championship club.

Using the Complex Position Player Profile depicted in Figure 11.8, construct a "Weighted OFP" giving more importance or weight to the tools of higher priority.

PITCHING RULE of 160 EXERCISE:

Can you draw any parallels between the pitcher's particular role and the Rule of 160?

In the Team Pitching Profile below, pitchers are in ascending order (1-5) and (6–12) of their importance to a championship club; as such, the requirements should move downward with each less-impactful role.

Can you detail each role's minimum requirements using the Rule of 160?

Maximum value is 240 (80 + 80 + 80)

TEAM PITCHING PROFILE:

1. STARTER	_____	6. CLOSER	_____
2. STARTER	_____	7. LH SETUP	_____
3. STARTER	_____	8. RH SETUP	_____
4. STARTER	_____	9. LONG or 6th STARTER	_____
5. STARTER	_____	10. LH MATCH-UP	_____
		11. LESSER SETUP	_____
		12. MANAGER's DISCRETION	__160__
		(Long-man, Situational)	

The Final Analysis

In the final analysis, the TOOLS of the players on the roster will help determine the success or failure of the club. The manager is charged with attaining maximum performance from the group as a whole. The overall lack of tools of his players will limit him, and success beyond the overall tool potential of the group is not a realistic goal for even the greatest managers.

The starting pitchers must offer the team a chance to win almost every night pitching quality innings deep into the game. The club must possess relievers that can maintain a lead, match up against the opposition's best hitters in critical situations of the game, and dominate late in the game to secure victory.

Defense should be a hallmark of the team, and excellent defensive ability must be evident in the middle of the field. The lineup should employ solid on-base-type offensive players, and it would be advantageous if they have speed as an asset. The lineup should also possess corner players who have the ability to drive in runs and hit many homers.

This is a general, simple description of a championship club—a well-balanced team that features many attributes and strengths with no glaring weakness. Anyone can attempt to design the perfect club with all five starters of "ace" quality, a bullpen filled with 100 mph arms with great out pitches and control, a lineup which boasts every position player who can play tremendous defense, and the capability of getting on base with the ability to hit 40+ home runs.

Is that a reasonable expectation? I think not. The theory of our design is to combine the player's primary importance of their position on a championship club with the type of secondary tools that are adequate at minimum. Because of our attention to the primary importance tools, we may not have the best secondary tools in the game, and that is fine with us. We are prioritizing the primary importance tools as much more integral to our championship quest. This theory has a realistic practical application in the competitive landscape of MLB.

Food for Thought

The manager should be able to employ a well-balanced lineup with on-base-type hitters and run producers. Can you construct a well-balanced lineup consistent with how you have prioritized the tools for each position? Eliminate the designated hitter, and construct a batting order using the eight position players (C, 1B, 2B, 3B, SS, LF, CF, and RF) and batting the pitcher ninth:

1. _____

2. _____

3. _____

4. _____

5. _____

6. _____

7. _____

8. _____

9. PITCHER

Key questions:

☐ Do you have speed in your lineup?

☐ How do you view the second base position offensively now that you have completed a lineup?

☐ Does your view of speed in premium positions change now that you have completed a lineup?

Summary

The Exceptions

In these scouting chapters, I have consistently dismissed the influence of the exceptions—players or teams that do not exhibit the characteristics of what's most common. I must admit, exceptions exist in Major League Baseball and some have had great success. The focus on what's most common and more probable, though, can lead to underestimating the impact of some exceptions. Evaluating baseball players requires understanding that you'll be incorrect on occasion. Indeed, most great scouts are incorrect more than they care to admit. Failure is a key component of every inexact science, and scouting is no different. *"Missing"* on a player is how we can learn to better shape player evaluation processes for future success.

We can strive to understand what we'd formerly believed was an exception and could actually be the rule based on what's most common. *Missing* is a key component of the successful future ability of player evaluation, but that's true only if we understand why we missed on a player's evaluation.

> When you are experienced and have achieved the level of Master Scout, then you can deal in exceptions. Otherwise, I would proceed with caution.

Becoming a Master Scout

Because the journey to becoming a Master Scout is never complete, you must constantly alter your process to fit what the game has most recently become. If properly reviewed, using a comprehensive framework to evaluate baseball players and teams will make your misses easier to understand. Always seek to know why you missed an individual player or team and determine if you should alter your player evaluation process due to a flaw in it or an issue with a particular area of your evaluation. That means implementing a personal "checks and balances" system for your player evaluation process to progress. It also means evaluating with full confidence your scouting process while having the honest ability to modify it when necessary.

This basic construct framework provides this outline to follow.

A BASIC CONSTRUCT FRAMEWORK OF SCOUTING:

- ☐ Complete understanding of what is *common* in the Major Leagues
- ☐ Use of a *professional grading scale*
- ☐ Breakdown of a player into a *set of now tools*
- ☐ *Prioritization* of characteristics of certain baseball tools
- ☐ Ability to *project* physical characteristics into the future
- ☐ Complete understanding of a *profile of positions*
- ☐ Use of a *championship standard* for each position
- ☐ Recognition of a *player's impact*
- ☐ Ability to *match a player's impact* with the proper role
- ☐ Ability to *scrutinize similar players for their level of impact* in their role on a championship club
- ☐ Ability to rate a player's *overall future potential* on a championship club
- ☐ Awareness that *it's not easy!*

It's Your Responsibility

Chapters 8 to 11 offer the foundation of a basic construct designed to recognize a player evaluation framework for acquiring championship players. It's also a framework built to understand what's most common among Major League players and a plan to direct attention to what's more probable. We use the laws of probability in our favor.

We recognize which tools are most likely to provide impact in a particular role on a championship club. We also recognize which seemingly flawed players could fit into a plan to win a championship by using their tools of impact.

Now it's up to you to finalize the details of *your* basic construct of a championship club following these steps. You have examples of what has been done and the benefit of my experiences and professional baseball lessons from my interaction with master-level staff.

Caution: In no way am I promising the exact way to evaluate players. The game of professional baseball changes too often to attempt to have all the answers well into the future. You must learn to recognize changes in the game and alter your basic construct accordingly—it's your responsibility!

Sample Scouting Report

This is an example scouting report. One I filed with the New York Yankees many moons ago. At that time, by our club, an OFP of 56 was considered a first-round candidate. I wanted to raise his OFP in the Scouting Instincts column but a 64 was the highest OFP I had ever recorded on an amateur player. I was still developing my confidence and conviction.

NEW YORK YANKEES
FREE AGENT REPORT

Overall future potential ___64___

Scouting instinct _____

Report No. ___1___

Scout Score _____ Raw Score ___64___ Territory ___SANTIN___

Player ___RODRIGUEZ___ ___ALEX___ _____ Position ___SS___
    Last name   First name   Middle name

Current Address _____
        City   State   Zip Code

Telephone _____ Date of Birth _____ Ht. _6'4_ Wt. _190_ Bats _R_ Throws _R_
    (Area Code)

Permanent address (If different from above) _____

Team Name ___WESTMINSTER CHRISTIAN___ City ___MIAMI___ State ___FLA___

Scout ___GEIVETT___ Date ___4/6/93___ Games ___1___ Innings _____

RATING KEY	NON-PITCHERS		Pres.	Fut.	PITCHERS	Pres.	Fut.	USE WORD DESCRIPTION
8—Outstanding	Hitting Ability	*	40	65	Fast Ball	*		Habits
7—Very Good	Power	55	35	60	Curve	*		Dedication
6—Above Average	Running Speed	*	65	65	Control	*		Agility ___VGOOD___
5—Average	Base Running		50	65	Change of Pace	*		Aptitude
4—Below Average	Arm Strength	*	65	65	Slider	*		Phys. Maturity ___EXCLNT___
3—Well Below Average	Arm Accuracy		50	60	Knuckle Ball	*		Emot. Maturity
2—Poor	Fielding	*	50	65	Other	*		Coachability
	Range		50	60	Poise			Comment(s)
Use One Grade	Baseball Instinct		65	65	Baseball Instinct			
Grade On Major	Aggressiveness		60	60	Aggressiveness			
League Standards	Pull ___ Str. Away		Opp. Field		Arm Action			
Not Amateur	X				Delivery			Date eligible ___1993___

Physical Description (Injuries, Glasses, etc.) Graduation ___1993___
TALL VERY ATHLETIC MUSCULAR BODY ON LARGE FRAME. ALL-PRO BODY IN ANY
SPORT. MUSCULATURE IS WELL-PROPORTIONED, DEFINED AND DEVELOPED. STRENGTH
IS VERY EVIDENT. BODY EXHIBITS EXTREME ATHLETICISM, EXPLOSIVENESS, VERY
FLUID ACTIONS TO MOVEMENT, AND STRENGTH. OUTSTANDING BODY AND ATHLETE.
BODY SHRINKS FIELD. EXCELENT STENGTH POTENTIAL. NO KNOWN INJURIES. NO
GLASSES.

Tools and Abilities SOFT-HANDED FIELDER WITH VERY GOOD INFIELD ACTIONS/INSTINCTS,
SOLID RANGE WITH QUICK ACTIVE FEET, FIELDS WELL BEYOND HIS AGE. VERY GOOD
ARMSTRENGTH WITH STRAIGHT CARRY, ALL-ANGLE THROWER WITH ACCURACY, GOOD TOUCH
AND FEEL. VERY GOOD RUNNING SPEED WITH INSTINCTS, PRESSURES DEFENSE, QUAL-
ITY JUMPS AND AGGRESSIVE TO STEAL. ALL-FIELD HITTER WITH VERY GOOD BAT-
SPEED, HAS BALANCE, SHORT COMPACT STROKE. POWER SHOULD BE VERY EVIDENT AS
HAS BATSPEED AND STRENGTH TO SWING.

Weaknesses BODY MAY OUT-GROW POSITION IN FUTURE, IS NOT A MAJOR CONCERN AS
PLAYER IS A SUPERIOR ATHLETE AND HAS ALL THE SKILLS/TOOLS TO PROVIDE IMPACT
AT SS. NEEDS TO DEVELOP PROPER HAND ACTION TO HIT, HANDS ARE QUICK TO PULL
TO INSIDE WHICH DECREASES EXTENSION OUT FRONT. HAS RAW HITTING TOOLS AND A
ATHLETICISM TO MAKE ADJUSTMENTS EASILY.

Summation SIZE STRENGTH TOOLS FOR STAR SS IN ML. YOUNG KID WITH BEAUTIFUL
BODY AND ATHLETICISM. DEFENSE WILL PROVIDE IMPACT ON CLUB AND WILL HAVE A
CORNER BAT AT PREMIUM POSITION. BEGINNING OF ORDER HITTER TO OFFER PRODUCT
ION IN ALL PHASES OF OFFENSE, INCLUDING STOLEN BASES AND BAT SKILLS. SU-
PERIOR ATHLETE WITH OUTSTANDING STRENGTH POTENTIAL. DRAFT STATUS-ML.

S-5

CHAPTER 12:

PLAYER DEVELOPMENT—PHILOSOPHY

Salt River Fields, Scottsdale AZ.
Spring Training home of the Arizona Diamondbacks and Colorado Rockies.
Photo Courtesy of Salt River Pima-Maricopa Indian Community

The Unheralded Minor League Staff

SIMILAR TO THE ANONYMOUS SCOUTS, MINOR LEAGUE STAFF MEMBERS complete their daily duties in relative anonymity. Many of them won't see their homes from mid-February to mid-September, spending more time with their assigned club than their own families. At the end of the professional season, some visit home only briefly. Then they move on to their next assignment in the Fall Instructional League, Arizona Fall League, or Winter Ball in Latin America or Australia.

These employees are not paid huge salaries. Many in professional baseball consider them drastically underpaid considering the valuable service they provide. The media tend to ignore this group while offering praise to the Major League coaches for the successes of young players. Without complaining, these staff members soldier forward to shape promising players and the future landscape of the Major League club, yet they are unheralded.

In the Middle of the Action

The Player Development Department holds a unique position within an organization—precisely in the middle of the Baseball Operations structure. Staff members work closely with either the Scouting Department or the Major League Operations Department. The front office, including club owners, receives daily game reports from all of the Minor League teams. These widely distributed reports include each manager's game notes, decision-making process, and opinions of every player's performance. The Scouting Department receives identical reports, making each scout in the organization aware of daily events in Player Development. Though the scouts might have tepid interest in the Minor League teams, they have laser-like focus on the progress of "their players"—individuals the scout has personally signed to the organization.

Player Development is the only department in which all of the daily activities are well-documented, disseminated to the entire Baseball Operations staff, and open for criticism by others. (No other department is required to detail its daily activities.) Amateur Scouting and Major League Operations have little interaction with one another in an MLB organizational structure, but the Player Development Department must effectively interact with all departments in Baseball Operations. That puts Player Development squarely in the middle of the action—a tough gig!

Player Development Department Goals

A Self-Sufficient Organization: Championship Standard

The Player Development Department should not exist to produce players who possess the tools and baseball skills to *adequately* participate at the Major League level. Rather, it strives to produce an entire roster of players that will comprise a championship club. Its goal is to provide players who possess the physical, fundamental, and mental skills to compete at a championship level at every position.

If this lofty goal were met, the Scouting and Player Development Departments would create a self-sufficient organization—one designed and constructed to fulfill all of the needs of a championship club. This could be considered the epitome of an unrealistic expectation of perfection, but anything less is to submit a plan designed for mediocrity. *This goal of self-sufficiency directly relates to a championship standard.* It's doubtful a club could win a championship unless it has built-in standards of operation reflecting the characteristics of a championship club. After all, the Scouting Department bases its player evaluations against a championship player standard. Those in the Player Development Department must operate this way daily to have consistency with a championship standard. Nothing less is acceptable.

A Championship Club: Impact and Consistency

Chapter 11 examined the characteristics of a championship club related to a player's tools for a particular role. It concluded that the more impactful the PRIMARY IMPORTANCE TOOLS, the more probable the chances of winning a championship.

However, the concept of "more probable" doesn't always translate into a championship; tools alone aren't the deciding factor. A championship club performs consistently throughout a long professional season to dominate the competition, and its potential is not analogous to consistent *performance.* What is the true measure of a championship club? *Performance through impact and consistency,* which are the hallmarks of success.

A Championship Player: Skills and Mentality

While directing staff meetings, I have asked many questions of staff members over the years. Here's one I asked during every Spring Training: "How do we define a championship player?" Typically, an awkward silence follows.

Many scouts and instructors use the term "championship player" to describe certain players. However, have they ever truly defined the term? Although I don't recall one player development instructor or Major League coach clearly define a championship player, I've received many responses in answer to this quest, noted in Figure 12.1 and 12.2.

Figure 12.1

CHARACTERISTICS OF CHAMPIONSHIP PLAYERS—COMMON RESPONSES		
Talented	Great make-up	Clutch player
Unselfish	Big tools	Responsible
Skilled	Makes others better	Accountable
Competitive	Hard worker	Makes adjustments
Professional	Leader	Disciplined
Team player	Good baseball intelligence	Respects others
Aggressive	Good baseball awareness	Dedicated

Let's organize this list in another fashion:

Figure 12.2

BASEBALL ABILITY	PERSONAL TRAITS
Talented	Competitive
Skilled	Team-player
Big tools	Aggressive
Makes adjustments	Great make-up
Clutch player	Makes others better
Good baseball awareness	Hard worker
Good baseball intelligence	Leader
	Responsible
	Accountable
	Unselfish
	Dedicated
	Professional
	Respects Others
	Disciplined

Through staff responses, I've learned that baseball ability is only part of the equation. The staff seemed fixated on the team aspect, consistently recognizing that winning a championship was a group effort. The championship player as described would make the entire team better, not only with his baseball ability but with his personal traits and dedication to a championship standard. Staff members could envision the championship player as an integral driving force of a team effort. He must perform an impactful role, but his mindset must fit in with a group of like-minded championship players—a critical goal of the Player Development Department.

Organizational Philosophy

The Cabin Story

In the early 1990s following the June MLB Draft, my duties as an area scout included professional scouting throughout the summer months. I'd spend time staying current with the amateur players in my area, with my main responsibility to complete my professional scouting duties. I was assigned to cover much of the California League (Single-A) and Pacific Coast League (Triple-A), and I was responsible for writing scouting reports on all of the players of my assigned teams. I would examine the schedule of these leagues and plan as much time as possible in Southern California for the California League or in Las Vegas for the Pacific Coast League. I especially enjoyed the California League because it allowed me to spend time in a special place— Lake Gregory. (Hey, there are some perks to the job!)

Close family friends Charlie and Keitha Slaton owned a cabin at Lake Gregory in the mountains above San Bernardino. Tucked into the trees overlooking the lake, this quiet space gave me time to compose my scouting reports during the day without distraction (no cell phones and certainly no Internet). In those years, the Yankee scouts weren't even using computers. We completed our reports on a typewriter or wrote them out. Each night, I'd attend one of the games of the San Bernardino Spirit (SEA Mariners), High Desert Mavericks (SD Padres), or the Palm Springs Angels (CAL Angels). After the game, I'd return to this cabin, organize my game notes, and ponder the players I had just scouted so I could write my reports the next day. What a great setup!

With local cable television options minimal, I rarely watched TV there. Instead, on my daily drive to the ballpark, I'd tune the radio to Jim Rome (esteemed UC Santa Barbara Gaucho) on the Mighty 690 AM station. I relied on "Romey" to catch me up on the major sports news of the day.

One night at the cabin, feeling bored silly, I turned on the TV, knowing the limited TV options were probably a lost cause. As I clicked through the channels of real estate seminars and old sitcom reruns, I was amazed to stumble on a local community cable show about professional baseball—the High Desert Mavericks Baseball Show. Because I was assigned to cover the Mavericks, I was thrilled to get inside information on its players.

Forget Romey. I instantly became a fan of local community cable access channels.

After discussing the latest Maverick games, the host announced a special guest—San Diego Padres General Manager Joe McIlvane. My excitement quickly turned to dismay. I would have rather listened to one of the Maverick coaches talk about the players he was working with or a particular player's fault they were correcting. Or I wanted to hear the Mavericks manager discuss which players he thought were Major League prospects. I didn't want to listen to a Major League GM talk about his club in San Diego. But I was wrong.

As the interview unfolded, Joe McIlvane was enlightening the viewers (possibly 10 of us) on the Player Development Department of the San Diego Padres, and he was only talking about the Minor Leagues. For his entire interview, Joe discussed almost every aspect of player development from an organizational standpoint and team vision. He stated his organizational philosophies and various player development philosophies of the Padres. I was mesmerized.

Although I can't recall one player development detail learned from listening to Joe, I do remember him educating me in a new way to think. Joe offered me the perspective of a professional baseball man who understood the journey of an amateur player from the June Draft to the Major Leagues. He spoke of the goals the organization had at the Single-A level for the High Desert Mavericks and how they differed at the higher levels of professional baseball. He spoke of what was important philosophically to the Padres and the type of player the team wanted to develop and eventually play in San Diego. I was utterly impressed with his organizational knowledge and the importance of "philosophy first." When he said each level may require a different mindset and philosophy, a light came on for me. The details of player development can only be judged by their ability to fit within the overall organizational and departmental philosophies. The lesson: First see the complete picture philosophically to make the proper decisions on the individual detail or strategy.

I'll fondly remember that cabin at Lake Gregory with its beautiful setting tucked into the trees and the limited but impactful TV options. No offense, Romey.

> The organization's overriding philosophy dictates the strategies and defines the details of proper procedure. Philosophy must come first!

What is Our Philosophy?

Whether we realize it or not, we all have general preconceptions on developing players or educational theoretical philosophy. In the context of the basic construct "know what we want to build," we must examine the endeavor from start to finish to identify the most important aspects of what's being built. Each stage of the process presents different challenges. Carefully examining all of the stages exposes our basic philosophy. We then "pour" our philosophical beliefs over the entire player development process to lay a foundation for the entire program. This philosophy is embedded into the foundation to shape "how we will build it." The strategies and details reflect the philosophical beliefs and strong convictions.

The following sections feature examples of teaching and player development philosophies. However, you have to make your own determinations about the elements and strategies of your process. You measure the individual baseball details against your philosophical beliefs and your strongest player development convictions. They only fit into your player development process when they are consistent with your philosophy. Key questions:

- ☐ What is the goal?

- ☐ What is your philosophy?

- ☐ How do you envision the process?

- ☐ What's most critical at certain stages of the process?

- ☐ How do you consider the philosophy's practical application?

Basic Teaching Philosophy

Physical/Fundamental/Mental: A Teaching Model

The many skills and abilities of a baseball player can be categorized into three specific areas: PHYSICAL, FUNDAMENTAL, or MENTAL. All of these have a natural order and progression.

PHYSICAL:

A player has a decreased probability of improving *fundamentally or mentally* if he doesn't possess the *physical strength or physical endurance* to handle the demands of daily professional play. A player's *physical* nature is extremely important in attempting to discern his *present capabilities.* Most scouts initially judge amateur players *physically* to ascertain whether the player is physically ready to sign a professional contract and can satisfactorily compete in professional competition and handle the daily activities without breaking down physically. If the player does possess the physical strength and endurance, the scout will be more confident in the player's potential to improve both *fundamentally and mentally.*

The PHYSICAL characteristics must be developed *first.* Key questions:

☐ Does the player have the physical strength to handle professional baseball?

☐ Does the player have the physical strength to handle a full season?

☐ Does the player have the physical tools to compete in professional baseball?

☐ Does the player have the physical endurance to complete the necessary repetitions to improve?

☐ Does the player possess the physical agility and flexibility to make adjustments in mechanics?

FUNDAMENTAL:

The player with the *physical* characteristics to handle the rigors of professional baseball has an increased probability of learning the *fundamental* and *mental* aspects of the game. Physical characteristics combined with proper fundamental technique make it more likely the player will perform consistently. Consistency of performance determines a player's upward movement into a higher level of play. He has a decreased chance of progressing through the system if he can't exhibit the proper fundamentals and technique associated with consistency. The mental aspects of the game are inconsequential if the player doesn't possess the reasonable proper fundamentals based on the level of play. Key questions:

☐ Does the player work hard enough to learn proper fundamentals?

☐ Does the player have the ability to repeat proper technique and mechanics?

☐ Does the player have reliable, repeatable fundamentals?

☐ Does the player have the aptitude to learn proper fundamentals?

MENTAL:

Mental skills are at a premium at the highest levels of the game. Major League players have proven they can physically handle the rigors of professional baseball and possess the physical endurance to improve their skills. These players have learned proper fundamentals and have honed their baseball skills into reliable repeatable assets of their game. They have personal drills to keep their baseball skills sharp and are prepared to play at a high level consistently. This consistency of play opens their minds to focus on the *mental* aspects of their individual craft as well as the complex team dynamics required to win a championship. They understand their strengths and lesser strengths, and they strive to maximize their impact by consistently performing their role on the team.

Championship players study their opponents to detect their weaknesses or their tendencies to take full advantage of strategies to address them. They know their role as members of a championship club, holding other players accountable to a "team first" attitude. They steer the group in the direction of a championship. Key questions:

☐ Does the player understand his strengths and lesser strengths?

☐ Does the player understand his role?

☐ Does the player study the opposition?

☐ Does the player recognize the strategy of the opposition?

☐ Does the player react when the team needs his leadership?

☐ Does the player think like a championship player?

The valid philosophical concept of PHYSICAL/FUNDAMENTAL/MENTAL follows the normal progression of a player's career. All of these areas are emphasized at each level, but some should be stressed more than others. Since there is a natural order of these areas, the overall teaching philosophy of the organization should reflect this concept.

PHYSICAL/FUNDAMENTAL/MENTAL EXERCISE:

This exercise examines your thoughts and beliefs on this concept and influences planning your developmental process by asking, "What percentage of each area (physical, fundamental, mental) would you use for a teaching emphasis at each level? See Figure 12.3.

Figure 12.3

	ROOKIE	A	AA-AAA
PHYSICAL	%	%	%
FUNDAMENTAL	%	%	%
MENTAL	%	%	%
	100%	100%	100%

Yogi Berra probably never completed this exercise, but he had a memorable theory when he said, "Baseball is 90 percent mental and the other half is physical."

Food for Thought

I have witnessed an instructor lose his job in the Major Leagues by working his players too hard physically. Many in the organization believed the Major League players were worn out physically and unable to perform to their maximum potential.

I have also witnessed an instructor lose his job at the Rookie Ball level because he'd often cancel early workouts to keep his players physically fresh for the game. Many believed the players weren't completing the necessary repetitions to develop their baseball skills well enough.

An Organized Progression

In education, a style of teaching called the *shotgun approach* happens when a teacher haphazardly shoots every bit of the information to be learned at the students. It's also called the *vomit technique* (no explanation needed).

Unfortunately, I have witnessed this technique often by professional baseball instructors. They blast technical baseball information with no coherent organization or progression to the material. Experienced educators present in an organized progression similar to the conceptual PHYSICAL/FUNDAMENTAL/MENTAL model. In this style, priority is dictated by the philosophical values of the team, which also guide the order of teaching emphasis. Teaching information in a logical progression allows access to the most complex concepts. The foundation consists of initial basic information from which to build toward advanced information. An organized progression requires beginning with the *simple* in preparation for the more *complex*.

The Bunt Defense Fiasco

After fulfilling my desire to save the New York Yankees money by staying in the cabin at Lake Gregory, I returned home to Huntington Beach, California, for a short time before my next assignment, Fall Instructional League (FIL) in Phoenix, Arizona. I was responsible for covering four MLB organizations in the FIL and to write scouting reports on each player—approximately 40 players in each organization.

A Fall Instructional League roster is comprised of young, inexperienced prospects of an MLB club. Many of these FIL players have recently signed a professional contract. They typically have great tools and solid future potential, but they can be inconsistent in their approach to the game or their performance of skills. I couldn't wait to scout the best young prospects in these organizations.

A good friend of mine, Earl Frischman, was scouting the FIL for the Minnesota Twins and reporting on most of the same teams I'd been assigned. We matched up our scouting days so we could spend time together. On the days we were scouting the same game, we'd meet early for breakfast, eating quickly so we could arrive at the ballpark in time for the players' individual early work sessions. We also wanted to talk to some of the instructors and gain insight into the players we were to evaluate. The FIL allows scouts to be in close proximity to the players and staff. On one particular day, we watched early work, received good information from a few coaches regarding certain players, and settled in to observe.

At this time of the morning, the entire group of staff and players reported in to the clubhouse to have a daily meeting and preview all of their team's FIL activities for the day. As we waited, Earl and I talked about golf and Romey's latest controversial remarks on the radio.

Earl and I watched the players walk closely by on their way to the field. As they passed, we'd judge their bodies with the "eye test" and get a good look up close before they went to stretch in the outfield. Tired of sitting in my lawn chair listening to Earl detail his latest 4 iron into the wind to a tucked pin, I walked around to stretch my legs. By then, the players had finished their stretching, played catch to loosen their arms, and headed to the infield for their team drill. One pitcher went to the mound while the others stood lined up in front of the dugout in foul territory. The position players were split into two groups, one on offense and one on defense. There were potential bunters at the plate and a runner at first base. A full defense took the field, including outfielders and everyone in position. All of the instructors appeared ready and eager to coach the drill as someone yelled, "Let's go!"

My first clue this drill was doomed occurred when the pitcher couldn't throw a strike to the bunter at the plate. He wasn't throwing at game-type effort because he hadn't completed a full warm-up routine for mound pitching. After four balls in a row, the instructors replaced him with the next pitcher in line. The poor strike-throwing results continued, although the second pitcher did throw a called strike with his third pitch. (Anyone involved in this type of drill knows the difficulty pitchers experience throwing consistent strikes at less-than-game speed.) The instructor coaching the bunters admonished that batter for taking a strike in a sacrifice situation. "Bunt the ball!" he screamed.

After a few more balls outside the batter's strike zone, a third pitcher was summoned. With his first pitch, he threw a strike right down the middle, and the bunter popped it up to the catcher. The bunting instructor furiously screamed, "Bunt the top half of the ball!" He then proceeded to walk out in front of the plate and lecture all the bunters on the basics of sacrifice bunting. This lecture lasted close to five minutes. Stopping the team drill to instruct only one segment of players left the others with nothing to do but wait. (This was a pet peeve of Felipe Alou's: Never stop a team drill.)

The third pitcher departed to the high-fives of his pitching comrades for his surprising ability to throw one strike. Then the fourth pitcher came to the mound with the now predictable strike-throwing difficulty and was quickly replaced after two pitches. The increased tension of players, especially the pitchers, mixed with the staff's embarrassment, was palpable. What a disaster.

Then a new pitcher strode to the mound and, to everyone's amazement, threw a strike. But the bunter missed the ball. The aware, energetic catcher fired the ball to the first baseman and caught the runner in a rundown between first and second. (Calling it a rundown is kind; it was more of a throwdown.) After five throws by the infielders, they still hadn't tagged this quick runner out. (Having two throws or fewer is the accepted measure of a successful rundown.)

So the infield instructor stopped the action and began to yell instructions to the infielders regarding the proper technique to retire a runner in a rundown. As he lectured the infielders, the remaining players stood around waiting. That's not completely correct. Tired of standing, the outfielders took a knee during this lecture.

As time slowly passed, Earl and I felt bad for all involved. We were former coaches, and we knew how everyone must have felt participating in a drill that had gone horribly wrong. The instructors gave up on the planned drill and sent all of the pitchers to the adjacent field for pitcher fielding practice. A coach proceeded to throw to the bunters to salvage the drill for the position players, but it was too little too late. A few minutes later, everyone moved on to the next activity on their schedule hoping for a better outcome.

At lunch time, a group of instructors stood near our lawn chairs. Earl and I could hear them discussing the infamous sacrifice bunting drill fiasco. I heard one instructor say, "I haven't had any time to practice sacrifice bunting with these kids." Another said, "I need to teach these infielders the fundamentals of rundowns."

Earl and I agreed with both of them. They had attempted a highly complex full-squad game-simulation drill without first teaching individual parts. This FIL team of young prospects performed in a youthful fashion. Not only was inexperience to blame; the drill was ill-conceived and doomed from the start. It became a valuable lesson in organized progression.

Begin with the simple, and then build to the complex.

An *organized progression* is a simple concept to incorporate into your philosophy of teaching proper fundamentals and your overall coaching strategy. It takes fully examining and understanding the entire landscape of the developmental program to plan an organized progression for teaching particular skills. What's needed?

1) The dissection of a championship player into a set of baseball skills

2) A proper plan of the path of instruction for each of the skills

Think of it this way: Math teachers wouldn't attempt to teach algebra before the student had learned addition and subtraction. Key questions:

☐ What are the foundational aspects of the skill?

☐ What should we teach first?

☐ How are we going to teach it?

☐ What are the more complex skills that come later?

"Plan your work and then work the plan." – Joe Kerrigan

Organizational Baseball Philosophy

Aim for a Championship Standard

A championship standard speaks to a high expectation of a *minimum guideline* from which to judge an aspect of the game or an individual player. This championship standard goes beyond the recognized norm when compared to the competition, for only the best in the game judge themselves this critically. It's a high bar by which to set your sights. However, it doesn't mean expecting Single-A level players to perform baseball skills perfectly at a championship Major League level. That would not be reasonable or appropriate. Yet some aspects of a young player's personal traits may be judged identically to those of a Major League player, such as work ethic, playing for the team, and more.

We also define each individual championship standard according to the level of play or the individual maturity level of the player. A championship standard may vary from level to level in the developmental process. To detail the philosophy of our championship standard, we can turn to the list of responses by past Player Development staffs and Major League staffs describing the individual characteristics of a championship player.

Use the list of Championship Player Characteristics in Figure 12.1 as reference.

Key questions:

☐ Should certain championship player characteristics be hallmarks of the organization's players?

☐ What should be the staff's approach to develop these championship player characteristics in young players?

☐ Can some of these championship player characteristics be compromised?

☐ What are the goals in developing these championship player characteristics at various levels of baseball?

CHAMPIONSHIP PLAYER CHARACTERISTIC: DISCIPLINED

A player who's disciplined is more likely to maximize his performance to become a championship player.

What is your organizational philosophy regarding the discipline needed to develop this characteristic in a young player throughout his career? For example, what is the approach of your overall program to reprimand a player who consistently breaks organizational policy (i.e., shows up late to the ballpark, is absent for weight training, etc.)?

Figure 12.4

Rate your organization between 0 and 10, with 10 being highest, based on these key questions:

How DISCIPLINED is your overall program at:	Rate
Rookie Level	
Single-A Level	
AA/AAA Levels	

In this philosophy of a championship standard, the Player Development Department should employ guidelines to develop the characteristics of a championship player. The overall philosophy should integrate the various levels of professional baseball and the different environment of each level of play. In effect, you're planning the developmental journey of a championship player regarding his baseball ability and personal traits. So detail your plan by implementing a strategy to recognize various levels of play and determine what's considered an acceptable championship standard. In the philosophy of the championship standard, you're building the

DNA of a player and the fabric of the organization or an acceptable level of player and staff behavior within the organization.

Organizational Consistency

Anyone involved in intense competition or performance relies on consistency of preparation, schedule, and routine. It allows the performer to focus on the competition or the performance itself. Professional baseball requires players to traverse upward through increasingly difficult levels of play. Throughout these levels, the Player Development Department must have consistency in its programs and levels of play to maintain a degree of familiarity for the player. There must also be an organizational consistency from Minor League club to Minor League club. That means when a player is promoted from Single-A to Double-A, he shouldn't have to learn an entirely new approach to the game.

This philosophy of organizational consistency allows for players to become familiar with the schedule, programs, and routine so they can focus on workouts and game performance. The next level of play brings the challenge of a higher degree of talent and baseball skill in the opponents, thus requiring them to make adjustments. The players' transition would be even more difficult if they're distracted by adjusting to new ways to operate within the organization.

Because the Player Development Department exists to serve the Major League club, its staff must conform to the prescribed direction of the Major League staff. No matter what the professional difference of staff opinion in baseball technique, the Minor League staff must follow the lead of the Major League club. This reinforces organizational consistency for the Minor League player when he reports to the Major League club. The Player Development staff prepares every player to be viewed positively at the Major League level, working in concert with the Major League staff. Higher levels (AA/AAA) in the organization should replicate the details of procedure and practices at the Major League level as closely as possible.

Lower levels (A or Rookie Ball) may alter the strategies or details of the common philosophy to better serve the developmental process.

Rookie Ball and Single-A players may not be developmentally prepared for advanced techniques or intricate information. However, they still have to adhere to the prescribed organizational philosophy.

Biggest Jump in Baseball

At the Minor League level, adequate simulation of the Major Leagues does not exist, with the difference from Minor to Major referred to as "the biggest jump in baseball." Thus the Player Development staff must trust the Major League club's direction in improving skill-level development for technique.

Often, Minor League competition doesn't offer the advanced skill level to take advantage of a player's vulnerability. His lesser strength may not be exposed. However, the intense competition, talent, and skill at the Major League level expose the slightest of weaknesses in any player. The Major League staff should be able to identify an issue and the Player Development staff must trust these opinions. They aim to solve a possible future concern.

The Making of a Championship Player

The rookie-level Pioneer League is blessed with many picturesque towns, one being Great Falls, Montana.

While working for the Los Angeles Dodgers, I oversaw the Player Development Department and all of our Minor League clubs. In 1999, the Great Falls Dodgers had a young team filled with youth and inexperience. Although blessed with talent and future potential, most of the players weren't ready for professional baseball. The Great Falls Dodgers had a number of high school players on its roster who'd been recently selected in the 1999 June

Draft. The team also had inexperienced players from our Latin Academy at Campo Los Palmas in the Dominican Republic. Most of the other Pioneer League teams were filled with former college players or second- or third-year professional players who were mature. When compared to competing teams, the Great Falls Dodgers as a group of players were in over their heads.

That summer, I left Los Angeles and arrived at the airport in Great Falls (yes, this city has one). I rented a car and drove directly to the ballpark in time for a game. I had not scouted every player from the June Draft, so I was excited to witness the tools of the new players and judge their potential for myself. I had only read their scouting reports or listened to scouts describe these players in our draft meetings.

I could hear the national anthem being played as I drove into the parking lot, so I quickly parked and ran right into the stadium—a cozy (nice way to say small) one with a crowd of about 800 people. The Dodger players looked athletic, and I could see why our scouts wanted to sign these young players. Their bodies were projectable in future strength, and they had good raw tools. There were three quick 70 runners in the middle of the field, and they looked especially athletic. I could envision any of these guys hitting at the top of a National League batting order in Los Angeles. The pitchers had above-average fastball velocity, and their size was consistent with a future Major League pitcher.

They were fun to watch. Some players were making position changes for the first time in their baseball careers. They showed aggression and enthusiasm, trying hard to play the game— sometimes too hard. Then I noticed miscues in decision-making, and the physical errors were piling up. The future Major Leaguers began to look ever more youthful. Their enthusiasm turned to panic when they faced a complicated turn of events.

Most of the hometown fans were biting their tongues. I could sense their frustration growing with each successive blunder. Finally, the game ended—a rough one for the boys.

I made my way to the Dodger clubhouse to say hello to the staff. As I got closer, I could hear the familiar loud angry tone of a professional baseball manager who had just lost a game in an ignominious fashion. It's a necessary part of the developmental process. Professional baseball is not to be taken lightly. People pay precious money to watch good baseball skills. They don't want to pay for a substandard product, and they certainly don't want to pay to watch errors and misplays. The ultimate responsibility of professional baseball players is to their fans.

As the meeting ended, I entered the close, cozy clubhouse. The room was quiet. The players seemed rushed to get out as quickly as possible. I sat down with the staff, and we discussed the relative youth of our team and how staff members were concerned with the baseball skill development and proper pregame routine of the players. With this youthful group, I knew the early work was critically important to give them the required repetitions to further their baseball skills. The players needed to practice more to become proficient as professional players.

One individual player was brought to my attention. This kid—a high school player taken in the most recent June Draft—wasn't working as hard as he could in his pregame sessions. But when I watched him that evening, I liked what I saw. He was an electric runner and an aggressive player. He played with high intensity and great energy for the game. It seemed odd the staff would ask me to help this player as he was flyin' around the field, but they insisted I speak with him the next day before workouts. I said okay.

I drove to the ballpark the next day, still perplexed about the whole situation. I'd never even talked to this kid, yet I liked the way he played the game. What would I say? Should I listen to the staff and reprimand this kid? How would I teach him a lesson about working hard?

I didn't know what to do, so I decided to ask him questions so I could get to know him better. The skinny youthful-looking player was waiting for me at the clubhouse. I introduced myself, and we proceeded to go down to the dugout to get privacy for a difficult conversation. I needed to prod this kid into working harder and help him gain discipline in his pregame sessions.

We talked awhile about his family and how much he loved his parents. He discussed the tough personal adjustment of moving far from home to play in Great Falls. Obviously he was homesick and missed his family and friends. I was amazed at his maturity as well as his intense love for his home and family.

We also spoke of the difficulty of playing against experienced players for the first time. He explained how his personal and baseball world had been turned upside down. His mature responses to my questions gave me confidence to boldly address the staff's concern about his work ethic in his pregame sessions. I had never witnessed his early work to evaluate him, so I had to be honest when I asked, "A lot of people tell me you don't work as hard as the other players. Why do you think some Dodgers people believe you could work harder in pregame drills?"

He said, "Mr. Geivett, I just get too tired if I work too hard before the game. I never had to work like this before a game at home. At my high school, we would just come out and play the game. I need to feel strong for the game."

I sat and stared into the distance. A lesson learned that day in picturesque Great Falls came from a youthful player, not me.

After an honest reflection of our program, I surmised that, in our effort to teach a championship standard work ethic, we forgot the obvious: Were we working them to death? No. However, the new high school player didn't have the physical background or stamina for such an intense workout schedule before a game. He wasn't accustomed to this physical standard. Young players have to build their stamina and increase their workload to feel physically capable to compete in the games. That meant starting slower with our June draftees and exercising patience when bringing them to a championship standard.

It was fortunate I learned from this high school player named Shane Victorino. Nicknamed the Flyin' Hawaiian, Shane has since won four Gold Glove Awards and played in two All-Star Games. More important, he has proven his value on championship clubs. This six-time post-season participant played for two World Series champions. He's never been accused of not working toward a championship standard. This skinny kid from Maui, Hawaii, just needed a few weeks to get accustomed to living away from home and understanding the rigors of professional baseball before developing into a championship player.

To summarize, we were correct in attempting to have players adhere to a championship standard, but we did it too quickly with high school players. As an organization, we needed to soften our initial approach and gradually build them to a championship standard. We wouldn't relinquish or compromise this goal, but we didn't need to achieve it in the first two weeks of a player's career.

Food for Thought

Would you answer the exercise questions in Figure 12.4 regarding a championship standard for discipline at the Rookie Ball level the same way after reading the Shane Victorino story?

The Philosophies Combined

A Developmental Puzzle

This chapter outlines the foundation of a player development philosophical puzzle. The teaching (PHYSICAL/FUNDAMENTAL/MENTAL, ORGANIZED PROGRESSION) and the organizational baseball philosophies (CHAMPIONSHIP STANDARD, ORGANIZATIONAL CONSISTENCY) combine to form an overall philosophy. You may add additional philosophies or omit some of these from your structure. The philosophical design should reflect the philosophies important to you as the foundation of your basic construct.

Either way, it's critical to build your structure on a philosophical base. After completing it, you fill in the details to design how to apply your philosophies. You can then analyze the individual characteristics of a championship player or baseball skill and develop your program of instruction at certain levels of play, ensuring they're consistent with your core beliefs.

Blending of Philosophies

The blending of these philosophies can be complex. The philosophies are not created equal for every level or set of circumstances and should not be applied evenly throughout a player's career. Often, there's one philosophical ideal that can't be compromised, given a particular set of circumstances or the level of play. One philosophy may be of supreme importance for the situation and should take precedence in any particular issue. That's entirely at your discretion.

I debated the blending of philosophies in Shane Victorino's case by asking these questions:

☐ Should I always maintain a championship standard philosophy, even with high school players who aren't ready to handle the physical nature of professional baseball?

☐ Should I make the high school player adhere to what's consistent organizationally with all of the other teams and players?

☐ Should I follow the philosophy of the PHYSICAL/ FUNDAMENTAL/MENTAL and ensure that every Rookie Ball player complete a high rate of repetitions of baseball skills from day one?

☐ Should I not worry about how tired these players are for their games?

In the Victorino situation, I relied on the teaching philosophy of an *organized progression*. This high school player needed time to adjust to personal and professional issues related to playing professional baseball. He didn't have the physical stamina to work at a professional level without feeling tired for the game; therefore, he had no chance of working at the championship standard level. It was up to the organization to allow the high school player to be indoctrinated into professional baseball over a few weeks. Only then would it be appropriate to add a physical workload aligned with a championship standard. We had to stay cognizant of players' individual differences. In this way, a realistic program can take theory or philosophy and make practical applications fit situations at hand. The program has to be uncompromising in its dedication to core philosophies but flexible to account for individual differences.

Summary

What is important to the organization? What is important to the Major League club?

Philosophies refer to the core beliefs of an organization—what's important. These core beliefs shape the foundation for the entire Baseball Operations Department. Organizational goals are set for a championship club, a self-sufficient organization, and a championship player.

In the Player Development Department, a detailed practical application plan for all activities in the Minor Leagues should reflect the intended characteristics for goals set forth by the Major League club. Player Development uses various teaching philosophies to make the practical plan more efficient. All of the teaching and baseball development philosophies are taken into consideration in every situation to ensure the use of the more appropriate philosophy. The Player Development program should be rigid in its philosophy and goals but flexible in its practical application to teach the individual player.

PHILOSOPHY:

☐ Realize that working in the Minor Leagues is a tough gig.

☐ Define a championship player.

☐ Adhere to a championship standard.

☐ Define your baseball development philosophies.

☐ Define your teaching philosophies.

☐ Understand how to blend your philosophies for different levels.

☐ PUT PHILOSOPHY FIRST!

CHAPTER 13:

PLAYER DEVELOPMENT – SUPPORTIVE MIND SET

Climb the Highest Mountain

THE SUCCESSFUL JOURNEY OF AN AMATEUR PLAYER TO THE MAJOR Leagues is an extremely difficult and formidable task, like climbing the highest mountain. The beginning of the climb requires *physical strength* and *endurance.* At mid-range, this massive behemoth rises in a pronounced fashion. To conquer this stage requires an even higher level of *physical ability* and *advanced technical skills* for the climber. A number of climbers won't have those and they'll cease to progress. Near its pinnacle, the climb becomes even more difficult. *Physical ability, advanced technical skill,* and *mental acuity* of the climber at premium level are necessary to continue this journey to the top. The mountain's highest peak is a point that's extremely difficult to reach. It's typically only seen by the most *physically gifted, technically skilled,* and *mentally aware* climbers.

That point in baseball is the Major Leagues.

Let's never forget the talent, skill, and intellectual ability required to achieve a successful journey to the Major Leagues. It's even more difficult when subscribing to a championship standard philosophy and aim to develop championship players.

As you move forward to study baseball from the players' perspective, keep in mind this simple fact regarding professional baseball: It's a difficult game to play!

Similarities and Differences among Players

Although similarities exist among professional baseball players, each one possesses a unique set of personal and educational characteristics. Players arrive from various backgrounds and life experiences; no two players are identical.

Some players have been blessed with a loving home life and thoughtful, supportive family members. They've been conscientiously nurtured in ways that have cemented their emotional security, so they come with a healthy sense of self-esteem. They've been conditioned to receive recognition—both positively and negatively—for their actions. They've learned the concept of *consequences*. In contrast, other players may arrive from an unfortunate set of circumstances and a less desirable upbringing.

Players also arrive with different educational backgrounds, degrees of intellectual capability, and a range of mental aptitudes. Educational achievement can vary, from graduates of prestigious universities to players who have never attended one day of class in high school. In fact, many players from Latin America have been forced into employment by their families' financial hardships and had to forgo their primary education at an early age.

In addition, learning disabilities such as ADD and ADHD are prevalent in professional baseball players. Some choose to medicate their condition while others won't in fear it could harm their baseball performance. Sexual orientation is an issue for some players, who often carry the burden of whether to "come out" in this macho profession.

Based on this diversity, the quest to design a comprehensive development program should maintain *organizational consistency* but not attempt to be a *one-size-fits-all* program. Maximizing efficiency when developing championship players requires recognizing individual differences of incoming players and designing a program with the flexibility to make adjustments that best serve each player. Although program details and strategies must change due to the characteristics of individual players, the organizational and departmental philosophies are the constants. Gauge each player to arrive at the most effective strategy to achieve your philosophical goals without compromising your philosophical ideals. Key questions:

☐ What are the potential personal needs of players?

☐ What strategies should be put in place for the general program?

☐ How do you best serve the players requiring special attention?

Food for Thought

If the journey to become a Major League player is a difficult ascension, then how much more difficult is it when the player has emotional or educational problems? And how much more difficult when he doesn't speak English?

Be an Advocate

The players' game deficiencies will be publicly identified by the staff, media, or anyone who cares to pile on—an overwhelming situation for a young player. He might be constantly told "You aren't good enough!" A young player could even believe the highest mountain is too tough to climb and lose confidence in his baseball ability. That's why *you* must be an advocate for the player.

Remember, the daily struggle to have a Major League playing career is a lonely pursuit. When a player steps to the mound or into the batter's box, he feels totally alone. In this pressurized endeavor, negative thoughts and self-doubt can creep in. No baseball player is immune from a lack of confidence. Professional players at every level (including the Major Leagues) typically lose confidence in their ability to perform at some point in their career. Where will they get their confidence when things are going badly if not from you, their advocate? The player benefits from feeling your confidence in him to develop his own self-assurance—possibly the biggest determining factor in his overall success or failure.

The Importance of Confidence

In 1995, as farm director of the Montreal Expos, my main duty was to evaluate the progress and future potential of our Minor League players. I loved to watch our kids play. We had some exciting young players at the lower levels—Vladimir Guerrero, Michael Barrett, José Vidro, Geoff Blum, Orlando Cabrera, Brian Schneider, Javier Vázquez, and Jeremy Powell—with tremendous potential. Many of our staff believed we lacked future Major League players at the upper levels of the Minor Leagues. I disagreed. I remained confident in our players in both AA and AAA leagues. We had a well-balanced system of potential Major League players at all levels.

True to what many in the organization believed at the time, Jeff Blair, a writer for the Montreal Gazette, wrote an article about our International League AAA club in Ottawa. He cited a Major League source in the organization as stating, "We don't feel there is anyone in Ottawa who can help our team in Montreal." Guess the destination of my next trip. Ottawa, Canada.

Pete Mackanin, later the manager of the Philadelphia Phillies, managed the Ottawa Lynx in 1995. As a young farm director with limited experience, I was lucky to work with Pete because he had outstanding baseball knowledge, an upbeat outlook, and a wonderful sense of humor. I was more worried about every little detail of our Player Development Department than was needed back in those years. Pete had a way of calming me with his dry wit.

As I walked into Pete's office that day, he was more reserved than his normal jovial self. I expected a joking, light-hearted veteran baseball man.

"Pete, is something bothering you?" I asked.

"Yes. The players want to see you in the clubhouse," he said.

"Are they all in there?"

"Yes. Bill, they won't do anything until they speak to you."

Pete explained to me they had read Jeff Blair's article in the Montreal Gazette and were upset— pissed off—about how they were publicly portrayed. I sat in Pete's office to compose myself. Hell, I agreed with the players. I would be humiliated if I were playing in Ottawa and someone high up in the organization publicly stated there was no player in AAA who could help the Montreal Expos. I pondered every angle to come up with an appropriate and plausible presentation for the players. I understood their anger, but I didn't have a wealth of experience in my role to give a proper response. I kept going back to this truth: I honestly believed some of our AAA players had value for our Major League team, and I sincerely had confidence in their ability.

So I collected my thoughts, told Pete to wish me luck, and entered the clubhouse.

Most of the players were sitting in their chairs in front of the lockers while the others were milling around the clubhouse waiting. I sensed their courage had limits because none of them approached me or even made eye contact. I attempted to show I was in charge of this meeting by curtly directing the players with "All of you, into the training room!"

There in the training room was an entire AAA team filled with ambitious players trying to either debut in the Major Leagues or *get back into it. In each one of their faces, I could see their embarrassment and disappointment in the organization. In effect, they were told in the Montreal Gazette article what they've been hearing their entire career, "YOU ARE NOT GOOD ENOUGH!"*

At that moment, I realized the players needed to be heard, not lectured to. So I listened to their complaints, their utter despair of playing for an organization with no confidence in their ability, and their requests to be traded to another organization. "Why did I ever take this job?" I wondered. I recalled the manager in the movie The Natural when the Knights weren't playing well, and he said to one of his coaches, "Red, I should have been a farmer."

Most of the players' gripes were understandable, and I took each comment as if I were listening to a member of my own family. I had to appreciate their painful struggle to respond in a fashion that would make sense to them. They deserved to be heard.

After they got out their frustrations, it was quiet. My turn. I spoke of the confidence I had in their baseball ability, and I told them I believed there were players in Ottawa who could help our club in Montreal. I informed them the coaching staff in Ottawa had offered me the names of the players who deserved to be in the Major Leagues.

Finally, I spoke of the recent conversation I'd had with the general manager of the Montreal Expos, Kevin Malone. He asked for detailed information on which Ottawa players were the best to serve particular roles on our club in Montreal. All true! They seemed stunned to hear there were players in that training room who had advocates in the organization. Someone had confidence in their ability to play in the Major Leagues. There was hope after all.

Once the meeting ended, the players were in much better spirits. Pete was his funny self again, so I figured the meeting must have helped the situation. Maybe I shouldn't have been a farmer after all.

In those years, I would throw batting practice to the teams I went to visit. The players in AAA wanted to hit when I was throwing, either to impress me or injure me with a batted ball (most likely the latter). Either way, it was fun for all of us.

After throwing to a group of Ottawa hitters and departing the mound uninjured, I took a spot behind shortstop to help shag baseballs during the next group of hitters. I remember watching the fluidity of movement in Chris Martin, Ottawa's shortstop. Then one of the other Ottawa players, F.P. Santangelo, came up next to me wanting to talk. (This was not unusual; most players at AAA wanted to talk to me during my trips into Ottawa regarding their careers.) F.P. was still upset by the article in the Gazette but was even more discouraged by his career path with the Expos.

Playing in his fourth season of AAA, F.P. had yet to reach the Major Leagues. He was scheduled to become a Minor League free agent at the end of the 1995 season and thought he should be traded to another team that appreciated his talent and recognized his present Major League value. F.P. then detailed his baseball attributes of uncommon versatility and his long history of playing on winning teams. Finally, he said to me, "I'd be the best double-switch guy in the National League." At this, I sarcastically but accurately replied, "F.P., you're hitting only .243 in AAA. How can you be that good in the National League?"

Unfazed, F.P. continued his attempt to convince me of his extraordinary ability to play multiple infield or outfield positions and switch hit—all excellent qualities of a premium utility player who's valuable in the National League. After he made his points (not all I agreed with), I gave him a clinical evaluation of the situation, pulling no punches. I told F.P. he had to raise his batting average so someone in the organization might have more confidence in his bat to compete at the Major League level, and especially to improve as a right-handed hitter.

In addition, he needed to work on his middle-infield defense at second base and shortstop to be considered useful at those positions in the Major Leagues. As he departed for his turn to take batting practice, he still seemed disgruntled and frustrated. F.P. had tremendous confidence in his playing ability and didn't care if he was the only person on earth who believed it.

As I stood in the outfield shagging baseballs, I thought about how confident or possibly delusional F.P. had been during our conversation. I left town with a better understanding of how sensitive situations can be at the AAA level—and how taxing. The Ottawa players had mentally worn me out.

Soon after the Major League trading deadline passed at the end of July, I made my next visit to Ottawa. Which players should be called up to Montreal when the Major League regular-season active roster limit of 25 players expanded to 40 on September 1st? Soon after checking into the hotel, I located my room and, as I opened the door, a ringing telephone greeted me. It was Expos' General Manager Kevin Malone. He said the Montreal Expos might need a position player because it looked like one of our three catchers, Tim Spehr, was headed for the disabled list. It would be a non-playing spot, an extra man on the bench, and the 25th player on the roster.

Kevin instructed me to call him during the game in Montreal for an update on Spehr's health and, if necessary, take my recommendation for the Minor League player to be called up. I examined all the statistics I could on the Ottawa Lynx and then headed to the stadium.

Upon arriving at the ballpark, I never told Pete or the staff of the potential need in Montreal, but I did ask for a progress report on all of the AAA players. Without asking the specific question, I wanted their opinions on which Ottawa position player deserved to go to the Major Leagues. Through the player progress update, I thought staff members would offer enough information to make the proper decision, and they did.

During the game I called Kevin, who told me the Expos needed a position player for the game the next evening. The Major League staff had a player in mind, but it wasn't the player I'd chosen from my meeting with Ottawa staff members. Disagreeing with the Major League staff opinion, I gave Kevin the name of the player I recommended. Kevin agreed with me and told me to inform the player he was going to Montreal.

This put me in a tough spot. I had basically overruled the Major League staff, and we were calling up a player who wasn't their choice. Would these staff members be upset? Would they harbor bad feelings toward me? Why did I ever take this job? Realistically, did I know anything about being a farmer?

After the game in Ottawa ended, I made my way to the club-house to inform Pete of the situation at hand. His office door was closed when I arrived. The coaches told me F.P. Santangelo had broken every light in the runway from the dugout to the clubhouse after he'd struck out. F.P. did not perform well and obviously took out his frustrations on the items most culpable for his failure—the lights in the runway. This setting was ripe for a practical joke, and I couldn't pass it up. As F.P. tried to leave the office after his disciplinary meeting with Pete, I told him to sit back down. It was my turn to have a chat with him.

I lectured F.P. on the proper conduct of a professional player, and losing emotional control is not proper conduct. I informed him that someone with the Ottawa Lynx front office had to take time out of his or her busy day to clean up the mess he'd created and replace the broken light fixtures. Others had to alter their schedules and add to their workload because a frustrated F.P. couldn't control his emotions.

I went on ad nauseam to back up my point and make him suffer. I informed both F.P. and Pete that not only would F.P. pay for the damage he did, but he would also pay a heavy fine for his childish A-Ball-type actions. Then I added more punishment to his list. He had to sign autographs for 30 minutes before each home game in Ottawa for the next 20 games, and for an hour on Sundays when we didn't take batting practice as a team. Pete would be responsible to make sure F.P. completed his required autographs, and I'd have a spy at the ballpark to make sure the punishment was fulfilled. I then described the details of the autograph booth for F.P. so fans would know where they could find him. I warned him that only legible autographs would suffice, and I would personally examine some of them from the Lynx fans.

An exasperated F.P. finally couldn't take it anymore. "Bill, I got it, you're right. It will never happen again. I've learned my lesson. I'll pay the fine, and I'll sign all of the autographs you want. If that's all, I would like to go see my family as they just got here from California today, and I haven't seen them yet."

His remarks only fueled my desire to continue my dissertation on why it's inappropriate to cause damage in our stadium, our home, and our sanctuary. In turn, my filibuster frustrated F.P. more and more. After I'd exhausted my comments, it was time to inform Pete of some surprising news.

"Pete, there is only one problem. F.P. won't be able to sign autographs tomorrow night."

Pete gave me a quizzical look. F.P. held his head down in disgust, refusing to look at me.

"Because tomorrow night, F.P. Santangelo won't be here; he'll be in Montreal," I said.

Pete and F.P. hesitated for a few seconds. Then it hit them both simultaneously. My statement could only mean one thing: F.P. Santangelo was headed to the Major Leagues.

Tears of joy welled up in F.P.'s eyes as he realized what this meant. It was a memorable call-up for all of us. I was happy to play a trick on someone, Pete was happy he didn't have to time F.P.'s autograph sessions with spies watching, and F.P. was happy he was finally going to be a Major League player. His years of toiling in the Minor Leagues, especially the four at AAA, were finally all worthwhile. He always had confidence he'd realize his dream of playing in the Major Leagues, and it was finally vindicated.

After we laughed and congratulated F.P., my mind quickly turned to my next issue: Felipe and the staff.

I told F.P. to be at the stadium in Montreal at noon, even though the game was scheduled for 7:10 p.m., so he could be as comfortable in his new surroundings as possible. F.P. and Pete looked at me as if I were crazy. I'll admit noon was a bit early, but I could not allow him to make a bad first impression for the Major League staff, as he had not been their choice for the call-up. He needed to report early to Equipment and Clubhouse Director John Silverman to make sure his uniform, equipment, and locker were in order. Feeling anxious about everything at this point in my career, I didn't want anything to go wrong for F.P. Also, my butt was on the line!

The next morning, I altered my schedule to attend the game in Montreal. Although I had arrived into Ottawa the previous day, I wanted to explain my decision-making process to the Major League staff personally. On the drive to Montreal, I was formulating the best wording to explain my position to the staff. I arrived at Olympic Stadium at around 1:30 and nervously walked into the clubhouse. "Silver" informed me that F.P. was all taken care of. He was presently hitting in the batting cage under the stadium.

I felt some relief, but my biggest concern was still ahead of me when I walked toward the manager's office. Felipe Alou was sitting at his desk as I entered his office. He looked up at me and smiled.

"I knew you'd be here," Felipe said.

He explained that the staff was hoping to add right-handed power to the bench, which is why someone other than F.P. was wanted. He'd always liked F.P. from managing him in West Palm Beach in the Florida State League (Single-A), but the staff wanted a powerful presence on the bench. I was relieved that Felipe wasn't upset, but I had still gone against the Major League staff recommendation with my opinion. It was a very uncomfortable situation for me. Felipe called me over to his desk to watch something. He took out one of his lineup cards and wrote in the number nine spot in the batting order Expos' starting pitcher that night, "Fassero." I felt good about Jeff Fassero, a dominant Major League starting pitcher who always gave the Expos a chance to win the game.

In the number eight spot in the order, Felipe wrote the name "Santangelo."

"Santangelo?" I gasped.

Now more uncomfortable than ever, I had to question Felipe on his thought process. "F.P. has never even taken batting practice in Olympic Stadium, and you want him to start the game? He has never played on the hard artificial turf here, and it's the first time he'll be in a Major League uniform," I said. "He has to be extremely nervous. The opposing starting pitcher is a lefty, Chris Hammond, and F.P. doesn't hit as well right-handed. I don't think F.P. is ready to start a game. Can't we give him one night to get used to the environment and then play him tomorrow when he's more ready?"

Felipe leaned back in his chair grinning at me, then paused and said, "Mr. Geivett, almost every day I drive into the stadium parking lot, and I stop to talk to the security guard. He offers me a great deal of information regarding some of our players. Today was no different. He said some new kid named Santangelo was here at noon. If he came here at noon, Mr. Santangelo is more ready to play tonight than anyone else on this team."

Damn it! Why did I say noon?

As the game began, I leaned against the glass wall on the Olympic Stadium press level where I'd watch the game. I needed something stable to brace myself against in case F.P. did something embarrassing in the game. The situation reminded of a saying of one of my favorite scouts, Jethro McIntyre: "This kid looks more nervous than a long-tailed cat in a room full of rocking chairs." Well, that is exactly how I felt!

As luck would have it, in his second at bat in the Major Leagues, F.P. Santangelo laced a triple to right field and slid headlong safely into third base. The partisan Olympic Stadium fans gave him a standing ovation in honor of his first Major League hit. F.P. played like a confident man on a mission that night to prove he belonged in the Major Leagues, and he did nothing to embarrass himself or me. I could breathe again.

It was one of my most emotional experiences in professional baseball watching F.P. slide into third base. He hit .296 that 1995 season in Montreal and went on to play in seven Major League seasons—the same number of years he spent in the Minor Leagues.

For a certain time during the mid-to-late 1990s, F.P. Santangelo was the best double-switch guy in the National League. He also signed those autographs he owed me, but he signed them in Montreal.

The Power of Confidence

F.P. Santangelo taught me the power of confidence. He convinced me that day shagging balls in Ottawa that he truly believed he was the best double-switch guy in the National League. He had *confidence* in his baseball ability and would not be denied a Major League career. His belief in himself allowed him to maximize his potential and never give up on his dream.

That's why you have to be your players' advocate and help develop their confidence in themselves. Players can easily believe the highest mountain is too difficult to climb and succumb to the ever-present negative forces in the game. You must respect the difficulty of the journey and support players along the way. If all they hear is "You are not good enough!" that's exactly what they'll believe.

Summary

The highest levels of professional baseball require the immense talent and skill of everyone involved. Players need advocates around them to succeed in their daunting journey to realize a career in the Major Leagues. No one can do it alone.

It's the responsibility of the staff and front office members to recognize their challenges and reinforce confidence in the players. Great staff members know how to highlight every success to help players believe in themselves.

Consider confidence the greatest asset a player has to overcome the challenges presented by professional baseball. It's the key to turn potential into performance. The key points are:

☐ Appreciate the difficulty of the journey.

☐ Treat all players uniquely; everyone is different.

☐ Be an advocate for the players.

☐ Support players' confidence—possibly the most important characteristic of all.

CHAPTER 14:

PLAYER DEVELOPMENT—ANTICIPATE THE PLAYER'S MINDSET

A Player's Predisposition Created by the Game

CHAPTER 12 DISCUSSED THE *PHYSICAL/FUNDAMENTAL/MENTAL* philosophy as it pertains to a natural order of progression in a professional baseball player's career. The professional player with a minimum of average aptitude will recognize this progression during his career while climbing the various levels. The majority of future Major League players understand the need to get physically stronger while playing in Rookie Ball or their first full season of professional baseball. They comprehend the importance of fundamental consistency in Single-A and AA, and they also analyze their strategies and the opposition's strategies at AAA and the Major Leagues. The future MLB player focuses in these areas to shape his career. Key questions:

- ☐ What's the natural posture of the player so you can understand what's important to him at certain periods of development?

- ☐ Do you think an established Major League hitter *will want* to fundamentally change his swing?

- ☐ Do you think an established Major League pitcher *will want* to drastically alter his throwing routine?

You may consider the last two as simple questions to answer, but I've seen Major League staff members attempt these situations while facing tremendous resistance from players.

In addition, it's important to consider the maturity level of the player and the natural order of progression in a player's career. That doesn't mean a Major League coach can't instruct an established player to make physical mechanical changes, but it must be done realizing the player's natural mindset or *predisposition*.

Mindset Changes during the Season

The player's mindset tends to change during a season no matter what the level of professional baseball or where the player is in his career. Figure 14.1 shows the philosophical model of PHYSICAL/FUNDAMENTAL/MENTAL within a full professional baseball season.

Figure 14.1

PHYSICAL		FUNDAMENTAL		MENTAL	
April	May	June	July	August	September

Early in the season, a player's body is typically strong and injury-free. The excitement of a new season has him energized about improving his skills. Feeling enthusiastic, he wants to work his butt off! Fortunately, he arrives in the proper physical condition to manage himself through the rigors of extra workouts and still play a game that night.

In addition, the early season schedule helps minimize physical wear on the player due to April and early May weather—typically rain followed by cancellations of games and on-field activity. When making adjustments to a higher level of play, the player focuses on working hard to be ready to compete at the more advanced level. He works assiduously in an attempt to get comfortable.

The player may also have worked all winter long on his *fundamental technique* and wants to see how his altered form produces results in the new season. He might hesitate to take on mechanical changes prescribed by the staff because he hasn't had an appropriate number of at bats or innings pitched to determine how effective his new form might be. As the season begins, he's getting his feet back on the ground.

As temperatures rise, though, the excitement of a new season has worn off by mid-May. Settling into a comfortable daily routine, the player takes a more tempered and even approach to his workouts. Having played the requisite number of games, he's now in a position to evaluate his performance and technique.

What happens next? He begins to recognize his baseball vulnerabilities and lack of consistency when performing aspects of his game, and he looks for guidance from a trusted staff member. Fundamental flaws are easier for him to work on at this point, given the full attention and cooperation of the player in need. Many lasting relationships between coach and player have been forged during the hard work of this stage of the season.

> Teaching can begin when the student has arrived.

The "dog days" of August and September can fatigue the baseball player's body. Add dealing with minor injuries and he can feel physically depleted. He has likely lost weight and isn't as strong as at the start of the season. Having maintained a heavy practice workload combined with a grueling schedule of games, he looks for chances for it to taper off at this juncture. He arrives at the ballpark for pregame drills hoping the manager will decrease the physical routine and show "mercy" on his players.

Still, he has a desire to learn and improve his game, but fielding a thousand ground balls won't be as enticing to him as it was in April. At this point of the season, he wants to *mentally* focus on technique and strategy. The immense *physical* repetitions have been completed to feel comfortable and the *fundamental* flaws have been tirelessly addressed. Because the player has exhausted all avenues of improvement in these aspects of his game, he's more receptive to *mental* challenges at this time.

Of course, this is a generalization about our philosophical ideal and the professional season. All of the developmental aspects of the PHYSICAL/FUNDAMENTAL/MENTAL are prevalent during every month of the season. At no time do I suggest slicing up the season and focusing on one aspect at a time. I'm simply describing the typical predisposition of the professional player as the long season unfolds.

Learning Styles

The Uniqueness of Learning

According to Dictionary.com, "Learning style is an individual's unique approach to learning based on strengths, weaknesses, and preferences." Simply stated, learning is unique to each person.

That's true for professional baseball players who possess individual differences in how they learn or process information. Some players can *hear* technical baseball information one time and incorporate the information into their game. Other players may need to *see* an example of a technique to process the information and replicate what they've heard and seen. Another group may learn best by *doing it*—actually performing the technical skill discussed and seen. In any case, each player has a unique way to absorb information. Examine and appreciate their individual styles, understanding it's not a "one-size-fits-all" approach.

Only "Telling" Isn't Enough

One of my biggest frustrations as a farm director was seeing a player continually repeat the same mistake over and over again. I'd question the staff member in charge of the player regarding the repeated offense. Let me be clear; I was never frustrated with the player—I was frustrated with our inability to get the player to make the proper adjustment. My frustration would reach its peak when I'd hear an instructor say, "I don't know why this kid is still making the same mistake. I've told him a thousand times."

"I've told him" is never a good excuse for the lack of proper performance in a player. Telling a player the information may not be the appropriate learning style to get this person to respond correctly. A master teacher examines how that player learns most effectively, discerns the best strategy, and solves the riddle. Master teachers never rely on *telling* their players information as their only approach; they appreciate the different learning styles and individual differences in how people process information.

> Hear it—forget it. See it—remember it. Do it—learn it.

In 1993, Sandra Rief, educational consultant and an authority on learning disabilities, published a study concluding that students retain:

- ☐ 10% of what they read

- ☐ 20% of what they hear

- ☐ 30% of what they see

- ☐ 50% of what they see and hear

- ☐ 70% of what they say

- ☐ 90% of what they say and do

If the Rief study is reasonably accurate, only *telling* the players baseball information would not be our sole course of action in an educational environment. Do you see why it's frustrating when a player makes the same mistake over and over? I consider it our fault!

Offering the player written instructions with printed information to read is a low probability strategy in retention (10%). Only telling the player so he'll hear the information isn't a strong strategy either (20% retention). Plus, I don't have confidence in players retaining baseball information when they both hear it and see it (50% retention). Does that mean instructors shouldn't give out written instructions or give lectures? No, because players all learn differently. I recommend using every potential learning style, understanding that some are more effective than others for various individuals. I respect Rief's research conclusions as guides to better understand the degree our instructional methods will affect performance and retention of instructions. More often than not, though, people require the use of *all* of the learning styles available to best serve *all* of the players.

The Critique

As Farm Director for Colorado in 2003, I was in charge of the Fall Instructional League (FIL) program. In one of our morning meetings, I asked the staff, "If we had a million dollars to add to our Player Development budget, how should we spend that money to improve our program?" Great ideas flowed freely on how to get the most "bang for our buck" when allocating this money. (Staff salaries came up quickly—not a surprise.)

Ideas: longer Spring Training, improved Spring Training facilities, mini-camps, an additional coach for each Minor League team, more player development coordinators, and more advanced video equipment. I took their responses and Assistant Farm Director Marc Gustafson created a priority list of how to disperse these hypothetical dollars for our program. We needed to be prepared. (It was wishful thinking but not too hopeful.)

My next question was "How can we improve our program without spending any money? This question didn't elicit the same degree of enthusiasm as the first one. Staff responses didn't flow readily. But in time, momentum developed and this issue surfaced: Our young players didn't understand how to play the game and their situational awareness wasn't at a professional level. These players were not like those who grew up during my generation. They hadn't learned the game by playing in pick-up games in city parks with "right field closed" or the "pitcher's mound as good as first." We developed our knowledge of the game by actually playing a "team game" while these kids had learned the game through private pitching coaches and swing gurus. They had grown up focused on individual mechanics and had spent more time in indoor batting cages than outside on a field. The staff believed the kids "nowadays" don't know how to play a team game. (When you're old, everything seemed better in the past.)

With increasing awareness as the goal, we debated practical strategies that might improve this situation. For the most part, the majority of the proposed baseball awareness strategies we discussed seemed the same as what we'd already been using with our players. The ideas of change meant investing more time and effort into our present modes of operation. Honestly, I wasn't impressed by our progressive thought process. Then Tony Diaz, one of our Rookie Ball coaches, spoke up.

Tony presented the idea of having our players critique and instruct their teammates about baseball skills. These players would have to know the physical and mental details necessary for their positions to properly critique other players. The Rief concept of learning and retention helped me realize Tony had a brilliant practical application. According to Rief, students would retain 70% of what they say and 90% of what they say and do. That means the probability of successfully retaining information would rise with this methodology. Perfect!

So our group planned how to add this style of teaching into the program. Butch Hughes, one of our veteran professional pitching coaches and a longtime college educator, was instrumental in turning our theory into practical application. We selected one or two players for each area of our team (pitching, situational hitting, base running, catching, infield defense, and outfield defense). These players were required to watch a game, focus on players at their corresponding positions, and critique them the next morning in the full camp meeting. This setup gave our staff time to ensure the players' critiques would be consistent with the staff's instruction.

The critiquers would each be armed with a clipboard and a printed form of specific aspects of their position, designed by the staff, to assist in organizing the presentation. They'd watch their assigned players in the game, scrutinize every aspect of their play, make their evaluations of the performances, and keep notes on both positive and negative aspects. The next morning, we'd begin our full camp meeting with game notes from the previous day. The critiquers would report to the entire group of players and staff, offering positional critiques of their area of expertise. The staff would then follow up after each critique to highlight additional points they wished to stress with the team. It was a solid practical application plan, built with sound reasoning and educational research as its foundation. Still, I felt apprehensive attempting something new. Although I loved the concept, I had never witnessed it used in professional baseball. One thing was for certain; I couldn't wait to see this in action.

But once we used it, I was struck by the critiquers and their intense engagement during the game. They were "all in" to perform their job, which became evident as they studied their assigned players. Players not participating in a FIL game are typically half asleep, but the critiquers were fully engaged. Other non-game players sat close to assist the critiquers and offer their opinions of the action to be evaluated. Even players participating in the game were discussing aspects of their play with the critiquers to ensure they understood their on-field decision-making process.

From the 1ˢᵗ inning, it was clear this exercise could have tremendous value as a practical application. One aspect underestimated by our staff was the power of having to speak in public—a strong motivator. No player wanted to be embarrassed when speaking in front of the entire camp. They wanted to make sure they had the information organized to offer the best critique possible.

I witnessed the critiquers interacting with their position instructors during the game, after the game, and before the morning meeting the next day. The power of public speaking created a surprisingly heightened awareness of the smallest positional details for the player to include in his critique. We proved Rief correct in her conclusions.

As the Fall Instructional program continued, players became more comfortable with the exercise. They were fully engaged in breaking down the details of the performances. I'd sit in the back of the room and marvel at the precision of the critiques and the effort displayed by the players. I also realized this new strategy transcended common baseball instructional practice. When the critiquer offered an evaluation of an individual player's game performance, we would have the player stand up to receive it. After listening to the critiquer, the player would either agree or offer a reason for his actions. This helped the players become more comfortable exchanging constructive criticism as teammates. Not only were they learning to offer advice to teammates, they were learning to accept constructive criticism from one of their peers. In effect, they were making each other better players.

As a bonus, the increased English language production helped our Spanish-speaking players, who tired of using an interpreter for their critique. They pushed themselves to use English to better express their ideas. They showed great courage!

This exercise was one result of our progressive thought process. Although we'll never be able to quantify its positive impact to increase the baseball awareness of our young players, we thought it helped. Clearly it made us push hard to improve a big weakness. Thanks, Tony, for this progressive idea.

By the way, I don't care what size market your club belongs to; you'll never get an extra million dollars for the Player Development Department.

They Become a Creature of Habit

The best players in the world rely on their discipline not only to develop their baseball skills but also to improve their consistency of performance.

Major League players have their individual routines for all of their baseball activities. Some believe the player's natural desire for routines is rooted in superstition, as the player looks to meticulously replicate identical procedures, which allowed him to have a good performance. I agree that professional baseball players are highly superstitious and that's why they stick with a consistent daily routine. But consider another rationalization.

Stability through Routines

High-level performers in any profession desire stability in their environment to better prepare for playing in the game, singing in a concert, or conducting a medical operation. Their successful performances depend on their level of comfort and peace of mind with their surroundings. Major League players may be particular regarding their daily *routines* because it's their primary strategy to limit distractions as much as possible. They may respond harshly toward any changes to their personal routines—even when it's out of their control, which makes some believe they are acting like "divas." So players seek an acceptable level of consistency and comfort, which makes them extremely particular about their routines.

What kinds of routines? Their needs may be as simple as the time they leave for the ballpark every day, the type of pregame smoothie they drink, or the brand of socks they wear. To the uninformed, the Major League players may seem like spoiled brats to be "picky" about these minute inconsequential details. In actuality, the player aims to maintain a level of consistency to afford the opportunity to perform to the best of his ability. No changes, no distractions, and everything the same every day. I'm sure Beyoncé would agree!

Game-Related Routines

A Major League position player's routines may also relate to game performance. Examples include the number of swings hitting off a tee in the cages, the type of batting practice rounds they take on the field, the amount and type of pregame ground balls and fly balls they field, or what to look for when watching video of the opposition's starting pitcher. Pitchers have individual stretching and training room procedures, specific numbers of throws a day from various distances, flat ground rituals throwing to a partner positioned in a catcher's stance, or when and how they review the scouting report and video of the opposition's hitters.

Major League players hone their individual routines by trial and error as they progress, relying on them to maximize their preparation and perform their best.

"Failure to prepare is preparing to fail." – John Wooden borrowed from Benjamin Franklin.

Assistance for Developing Consistent Habits

As he matures in his career, a professional player naturally gravitates to the concept of consistent preparation and its importance to consistent performance. Younger, less experienced players may need assistance from the Player Development staff to arrive at the same conclusion.

Here's what I say about the immature unprofessional player: "You can lead a horse to water, but you may have to dunk its head in it to make him drink." Having a routine clearly isn't important to a young player who reports late to the ballpark, skips early work, can't find his helmet for batting practice, or misses the team bus. Because of that, the staff prescribes his routines. He has to follow organizational directives on how to wear the uniform, stretch, lift weights, play catch, warm up in the bullpen, take batting practice, and every other rudimentary activity to prepare for the game. It's all part of player development.

A Player's Personal Discipline

This chapter has addressed players' potential predisposition at certain points in a season or career, emphasizing how your overall process must have flexibility to account for the individual differences of players. Yet no matter how much effort you put into a player's development, his success or failure may ultimately be a function of his personal discipline. Key questions:

☐ Does the player work hard?

☐ Does the player focus on consistent routines?

☐ Does the player abide by the program?

☐ Does the player listen to staff members?

☐ Does the player study the game?

☐ Does the player do everything in his control to make himself better?

☐ Does the player play for the benefit of the team?

☐ Does the player have off-field habits that are detrimental to his career?

Be sure you have a philosophical understanding of the specific championship player you're attempting to develop. Your championship standards should guide each player to comprehend acceptable behavior in the organization.

Organizational Rules—Who Enforces Them?

That said, professional baseball players won't always act in accordance with organizational rules and guidelines. They will make poor decisions. When the player graduates from first-time to repeat offender, it's time to stop the pattern.

When dealing with repeat offenders, I have never much cared about the player's individual differences in characteristics, nor did I show much compassion. The professional player can only develop into a championship player by conforming to established organizational acceptable behavior consistent with a championship standard.

I've not heard a Major League manager admit he had a lot of rules for the players; in fact, most managers state the contrary. The Major League coaching staff is paid to win championships, not babysit undisciplined players. There's no patience in the Major Leagues for a lack of discipline in a player; the stakes of earning a championship are too high. Typically, veteran players are first to witness substandard player behavior, and they get upset with their undisciplined teammates. They have no appetite for a player "in their clubhouse" who doesn't work hard, play for the team, or has bad off-field habits. Acceptable player behavior isn't taught in the Major Leagues; it's developed into an individual player's characteristics in the Minor Leagues.

The characteristics of discipline are directly associated with the longevity of a player's career. Scouts look to acquire the impact tools of players combined with the body and athleticism for longevity. Minor League staff members develop discipline in their players to maximize their probability of impact and longevity. Major League players who don't conform to the accepted standard of behavior are sent down to the Minor Leagues until they prove they can act appropriately. Or they may be traded to another team or released from the Major League roster. Make no mistake; even though managers don't post player rules in the Big Leagues, they exist.

Return to Chapter 12 and answer the Championship Player Characteristic—Disciplined again. Did *your* philosophy change?

Housecleaning

In 1994, the young Montreal Expos players in our Fall Instructional League program in West Palm Beach, Florida, were less disciplined than what I'd been accustomed to and expected. Players for the New York Yankees, my previous organization, were known for a businesslike approach and its intense demands on the players. George Steinbrenner's military and football background formed the foundation for the type of player development program he desired. Bill Livesey built it for him. A proper code of conduct for the players was widely administered with the Yankees, and it fit tightly into all aspects of the Yankees' player development program.

In contrast, the young players with the Expos presented a culture shock for me. Some of these players had no concept of a professional approach to their job or what's considered acceptable behavior. They were out of control.

Earlier that summer, the veteran players of AAA had forewarned me about this group of rambunctious youngsters. They were hearing surprising stories of their juvenile actions that had traveled throughout the organization. Remembering the far-off goal of a championship standard, I couldn't idly stand by and watch our hardworking players face the daily distractions of those players who didn't conform to a professional standard. It was time to dive in and change the environment. After gathering as much information as possible on our less-than-disciplined players, it became clear I had to deal with two main culprits: Brad Fulmer and Hiram Bocachica.

Brad was a surprising target. He was a 4.2 GPA student at the prestigious Montclair Prep High School. He had accepted a scholarship to attend Stanford University before deciding to sign a professional contract with the Expos. As a Yankee area scout, I had scouted Brad and thought of him as a gifted hitter with tremendous instincts at the plate, excellent bat speed, great hand-eye coordination, plus raw power. As part of my scouting duties, I had completed a home visit with the Fulmer family and found them to be wonderful people. I liked Brad a lot in that visit; he was polite and respectable. Because he was brilliant academically, I knew he must have great self-discipline.

Drafted in the second round in 1993 but negotiating a signing bonus consistent with a first-round pick, Brad had been a professional player for more than a year and should have developed a disciplined approach. I surmised that I had an "Eddie Haskell" (millennials, google him) on my hands. Fullmer never did anything malicious or really bad, but he could have been much more focused on improving his game.

For Hiram Bocachica, I had no personal background history other than watching him play in games and scouting him that same season. A newly signed 1994 first-round pick out of Puerto Rico, Hiram had tremendous athletic ability, a strong compact muscular body for his age, and explosive quickness. Fun to watch, he had outstanding potential by nature of his impact tools and strong athletic body.

*These two kids were loaded with talent, but they also had defi-
ciencies in their games.*

*We knew Brad's bat would ultimately be his calling card to
the Major League level, but he needed to become proficient on
defense. His passion for the game revolved around hitting a
baseball, and that is where he wanted to spend all of his energy.
As his shoulder injury worsened, we were searching for a defensive position for him. Hiram struggled defensively at shortstop.
He could turn a sure single into an out with an unbelievable
defensive play during one inning, and then he'd boot a seemingly routine ground ball the next. It would take a lot of instruction, hard work, and discipline for these two to improve their
lesser strengths.*

Higher Standards

*One morning, I told the staff we needed to raise our organi-
zational standards for the players to what should become a
baseline for acceptable behavior. I explained that a player with
mediocre work habits and poor self-discipline would hide among
the masses, thus making it difficult to detect their shortcomings.
We needed to raise our expectations to expose those players who
weren't conscientious or disciplined. It was time to put on a little
heat! We put in place a strict dress code to and from the ballpark; we added regulations for hair length and beards; we stated
that uniforms were to be worn in a required fashion with a cap
at all times when on the field. We also made daily early work
mandatory and extended workouts into the late afternoon with
weight room requirements following the workouts. We enacted a
curfew and increased intensity of the drills.*

*I knew this would shock the players, but it would lead me to
identify those who needed to develop the required discipline or*

mental toughness to become a Major League player. I had to learn more about the characteristics of our young players.

In the FIL program, typically a few veteran players attend to rehabilitate from their injuries. One of them thanked me for what I was doing with the program. The veteran told me stories about the most influential man in his career, John Boles. "Bolesy" was a longtime professional baseball executive, farm director, and eventually a Major League manager for the Florida Marlins. He said I reminded him of Bolesy and was putting in place rules he remembered when he started his career under Bolesy.

I couldn't have been more flattered. John Boles was one of the best player development men in professional baseball. In fact, I had just spent an entire day with Bolesy at his home in Sarasota, Florida, before coming to the FIL. He had graciously accepted my request to interview him on all aspects of professional base-ball player development. I expected his lovely wife Rosemary to kick me out of the house at some point, but she allowed me to stay and ask player development questions all day. By the way, dinner was fantastic.

Consequences

The next morning before our staff meeting, I was greeted by the player development instructor in charge of the player curfew check the night before. We had two violators, Brad Fulmer and Hiram Bocachica. (That didn't take long.) In the meeting, I asked the staff for recommendations on suitable punishment for these curfew violators. (Yes, I should have detailed punishment and consequences for violating team rules beforehand, but I hadn't figured that out yet.) The consensus was to either make the play-ers run until they dropped or have them pay a monetary fine.

As a key component of a player's physical conditioning, I believed running should never be viewed as a negative consequence to poor decision-making. I didn't agree with a monetary penalty either, as players in the FIL program didn't receive a salary for their time there. Plus, these guys were high draft picks and had plenty of money. They wouldn't learn their lesson by paying a relatively small amount of cash as a penalty.

Someone suggested sending them back to the hotel for the day, denying them a day of working on their baseball skills. I was intrigued by the idea, but I didn't want them to get off so easy—a day of lounging around the pool at the hotel! I instructed the staff to tell Mr. Fulmer and Mr. Bocachica to remain in the clothes they wore to the ballpark and sit by their locker until further notice. I then asked our Minor League Equipment Coordinator Mark Rego if he could use help cleaning the clubhouse that day. With enthusiasm, he assured me he could find plenty of work if I gave him a couple of helpers. Looking back, he must have had revenge on his mind after dealing with those two in the clubhouse for a while. The players were then summoned to my office.

Discipline

I yelled and they listened. I wanted to impress upon these youthful players the need to become more meticulous about the details of their careers. I spoke of how they both had obstacles to overcome, which would require them to be detail-oriented in their work. They needed a professional approach to maximize their potential impact as Major League players. They also needed to get serious about their careers and take advantage of the physical gifts they possessed, and make every day meaningful in developing as a player. Every day they spend in the Minor Leagues was one less day they get to spend in the Major Leagues. Lastly, I *wanted to make sure these two high draft picks understood the reality of their situation. I said, "A group of scouts watched a few games, had some meetings, and decided to give you guys a bunch of money. That's what happened; they just gave it to you. But you can't buy a Major League career with your signing bonus money or impress your way into a Major League clubhouse with your draft status. The Major Leagues have to be EARNED! You two have lost the privilege for the day to earn it. You won't get closer to the Big Leagues today."*

After giving them the assignment to work in the clubhouse, I made sure they understood that any disrespect shown to Mr. Rego would be taken as a personal insult to me and to my position as farm director. So off they went, Mr. Rego and his two understudies who didn't look happy. A few minutes later, Rego leaned his head into my office doorway and asked if this was a joke or could he really work them hard. I replied, "Bury them."

An hour later, I called Rego to my office for an update on our new clubhouse employees. He said he was surprised they were completing every task he gave them, but they were saying terrible unrepeatable things about the farm director.

I just laughed. One day they'd figure it out.

I went about my business until I was interrupted by a knock at my office door. It was Brad. Did he come to complain? Was he going to stop working and make me send him home? Did he want to go home anyway? I should have known "Eddie Haskell" Fulmer would do something to drive me crazy.

Then he said, "Mr. Geivett, I'm supposed to vacuum and dust all of these offices. You can stay in here if you like, but I'm going to get my work done."

He got me. I loved that kid. As I departed my office that day, I left to the sound of Brad singing and vacuuming as if he didn't have a care in the world. Then I wandered over to check on Hiram. He got the raw end of the deal, as he had to clean the players' restroom in the clubhouse—not pretty. (He must have done something terrible to Rego that summer.)

He saw me, looked up and said, "This is bullshit; this is professional baseball; this is not the army!"

I could barely contain my laughter.

"In the army, people try to kill you. Here, people are hoping to pay you millions of dollars. Follow the rules!" I replied.

In the End

Brad Fulmer went on to play in eight Major League seasons, but I believe a lingering shoulder issue never allowed him to display the true Major League ability he possessed. Hiram Bocachica also played in eight Major League seasons at various positions. My career took me to other clubs, and I lost contact with both of these players, but I still followed their careers closely on TV and read their statistics daily.

In 2013, I was at Spring Training watching a game between the Rockies and Giants at Scottsdale Stadium. Feeling a tap on my shoulder, I turned around—Hiram Bocachica. The young kid I remembered from West Palm Beach had grown into a mature man. He was working as a player agent and attending the game to visit one of his clients. As we fondly reminisced about the Expos players from the years we were together, I felt as if I were talking to an old friend.

Just before he got up to leave he said, "I always wanted to thank you for what you did for all of us players. You gave us discipline, and we had none. You and the staff were exactly what we needed."

Summary

This chapter has featured many generalizations. I've examined professional baseball players broadly in an attempt to determine commonalities of perspective. Yet I understand there are no etched-in-stone rules and regulations for every player, and no two players should be viewed as identical.

As time goes by, the game of professional baseball will change, and the players will change, too. I have witnessed many shifts in the game during my career. Advances in technology and the "wired" world have offered additional resources to baseball instruction. Players have more information at their disposal and, as a result, have increasingly relied on it as an integral element in their preparations.

You'll identify many changes during the course of your career as well. It will be your responsibility to know the current landscape of professional players and have your own opinions on the characteristics of how they process and learn information, the learning tools they prefer to use, and how they're *predisposed* at certain points in their career. One thing is certain: To be a quality staff member in the Player Development Department, know your audience!

- ☐ Understand the player's predisposition.

- ☐ Have a strategy for different learning styles.

- ☐ Hear it, see it, do it.

- ☐ Tap into the power of daily routines.

- ☐ Teach players a disciplined approach.

CHAPTER 15:

PLAYER DEVELOPMENT—THE STAFF

The Staff Perspective

Hiram Bocachica was not quite 40 years old when he greeted me at that Spring Training game in Scottsdale mentioned in Chapter 14. Evidently, he'd matured enough to recognize the benefits he'd gained from the unforgiving strategies employed by the Expos' Player Development Department. Although he hated us when he began his career, he had gained an appreciation for us teaching him a degree of discipline that led to enjoying a successful career as a Major League player.

Truth be told, we never cared much about what Bocachica wanted, liked, enjoyed, or thought. He had just turned 18 and some of what he desired then was detrimental to creating a long, productive Major League career. We had a responsibility to someone other than this amateurish kid. Instead, our player development contract had been with the 40-year-old wise, mature Hiram Bocachica.

Our Contract with the Future Player

This understanding of how to view the contract helps staff members maintain an unemotional perspective and determine right from wrong when faced with complex circumstances involving a young player's development. Even if we resort to acting out of character, we should employ any means necessary for the player to solve his issues. Our responsibility is to put the player on the path to Major League success, even if the player hates us for how he's treated. We're not his buddy; we're the guardians of his future. We must believe these words: "I don't care what he thinks of me now; he'll appreciate me later."

Bill Livesey required his staff in the New York Yankee Player Development Department to be hardworking, caring, and attentive. Admittedly, these are broad characteristics, but they're an excellent set of requirements. I believe Mr. Livesey's basic fundamental requirements provided the foundation for great player development instructors and an excellent standard by which to judge interactions with players. All players they teach and instruct will (at some point) respect the managers and coaches who can maintain these traits throughout their careers.

Even if the player doesn't recognize it at the time, we must believe he will someday—as Hiram did.

The Role of a Surgeon—and Staff Members

Whenever a patient enters an operating room, the impending medical procedure could result in improved life or possibly death. The surgeon is trusted to have the specific skills needed to administer the right medical treatment for the patient's needs. The successful surgery may extend that person's life, or an unfortunate set of complications during the surgery may diminish it.

Surgeons have studied their craft for years, continue their education throughout their careers, and stay current with progressive techniques to better serve their patients. Effective surgeons are never complacent in preparing for or exercising their craft. They continually seek to improve both their knowledge and skill. In this high pressure occupation, a patient's survival may be at stake.

In our world, Player Development staff members aren't held to life-or-death consequences for their actions, but they play a significant role in whether players have long careers or short-lived ones. Similar to how a surgeon cares for a life, the staff member must care for a professional player's career. The developmental experience for a successful Major League player has likely been filled by staff members who have provided the proper guidance, instruction, and personal mentorship along the way. Hardworking, caring, and attentive staff members have directed the player through all of the *physical, fundamental,* and *mental* adjustments for the player to maximize his potential. These selfless staff members would have spent long hours of study to perfect their craft and turn the players' dreams of a Major League career into reality.

In contrast, ineffective staff members may have promoted ineffective techniques or created situations detrimental to a future player's development. Stuck in their old ways, they view situations from a limited perspective, only using routine techniques and ignoring innovative strategies.

Advanced study and progressive thought are key components of a successful medical career, just as they are for a career in player development. As in life, the player only gets one chance. In player development, we're encouraged to learn throughout our careers while embracing new techniques and analyses. Advanced study and future technology provide better methods to instruct players. Let's be open to searching for and recognizing new and improved processes. By our actions, we can extend a player's professional career—or diminish it.

Negative Comments

Managers and coaches tend to heap praise on their players for the team's success. It's also common for them to place blame on their players for the team's failures.

You've heard negative comments such as these: "You can't win the Kentucky Derby with a donkey"; "Even the best mechanic needs the proper tools"; and the infamous "You can't make chicken salad out of chicken shit."

I won't deny the validity of these in some cases, but let me speak to the underlying spirit of defeatism they convey. If we subscribe to these negative comments, we're admitting to our own limitations and lack of effectiveness in developing Major League players. We have resigned ourselves to mediocrity. In effect, we're stating that we don't possess the talent or ability to improve player performance.

The best player development instructors will embrace the biggest challenges and look for complicated issues to solve. They understand there are no perfect players, and this fact excites them. They believe that any instructor of lesser knowledge and skill can coach a mature, intellectually gifted and talented player. Where's the difficulty or challenge in instructing these near-perfect players? The best instructors thrive on solving the issues of flawed players by exercising their advanced coaching skills and applying their expertise. They relish the opportunity to make a difference in players, careers, and organizations with an attitude of "let's fix this!" instead of "this kid will never play in the Major Leagues."

Positive Posture

What is a positive posture? It's a predisposition to problem-solve, focusing on creating successful outcomes rather than defining what's regrettably most probable. It's an outlook of hope and potential combined with an intense desire to find better ways to teach individuals.

The best instructors want a challenge. They believe they can influence any player, no matter the circumstances or deficiencies, and they can make a greater difference than a mediocre staff member. They take a positive posture and combine it with a supreme level of confidence in their ability to teach. The last thing they want to do is admit defeat or failure in a player's progress. They chose professional baseball coaching to develop athletes into championship players.

Personal Accountability

Dave Snow, the illustrious former collegiate baseball coach at Long Beach State University and professional instructor, sarcastically refers to the great American pastime as "the art of placing blame on others." Often, many in professional baseball blame others when situations don't go their way. Unfortunately, I can say I've worked with people in professional baseball who have used this blaming technique.

Notwithstanding the various factors that affect performance and outcomes, an extremely important characteristic for a strong staff member is *personal accountability*. That means we hold ourselves accountable for the performance of the team and its players. The result of the game or their performances, both positive and negative, should be considered as our own personal success or failure. WE MUST OWN THE RESULTS!

Looking into a Mirror

More than that, we take the position that team results and player performances are the direct manifestation of our own baseball knowledge, preparation, and strategy. We see action on the field as if we're looking into a mirror—one that offers individual, personal, and honest self-reflection. Even if the reflection is negative, we blame nobody except ourselves.

The great managers or coaches learn to examine the reflection, understand the issues of the team or player, and make the necessary corrections. They scrutinize the smallest imperfections, all while strategizing how to adjust the *reflection* to their satisfaction. It's how they hold themselves personally accountable to the image.

Great managers and coaches carry personal confidence knowing they can make a difference with any baseball issue and fix any team problem. They understand and live by the concept "when I look to the field, I'm looking at my work."

Common Issues

The Road to a Successful Career

The journey of a successful Major League player is long and difficult; likewise, the journey for the successful player development staff member is long and challenging, too.

Adhering to the philosophies of the organization and the department isn't simple, given the multitude of complex situations that arise while instructing young players. I have seen many instances of well-intended actions by hardworking, caring, attentive player development employees being viewed as inconsistent within the philosophy of some aspect of the organization.

I hesitate to relate negative experiences in describing practical application characteristics of player development, but the importance of the following traits can't be dismissed. Failure to understand and operate under the following basic concepts is why good staff members lose their jobs.

Winning versus Development

In the immortal words of former NY Jets Head Coach Herm Edwards, "You play to win the game. Hello? *You play to win the game!*" Coach Edwards' simple statement addresses the goal of athletic competition at the highest level of play in any sport—that is, you play to win the game.

We're all born with a certain level of competitiveness, but people who excel in athletic competition possess a heightened desire to win. It's coded into their DNA. But since the Minor Leagues are not the highest level of competition in professional baseball, they can be appropriately described as "developmental leagues." That means these leagues develop the advanced baseball skills of each player so they can successfully compete against the world's best Major League players in the future.

In the Minor Leagues, though, Player Development staff members won't find a more contradictory concept than *winning vs. development.* As some argue, "How can he learn to be a championship player if he's never won?" They stress competitiveness, game strategy, and an intense desire to win the game. Others argue that advanced baseball skills are the priority to be developed for a future Major League player to ever become a championship player. How can he be a champion if he doesn't have the necessary skills? In their daily routines they emphasize baseball fundamentals, improved technique, and an intense desire to work on baseball skills.

I've heard Minor League managers make comments about winning vs. development in *confidential conversations* with statements such as these:

- ☐ "I develop players before the game; during the game we play to win."

- ☐ "The first six innings are for the player's development; the last three are mine to win the game."

- ☐ "Players should worry about their skills; my job is to worry about winning."

Many player development staff members make statements about winning vs. development in more *public forums,* saying things such as:

- ☐ "My job is to teach my players Major League skills, not win Minor League games."

- ☐ "I don't like to sacrifice bunt as a strategy, but I need to develop their bunting skills."

Most would agree that *both* winning *and* development are critical to attain their goal of developing championship players. Managers and coaches wrestle with this issue in their daily decision-making. They want to act in the best interests of the players and the organization. Many Minor League situations set up interesting debates on the proper course of action, with no clear right or wrong answer. As a way to assist staff members, I believe direction should come from the front office and coordinators to clarify basic departmental and organizational philosophy. But often no distinct guidelines and direction exist.

Staff decisions on playing time, positions, batting order, and in-game situations all affect the development of a position player. The staff also help to decide on the role (starter or reliever), usage (relief role), innings, pitch counts, and pitch mix (pitches to be used and how often) for each pitcher on the team. Therefore, they must understand basic departmental philosophy to act appropriately when no guidelines have been detailed. Conversely, they may have no decision to make, as the following story indicates.

Vermont Expos

We were fortunate to have the highly respected Jim Gabella as our manager for the Vermont Expos in the New York-Penn League in 1995. Jim did an outstanding job of managing young players. Under his leadership, the team started the season strong and stayed strong all summer.

I suggest Jim was more of a "development man" than a manager solely fixated on winning Minor League games. He was a great instructor in many phases of baseball and a gifted teacher with a tremendous work ethic. He placed the organization's goals at the top of his priority list, never once going against the guidelines of the Montreal Expos' Player Development Department. That season after Jim had two weeks to get settled into the season, I made my way to Burlington, Vermont, to watch a game.

Centennial Field (constructed for baseball in 1922) was the home of the Vermont Expos, and in 1995, attendance was excellent. The sights and sounds of the crowd during the game are still vivid in my memory. The historic stadium, beautiful sunset, hot dogs, and the undying love of baseball from fans of every generation seemed like the perfect setting for a Norman Rockwell painting—a slice of Americana. The game itself was close. Its verdict hung in the balance with every pitch—until the 8th inning when the Expos rallied to go ahead of the visiting team. Fans screamed in excitement when the Expos scored. They showed support for their team until the last "out" when the home team prevailed. It reminded me of the love I have for the game and my good fortune to have a career in professional baseball.

Soaking up the last few minutes of this extraordinary night, I waited for the near-capacity crowd to exit the stadium before I left my seat. Soon after, I made my way to the clubhouse to congratulate Jim Gabella. When I entered his office, he was speaking to the media regarding the Expo victory, so I quickly left and went into the coaches' office. They were celebrating the victory and recounting each aspect of the battle. Feeling upbeat about the team, they thought it had a great chance to win a championship that season.

We talked about the unbelievable support from the Vermont Expos' owner, Ray Pecor, and how Kyle Bostwick was a bright young front office member who graciously helped the staff any way he could. It seemed as if the world revolved in perfect harmony in Burlington that summer, and I could momentarily forget my typical worries as a farm director.

The Interview

Returning to Jim's office, I could see he was still tied up with an inordinate number of media representatives for such a small town. I mouthed the words, "Great job; I'll see you tomorrow" and headed out to visit our athletic trainer. With him, I checked the post-game injury report then departed for my hotel.

As I turned the car key, I was surprised to hear Jim's voice on the radio. He was being interviewed by the Vermont Expos' announcer, discussing the turn of events needed to secure the win. Because they were still talking when I arrived at my hotel, I sat in the parking lot and kept listening. Jim came across as professional as I could have ever imagined—a great representative for the Expos. After the post-game recap and before a commercial, the interviewer said Jim would answer questions from callers after the break. I decided to wait longer, thinking maybe I'd disguise my voice and call in myself. Better not, I thought. I have enough problems without creating another one.

Feeling sure the comments would be positive, I expected to hear the callers say how much they loved our team. After all, we were playing great, and the fans at the stadium had been so happy. The first two callers asked innocuous questions about how Jim prepared his players prior to the game as well as other questions geared to scheduling and logistics. The two calls were upbeat and complimentary, progressing as I thought they would.

However, as soon as I heard the abrasive, aggressive voice of the third caller, I became suspicious of his intentions. He had a raspy voice and cynical tone that generated bad feelings inside me. Suddenly, I forgot about the great day and regressed into my "worried farm director" mode. (Things can change quickly in this racket.)

The caller started by complimenting Jim on his team's early success. Despite that, I still felt uneasy listening to the sound of his voice. Then he told Jim, "I was at the stadium tonight, and the game should not have been close. You guys should have killed them. I kept score of the game with your player roster in hand to better understand you and your decision-making. I couldn't believe what I saw. You had three opportunities to pinch hit late in the game, and you didn't do it. You kept two consecutive right-handed hitters in the game to face a right-handed reliever, while you had four left-handed hitters on your bench. Am I to believe you know how to manage a baseball game?"

This raspy-voiced caller was looking for trouble. He put Jim in a bad spot because, in all fairness, he was correct. In this tight game, we had several opportunities to put in a pinch hitter, but Jim did not remove one single hitter. Let me explain why. Before the season began for the Vermont Expos, we had instituted a "no-pinch-hit rule" for our Rookie Ball managers. Thus, Jim was not allowed to pinch hit because of organizational policy. Most of these kids were new to professional baseball and new to the organization. We wanted them to compete in all situations to better understand their strengths and lesser strengths. How would we learn about our players if they weren't given an opportunity to fail? It's Rookie Ball after all, not a "win-at-all-cost" league. We told our Rookie Ball managers we would eliminate the rule during the month of August if they were in contention for the playoffs, but for the majority of the season they couldn't replace a hitter as a strategic weapon.

How would Jim answer this question? Clearly, his ability as a professional baseball manager was called into question. Would he blame the organization for instituting a policy that might negatively affect the outcome of a game?

Jim responded by thanking the caller for his support of the team, and then congratulated him on his baseball awareness to recognize the specific situations he saw in the game that night. Then Jim asked the caller this series of brilliant questions:

"Sir, don't you think our right-handed hitters should be allowed the opportunity to hit against right-handed relievers? How could a right-handed hitter develop into a Major League player if he was replaced for a pinch hitter every time he was up to face a right-handed reliever? Do you think our scouts would sign a

right-handed hitter they believed couldn't hit right-handed pitching? Should I assume our players will fail, or should I provide an opportunity for us to understand their strengths and weaknesses? Our organization is in the process of learning what these players can do and what to work on in order for them to get to the Major Leagues. How does pinch-hitting, for them, help achieve that?"

The caller fell silent. He'd never factored the Major Leagues into his thought process. Rather, he was focused on the winning strategy of that night's game. After a long pause, he thanked Jim for explaining his thoughts.

Jim had helped expose a fan to the developmental perspective and educated him that there's more to Minor League games than determining a winner each night. In the responses Jim gave Mr. Raspy Voice, he explained the developmental aspects of the decisions he had to make as a Minor League manager. He emphasized how these games have more to do with the future than the present. In fact, Minor League games are funded, produced, and managed for the future of a Major League organization. Winning today is not the overriding concern for a Minor League club in most organizations at the Rookie ball level.

The next day, I told Jim I'd heard his interview on the radio. I thanked him for his responses, which described the reasons for our Rookie level no-pinch-hit rule without ever stating that we had one. He laughed and said, "I wish people actually knew how much thought goes into all of these decisions we make."

For the record, Jim Gabella guided the Vermont Expos to the best regular season record (49–27), and was voted New York–Penn League Manager of the Year in 1995. His team competed in the championship finals. Jim taught his Vermont Expos team how to win while always making good daily decisions for the future of the Montreal Expos.

Food for Thought

Do you favor the importance of winning *or development* in the Minor Leagues?

Does your opinion change from the Rookie ball level to higher levels?

If a player struggles in certain aspects of offensive baseball (e.g., sacrifice bunting, base-hit bunting, hit and run), should the manager force the player to attempt to execute these skills in games even though the player struggles with them and it could be detrimental to the team's success?

The difference between leading off and batting ninth in a lineup can be as much as 100 plate appearances in a full Minor League season. Should a manager consider this fact to maximize the number of ABs (at bats) for the better prospects during the construction of his lineup, or design a lineup solely to win the game?

We all have varying opinions about *winning vs. development,* so I won't attempt to offer a formula for how to make those decisions in the Minor Leagues. You can decide depending on your philosophy. What's important is the conscious exercise of examining the situation and projecting future ramifications of your decisions. For example, am I providing my organization a brighter future with my actions, or am I only thinking about my team today?

During the game that I watched when Jim Gabella declined opportunities to pinch hit, I witnessed the opposing manager pinch hit for a second-round pick who had just been drafted and signed. It begs the question:

Was the manager thinking of the future of his Major League organization or strictly trying to win a Minor League game?

> "Life must be understood backwards. But it must be lived forwards." – Danish philosopher Søren Kierkegaard

Summary

The meaning of this quotation may be debated until the end of time. Some believe Kierkegaard was saying, "We can only understand our life as we look back with the benefit of hindsight." Maybe, maybe not. I don't profess to know Kierkegaard's true intention, but I believe it to have more substance than simply describing the art of learning from past experiences. Is the understanding of life only determined at its end by the summation of a collection of one's experiences? I think not. A great philosopher would not attempt to persuade people to think in such a limited fashion and believe we could only understand life after it had been lived.

In my estimation, Kierkegaard was hinting at the importance of a preconceived philosophical understanding of life prior to living it. "Life must be understood backwards" speaks to an end-of-life perspective. An end-of-life understanding of yourself would be, first and foremost, a philosophical compass to guide you through difficult experiences and decisions while living. It's a plan that's designed by your final perspective.

Define Your Final Perspective

This interpretation of Kierkegaard's quotation could be applied to a player development career. I'm not stating we should plan for the exact jobs we hope to attain or the titles we wish to acquire—decisions out of our control. But we *can* plan our thoughts, actions, and deeds.

What if you work in the Player Development Department according to the perspective of the end of a career? What would you say that will be important years from now? To answer that, define your characteristics, posture, style, intentions, perspective, communication, and participation with the "end-of-career perspective" that suits you. Construct a contract with your 80-year-old self. By planning for the outcome you want, in the final analysis, you will have a higher probability of success.

- ☐ Make a contract with the 40-year-old mature man, not the young player.

- ☐ Strive to be hardworking, caring, and attentive.

- ☐ Be a surgeon who cares and continues to study.

- ☐ Adopt a positive posture.

- ☐ Know that the result is your reflection.

- ☐ Understand the ramifications of winning vs. development.

- ☐ Define your final perspective.

CHAPTER 16:

PLAYER DEVELOPMENT—THE
PRACTICAL APPLICATION

The Real World

EVEN THE BEST PHILOSOPHIES AND PLANNED PERSPECTIVES WILL BE challenged by professional baseball. Many perspectives come together to produce the best possible outcome for the organization, and these perspectives must be recognized and considered. Every decision is an organizational one.

Sense of Urgency

Unless something dramatically changes in our natural thought process, human beings will forever desire instant gratification. Especially prevalent in youth, young people tend to gravitate toward the "now" in their decision-making. Young professional baseball players are no different. They hope the coach provides the information, drill, or strategy to instantaneously "fix" the player's performance deficiencies. They want coaches to help them experience immediate positive results; they want to get better now!

However, the pragmatic player development staff members understand that marked improvement in baseball performance may be a long, arduous process requiring uncommon patience on behalf of the player. They're aware that *fixing* fundamental flaws may involve the player's current level of performance getting worse before it gets better. This reflects an inherent dichotomy between the player and instructor, built into the development of advanced baseball skills.

To make matters worse, those in the front office and Scouting Department anticipate that a player's performance level will steadily improve, not regress, on his road to the Major Leagues. Typically, their trusted measure of progress is current statistical information. The *now* statistics play a huge role in the perception of many people in the organization. As a result, player development staff members often feel surrounded by an inappropriate sense of urgency for the player to improve. There can be a lack of appreciation for the proper sequence of events required to solve fundamental mechanical flaws.

Realistically, instructors can't always use their desired methodical approach to teaching baseball skills without external influences. No one operates in a vacuum; everyone works in an organization filled with interested bystanders, including the emotional player. Instructors must understand this circumstance.

The design of their instructional strategy must consider the individual characteristics of each player. It must relate to his career path and correspond to an appropriate timeframe. Problems must be fixed within a timeline that's acceptable to all perspectives.

This sense of urgency in the player and certain others in the organization will never go away, and the player development staff member must learn to live with that. This sense of urgency is part of the "checks and balances" of the job and should be integrated into each instructor's timeline—more appropriately deemed a *deadline.*

Patience has a short shelf life in professional baseball. Everyone in the organization wants to see progress in the development of baseball skills in the young players. If changes take too long, is it the best way to proceed? Any lack of patience in others should drive your own sense of urgency to solve issues with the player you're working with. To put it bluntly, fix the guy!

Proactive Communication

I often hear player development staff members say, "The office never talks to us"; "If anyone cared what we thought, they'd ask for our opinion"; "The Major League staff could help me do my job better, but no one ever calls."

It is understandable people feel slighted when others in the organization don't communicate regularly or effectively. Occasionally, the failure of others to communicate forces us to initiate better communications for the good of the organization. Let's be proactive. Remember, effective communication in an organization isn't solely up to the bosses; it's the responsibility of everyone in the organization. So be aggressive and have a well-organized plan to communicate effectively and regularly.

TIPS:

☐ Categorize the main issues of *your* job.

☐ Create individual staff member "go to" lists in each aspect of the job. By seeking out opinion or openly discussing strategies, you can gain their assistance with certain issues.

☐ After you execute a decision, inform people who might be affected or have offered help. Inform the people on your "go to" list. Tell them what has transpired while explaining the thought process.

☐ Offer subsequent updates as the situation develops.

Don't allow yourself to be the victim of poor communication. If a void exists, lead the communication yourself in your area of the organization. Make effective communication *your* responsibility. Understand that leaders have their own duties and areas of focus and won't always communicate how or when you'd like. Don't allow that to affect your process. Be the example of proper organizational communication and others will follow. When you do, you'll have gained a reputation as an effective communicator and earned the trust of many in the organization.

Benefits of Proactive Communication

A powerful example of proactive communication came from Jerry Weinstein while he was manager of the Modesto Nuts in the California League and I was Farm Director for the Colorado Rockies. Jerry would regularly call the individual area scout who signed the players on his team to offer a progress report. Even though the Rockies had no organizational guidelines or set prescribed number of phone calls to area scouts by Minor League managers, Jerry felt compelled to inform the scout what was happening.

Jerry would call area scouts to discuss any issues facing the personal progress of their players and describe the strategy for improvement. As a result, a strong bond grew between Jerry and the scouts. They trusted him and his motives regarding teaching methods with their players because they'd been informed every step in the process.

At times, the scouts also assisted in developing their players because they could relay to the player ideas consistent with the player development staff. Some might label Jerry's proactive communication "covering your ass" or "playing politics." I saw it as taking advantage of the available resources and communicating well for the betterment of the organization. In the long run, his approach strengthened the relationship between the Scouting and Player Development Departments.

Offer Your Opinion

The daily staff meetings of the Spring Training Player Development Department can be monotonous. The repetitive schedule of field activities typically dominates the agenda. Occasionally, they discuss serious issues facing the department and problems that need quick resolution. In my role as a farm director, I'd ask for staff input to gain their perspective and allow them the opportunity to state their opinions on departmental matters. I wanted input from everyone to help me understand how decisions might affect their jobs as well as formulate a proper course of action for our department. It was intended to stimulate a conversation that would develop into a constructive debate and create a consensus opinion. The healthy debates that followed gave people in our department a better understanding of issues and potential effects of each proposed solution. Engaging them in meetings became a positive process for our department. If they didn't participate in the discussion, the department would gain nothing.

At times, staff members wouldn't speak up on an issue but would meet with me privately. They'd offer great solutions—ones I thought necessary for our staff to debate. But why didn't these individuals offer their solutions in the meeting? Were they intimidated to speak? Were they afraid to defend their position? Either way, I was happy for them to participate in a fashion that felt comfortable, but their solution still required debate amongst the group. I would direct them to offer their solution in the next staff meeting. The department needed them to offer their opinion.

The Gulf Coast League

In 1994, I was summoned to report to the New York Yankees (NYY) mini-camp for the Gulf Coast League (GCL) Rookie-level team at our Minor League complex in Tampa, Florida. We'd prepare our young Yankee players for the summer season and indoctrinate them into the organization. My duties were not only to scout the players and file evaluations on them but to help with the workouts as an instructor.

The GCL staff had been together during the extended spring schedule and had been operating under the organization's player development guidelines. I asked a lot of baseball questions of the staff to make sure I was completing my duties. I didn't want to do anything inconsistent with the departmental philosophy for instructing Rookie-level players.

Every day following our workouts, I'd go to Mr. Livesey's office to discuss my player observations and ask questions about NYY player development philosophy and operations as they applied to Rookies. *If I drove everyone around me crazy with my unending questions, I didn't care.*

One morning we were performing Pitchers' Fielding Practice (PFP) on the diamond with all of the pitchers and infielders. I was standing with Hoyt Wilhelm, our GCL pitching coach, watching the players execute different defensive situations. Hoyt, a Baseball Hall of Fame inductee and renowned pitcher in his era, had always been standoffish toward me and never seemed inclined to talk. (I found out later, he thought I was George Steinbrenner's spy sent in to evaluate the staff members.) But I didn't let it bother me. I questioned Hoyt on all aspects of pitching to no end.

As the drill progressed, we transitioned to hitting a comebacker to the pitcher, with less than two outs, and trapping a runner between third base and home plate. I noticed the pitcher would field the ball, read the runner, and throw to either the third baseman or the catcher but would never leave the dirt of the mound. It was like nothing I'd ever seen before! Typically, the pitcher would be instructed to run toward the runner with ball in hand in an attempt to drive him back toward third base and initiate a rundown. Surely a staff member would correct the pitcher on the proper technique in this situation, but nobody said a word. To my amazement, the drill continued.

I asked Hoyt, "Is this correct?"

"Yes," said Hoyt while never allowing his eyes to leave the field.

"Is this the way we've always done it with the Yankees?"

"No."

"How come the pitcher never leaves the dirt?" I probed.

"I don't know; that's the way we do it," he answered.

It was obvious Hoyt was uncomfortable with this question, but I needed an answer. Was this technique part of a philosophical belief? Was it a unique way to teach a foundation of defense to young players? I couldn't stop thinking about it for the rest of the day's workout. What organizational stance had led to this break in the traditional response by a pitcher when fielding a come-backer with a runner caught in a rundown between third base and home plate? What was it? It was driving me crazy.

As I entered Mr. Livesey's office following the workout, I discussed my still-developing player evaluations as I did every day. But all the while, I wondered how to ask about the recent rundown scenario. I didn't want to appear unaware of an easily understood philosophical reasoning explaining this technique, but I honestly couldn't figure it out. I could wait for the morning meeting to ask the group of coaches, but Hoyt was the GCL pitching coach, and I had already asked him.

After finishing my player evaluation discussion with Mr. Livesey, I conjured up the courage to ask him the question that would solve this mystery. I explained what I'd witnessed on the field and asked politely why we would teach this technique, which was foreign to me. Mr. Livesey looked squarely at me and replied, "That's the way we do it in the Major Leagues."

"Thank you" was all I could say. Then I left the office.

In player development for the Yankees, it was our job to prepare the players for New York. How they wanted it done in the Big Leagues had to be taught in the Minor Leagues, no exceptions. I understood the importance of organizational consistency and received a satisfactory answer to my question. Once I had learned why we had implemented the technique, I had no further questions. My job—a lowly area scout and part-time instructor—was not to debate or change the way we operated. It

*was to perform the tasks as directed by the organization's lead-
ers. I never discussed the subject again.*

When you're faced with a situation in which you disagree with a
particular strategy or don't understand why something is being done, ask
someone! You'll likely gain a different perspective of others higher than
you in the organizational chain of authority. This helps with understanding why.

Again, either in a meeting or talking with the appropriate leaders,
know you're responsible to act for the betterment of the organization. There's
no positive outcome from failing to discuss the issue with authorities.

Player Evaluations

Player development staff members assigned to a Minor League club
watch their team play in 142 games during a regular season. A majority
of their players spend the entire season with that same team. Managers
and coaches consistently instruct their players on physical baseball skills
in early work sessions and counsel them in mental preparation for game
competition. They have the opportunity to witness the players' best performances, see how their tools can positively impact games, and note how
they mentally handle success. Conversely, they see their players' worst performances, notice how their tools can be limited in games, and evaluate
how they mentally respond to the ever-present adversities. They're able
to witness their intensity levels while working on skills and examine the
degree of dedication exhibited by each player to become a champion. Staff
members acquire an idea of each player's strengths and lesser strengths in
all aspects of the game. They should know a player's future ability better
than anyone!

A Scout's Role

How can a scout watch the same players for five games and see some pitchers only pitch once yet somehow be considered an expert on a player's future ability? The answer: Scouts are trained to study and develop their skills of projection.

Conversely, managers and coaches are trained on teaching a player baseball skills. Just as a scout needs to understand the player development strategies of an organization, a manager or coach must have a basic understanding of scouting principles. Staff members aren't required to be great scouts as well as great instructors, but any scouting ability can help them in their careers as instructors and potentially raise their ceiling to a Major League team.

Player evaluation becomes increasingly more important in the highest positions in the organization. The higher the job on the flow chart, the more impact those staff members have on the player personnel decisions of the organization. That's why it's important for staff members to immerse themselves in the principles, practice, and science of scouting. A staff member shouldn't be promoted solely because of an ability to evaluate baseball talent, but a lack of scouting skill can be a hindrance to getting promoted. Front office decision makers always look to staff members for assistance in shaping the player personnel and rely on those who can evaluate talent that adds to the discussion of a player's future value to the organization.

What to Expect of Young Players

The difficulty in projecting the future of young players is that their bodies and baseball skills are still developing. A Rookie Ball staff member typically works with a player who has not yet developed his body's strength potential or refined his baseball skills. As each year passes, the majority of young players get stronger, and most show considerable improvement in their skills. In addition, many 18-year-old players won't have the maturity of a veteran player. They may exhibit wide emotional swings that can negatively affect their focus on the task at hand. Others struggle in decision-making and don't have a clear professional perspective. To put it bluntly, they screw up a lot.

These factors add up to incorrectly projecting a younger player's baseball ability.

Wipe the Slate Clean

Player development staff members can take solace in knowing young players will get stronger, improve their baseball skills, solidify their emotional security, and make more mature decisions. But when? Well, I can't answer that question. Each player develops physically and mentally at an individual rate. Staff members can be overwhelmed by the young players' immaturity *(body, skills, decisions)* and allow that to have an excessive negative impact on their projections. Still, they must recognize this maturation process is a normal part of a player's evolution. If they don't recognize the process, they may be doomed to make mistakes when evaluating youthful players. Also, if they carry that opinion into the future with no admission of a player's progress evident, they risk compounding their mistakes. In fact, it's wise to anticipate there will be acts of unprofessional or immature behavior in a Rookie Ball player. Likewise, it's wise to anticipate his progress.

How can we protect ourselves from repeating mistakes in the evaluation of younger developing players when we've held a past negative opinion? Every Spring Training, we can wipe the slate clean.

That means we evaluate all young players with the fresh eyes of a new year. We look for progress in the player, not evidence that supports a past negative opinion. We can be optimistic that past lesser strengths may have evolved into improved physical or personal characteristics and baseball skills. The majority of young players will improve in all aspects, but we must be open to the possibility or we could miss it.

> The player can make a great deal of progress during the winter, so we must wipe the slate clean to correctly evaluate in the spring.

Position Changes

Scouting Department personnel make the initial effort for the organization to acquire a player. They assess the degree of impact a player is likely to have on the Major League club by examining his present attributes and projecting them into the future. Scouting is not an exact science. The scouts are relatively accurate but will never bat 1.000. A player's characteristics may develop well beyond the estimate of a scout or never change to the degree previously envisioned.

Still, the Player Development Department has the responsibility to supply impactful players to the Major League club. Occasionally a player's tools or characteristics won't be consistent with the Scouting Department's original evaluation. If a player's body develops tremendous size and strength, it could limit his range and effectiveness on his defense in the middle of the field. If a player's bat doesn't progress as projected, it could limit his impact as a corner player. Overall, the goal is to put the player in the position that will have the most impact at the Major League level.

It's a matter of managing the inventory!

> "If we do the best thing for a player's career, we are doing what's best for the organization." – Major League Manager Davey Johnson (Mets, Orioles, Dodgers, Nationals)

With this statement, Davey Johnson was offering an experienced Major League perspective on position changes. He meant the more impactful we can make a player, the more valuable he will be in the industry, and the more valuable he will be to the organization. By positioning the player to be the most impactful at the Major League level, we improve the probability of his adding value to our inventory of players, thus strengthening the organization.

Going beyond the fundamental aspects of scouting and projection, the player development staff members must also understand a championship player profile to accurately assess the probability of a player's impact at the Major League level.

If It Doesn't Work, It Was Your Idea

A great scout and a tremendous leader, Ed Creech was the scouting director for the Montreal Expos in 1995. I really enjoyed our working relationship. His small-town stories about his home in Moultrie, Georgia, always made me laugh.

Ed asked if I would see a few players that his scouting staff liked ahead of the 1995 June Draft. They were under serious consideration to be future Montreal Expos. As farm director, I had a busy schedule but said I'd find time to scout a few players. Besides, it would be nice to get away and do something different from my regular duties.

I told Ed I didn't want any information about the prospects I'd watch or what our scouts thought of them. Instead, I wanted to scout the players with an open mind and offer my own clinical evaluation void of other perspectives. Ed agreed, and then wrote out a list of amateur prospects scattered throughout the country. The list had a surprising number of players, and I knew I could never find time to see them all. As I looked to determine which prospects might fit into my schedule geographically, I noticed one played in Alpharetta, Georgia, a suburb of Atlanta. My travels regularly took me through Atlanta, so I offered to scout that kid on my next trip if his high school game schedule fit into my travel plans.

My next time in Atlanta, Ed offered to take me to the game so I could scout shortstop Michael Barrett. I figured Ed must really like Barrett because he wanted to be at the game with me. I didn't make a final call on the picks—that was Ed's job—but I knew scouts like to have others on their side when making important selections.

As directed, I flew in on a morning flight from West Palm Beach, and Ed was there to pick me up. I thought it odd to arrive so early for a four o'clock game, but maybe we'd watch Barrett hit earlier in the day or something. I said, "Ed, it's pretty early; are we going to watch him hit?"

"No. We're going to get some southern food," Ed replied with a big grin. (You can take the boy out of Moultrie, but you can't take the Moultrie out of the boy.)

Thanks to Ed, I developed a fondness for greens, grits, and okra that day. The fried chicken was the best I had ever eaten. Ed seemed to be in heaven, feeling content in his native state. I suspiciously wondered if he really liked Michael because he was a good prospect, or because the kid was from Georgia. Either way, I was determined to scrutinize this kid judiciously and not let Ed's Southern hospitality or the delicious fried chicken cloud my judgment.

Michael

Michael Barrett appeared to have a solid body with good size. He seemed athletic and had excellent baseball actions with fluidity of movement. He was not extraordinary physically but had no apparent weakness. He had a good glove and solid arm strength with accuracy. But I was concerned about his future range for the shortstop position as he matured and added muscle to his frame. While he was completing the defensive plays of the drill, I wondered about moving him to third base. His raw defensive actions were certainly good enough to play third base at the Major League level someday, but could he provide enough offensive impact? Where could he have the most Major League impact? I needed to see him hit.

Unfortunately, the game that day did not help me much. After a base on balls and a first pitch pop-up in the first two at bats, I told Ed I'd need to see Michael hit more to have a reasonably confident opinion of him. Ed asked if I could stay another day to watch him practice, but I couldn't. No matter how good the fried chicken was, I needed to leave. Then Michael singled to right field and flew out in his next two at bats, but he didn't get to hit again. I thought I got a decent gauge on his bat speed and swing mechanics, but I wanted to determine his raw power as a potential third baseman. When the game ended, to my surprise, Ed set up a private workout with the coach. Michael would take batting practice on the field, a perfect scenario.

As the other scouts left the ballpark and drove away, Ed and I just laughed. Little did they know we had a private workout to start soon.

The coach began to throw pitches to the plate, and Michael sprayed line drives all over the field. The kid could hit! Michael had excellent hand-eye coordination and made solid contact with every swing. He had good pop in his bat—but was the raw power enough to be a future corner player? It was close, but not quite the raw power I had hoped to see. I believed it was slightly shy of a championship corner power bat. He had the tremendous *hitting characteristics of a Major League player, but I wanted to see more raw power. Could he hit future home runs? Would that great swing and hand-eye coordination lead to future run production even though he may not hit an extreme number of homers? More than likely. I thought highly of his bat potential, and he should get much stronger in the future, but would the power be enough for a corner player on a championship club?*

Following the workout, we spoke to the Barrett family, and I couldn't have been more impressed. This excellent student and great kid seemed driven to succeed at whatever he tried to accomplish. I was sold, and I already knew Ed wanted to draft the kid. This was the only time he had ever bought me lunch.

Ed selected Michael Barrett in the first round of the 1995 June Draft with the 28th pick. We allowed him to play his normal position the first summer, and he was honored as the All-Star shortstop of the Gulf Coast League. He had an outstanding season with his bat and glove at the Rookie Ball level.

Decision Time

After the season, Michael participated in our FIL program in West Palm Beach. This allowed me to watch him every day and evaluate him extensively. He was a staff member's dream—a mature kid for his age, extremely intelligent and a tremendous worker, and he combined those characteristics with a thirst for baseball knowledge.

Clinically, I remained worried about the level of foot quickness for the middle of the infield and the lack of plus raw power in the bat for a corner position. Taught by Bill Livesey, I learned to insist on impact for an athlete to fit into a championship profile. There was only one place to position Michael to potentially provide the most Major League impact: catcher.

Allow me to review the circumstances so far: First-round pick and All-Star shortstop his first season; staff loves this kid who has no glaring present statistical weaknesses. Do I really want to attempt such an extreme move? Am I being too aggressive too early in his career? What am I thinking?

The next two weeks I watched Michael, intently focused on projecting his tools and physical characteristics into the future at the Major League level. Still, I needed to be 100 percent certain, no matter which way we proceeded. This move cannot be an experiment. The organization had made a huge investment in this high-level prospect. Should we take the safe choice and move him to third base? That would be a hell of a lot easier if I wanted to sleep at night.

After making my final evaluation, I had to talk to one extremely important person before I brought it up to the front office staff, player development staff, or the Major League staff. I'd better talk to Ed Creech.

We were nearing the end of the FIL program when Ed came into town. We had numerous phone conversations, but I never wanted to discuss the subject over the phone. The discussion was too serious. Besides, I needed the time to make my final evaluation of Michael. The morning he arrived, Ed sat down in my office for his FIL update, and I proceeded to review all of the players in the program—an upbeat meeting. As Ed stood up to go outside and watch the players' workouts, I stopped him. "Ed, we need to talk."

Then I told him I thought we should change positions and make Michael Barrett a catcher. Ed sat silently. I explained my analysis in tremendous detail, making sure he understood my intentions were in the best interests of the player and the organization. He just looked at me with a blank expression. I spoke of Michael's attributes—his great glove, tremendous intellect, undeniable work ethic, strong accurate arm, and good bat. After exhausting my clinical examination and explanations, I paused to let Ed speak.

Finally, he said, "Before the draft, an Atlanta Braves' scout asked Michael if he'd ever caught, and what did he think of becoming a catcher."

I felt relieved. Someone had thought of that before me! It added validity to my evaluation, especially coming from a Braves' scout. Everyone in professional baseball had seen the Braves' success with players from Georgia. And no Major League organization knows players from Georgia better than the Atlanta Braves.

I asked Ed, "What do you think?"

"I don't disagree, and I'm okay with the move. But let's make something perfectly clear."

"What's that?" I asked.

"If it works, it was OUR idea. If it doesn't work, it was YOUR idea."

We laughed.

Done Deal

In our next staff meeting, I brought the idea to our entire group of player development instructors. I saw quizzical looks at first but there was no resistance to Michael Barrett becoming a catcher. I suggested the staff think about it and watch Michael the next two days then we'd discuss it again. It didn't take the full two days. After the first day, most of the staff said it was a very good idea and we got set to embark on a serious position change. But time was running out in the FIL, with only two days left. The players would be leaving to go home, so I had to quickly design an off-season plan to help Michael make the transition because I didn't want to tell him "We're going to make you a catcher; see you in Spring Training."

Fortunately, Jerry Weinstein agreed to let Michael spend time with him in San Luis Obispo, California, where he'd train during the winter. We set up a meeting on the last day of the FIL to tell Michael he'd become a catcher. He took the news well, telling me about the Braves' scout's desire to also make him a catcher. We began the journey.

I received a tremendous amount of criticism early in the position change process from inside and outside of the organization. I didn't care; we were doing what was best for the kid. We had made the decision as a group of professionals with careful thought. As fate would have it, Michael Barrett played in 12 seasons as a catcher in his MLB career.

"Our" Decision

In 1999, I was at Spring Training with the Dodgers, and we were playing the Montreal Expos in Jupiter, Florida. It was great to watch my former Minor League players with the Major League Montreal Expos, now all grown up. As I made my way to the parking lot after the game, I heard someone calling my name. Michael stood by the locker room door and waved to me to come over. We chatted about our families and commenced with the usual small talk of old baseball friends. Then the conversation turned to his career.

Michael said, "You know, I was a little surprised and confused when you wanted to make me a catcher. I need to tell you that after my time in the Big Leagues, I know now what you did for my career. Your decision guaranteed me 10 years in this league, and I wanted to thank you for that." After experiencing the highest level in Major League Baseball, Michael must have recognized the best position in which he could impact the game was as a catcher.

I drove away reminiscing about our entire decision-making process. Did I still possess the courage to make such a drastic position change with a high-profile player again? I honestly didn't know. The decision to totally reshape the direction of a player's career is an extremely serious exercise. Maybe I'll go get some fried chicken and grits to think about it.

Summary

Embrace the different perspectives to discern the best possible plan. Be sure to:

- ☐ Have a sense of urgency.
- ☐ Communicate proactively.
- ☐ Offer your opinion.
- ☐ Wipe the slate clean.
- ☐ Rely on the profile for positive position changes.

CHAPTER 17:

PLAYER DEVELOPMENT—THE DNA
OF THE DEPARTMENT

Organizational Philosophy

It's important for a Major League club to create an overall organizational philosophy or belief system that defines the leadership's desired attributes for the company. What do we stand for? What characteristics do we wish to exemplify? Once identified, this stringent set of philosophies can shape employee activities and decision-making throughout the organization and its various departments. Likened to an organization's DNA, it takes an unapologetic stance for what's acceptable or unacceptable behavior for members of the club. This thinking embodies the principles and priorities of the organization with a desire to manifest into an organizational identity. To create this organizational identity, the philosophies must be well-defined, clearly communicated, and positively reinforced throughout.

A Public Agenda

These philosophies are also announced as a *public agenda* to be saturated into every level of the organization. All staff members must be keenly aware of what's important to its leadership to act congruently with its direction. If not, the philosophies will lower in probability of becoming hallmarks of the company and will likely fail to develop into reliable organizational characteristics. To successfully fulfill their daily duties in alignment with the organizational philosophies, employees must be guided by unequivocal, undeniable messages from their leaders. The stories that follow are examples.

The Ultimate Fan Experience

The Colorado Rockies have always strived to create a great fan experience for their loyal customers. This desire is prominently displayed in the club mission statement and embraced by its employees. Substantial financial resources and focused leadership have been exhibited by Dick Monfort (owner), Keli McGregor (former president), Greg Feasel (COO), and Kevin Kahn (CCO)) in an effort to make Coors Field the best possible venue for fans of Major League Baseball. In my career, I've never witnessed the level of thought and care that rivals the Rockies' in ensuring baseball fans enjoy their time at the ballpark. From the purchase of tickets, parking, security, and concessions to in-game entertainment and ballpark departures, each interaction with fans has been extensively examined. Because of this dedication, the team's leadership has successfully embedded its desire to deliver the best fan experience into the DNA of the organization.

In 2005, then-President Keli McGregor requested an update on the progress of some of our young players in the Minor Leagues. He asked me to meet him on the main concourse of Coors Field an hour before the gates were opened. It seemed like an odd place for a meeting, but I didn't question it. I arrived a few minutes early to show respect to the boss. Not surprisingly, Keli was already waiting (not out of character for him).

We walked around the stadium while I informed Keli about the latest performances of certain Minor League prospects. Truth be told, he didn't have many questions. I think he only wanted to know when I projected these players could help our Major League club. As we talked, I could see Keli surveying the conduct of our stadium staff as they prepared for the evening game. He was making sure everything was prepared for our customers' entrance in what must have been a standard survey trip for him. Workers were setting up concession stands, ushers were getting last-minute instructions, and ticket takers were readying to greet the fans already lined up outside the stadium. Keli said hello to all the part-time workers and called to some by name, which appeared to brighten their moods.

Picking Up Trash

As we strolled the concourse, I noticed something peculiar. Keli had a tendency to pick up trash he saw on the ground and throw it away. Even the smallest piece of refuse found the nearest receptacle as we walked the park. To Keli, the mission to provide fans with the best fan experience wasn't idle chatter; it was a philosophical guide. He wanted Coors Field to be a special place, and trash lying around didn't indicate "special." Indeed, it was unacceptable. For Keli, there was never a job too small or a person too insignificant to make a difference.

Leading by example, Keli chose actions that reflected the Rockies' organizational philosophy of providing a great fan experience. There were no established guidelines regarding the removal of waste from the stadium floor by employees, but he did it every day. Without Keli ever speaking a word, I completely understood his passion and leadership for the fan experience. To achieve the organizational objective, the president would happily assist the janitorial crew if necessary. It was only then that I truly understood the entire organization's focus on the fan experience.

Taking Keli's lead, I tried to apply this organizational philosophy in a more pronounced fashion in the Player Development Department. I asked our affiliate front office staffs to increase *opportunities for Minor League players to interact with fans. They might add speaking engagements with their local schools and even set up autograph sessions at the end of home stands. I wanted the young players to understand the importance of interacting with fans and have more chances to practice their interpersonal skills. The player-fan relationship has great importance; after all, the fans pay the bills—a key concept for the players to grasp. It's not only through playing well and winning games that players offer fan enjoyment; they should adhere to the organizational philosophy and make fan experience a part of their daily thoughts.*

As for me, I never again passed a piece of trash at Coors Field without picking it up.

Former Colorado Rockies President Keli McGregor.
Photo courtesy of the Colorado Rockies

L.A. Dodgers' DNA

Late in the 1998 season when I was Assistant GM with the Los Angeles Dodgers, I grabbed my notebook and headed downstairs for a staff meeting. The entire Major League coaching staff and the lead Baseball Operations front office employees were meeting in Dodger Stadium to pass judgment on our Major League players. We also discussed a few Minor League players of interest, but we focused on our current 25-man roster and how to improve the team.

A group of 20 high-ranking officials with varying experience in the organization would decide on future player personnel of the Los Angeles Dodgers. Glenn Hoffman (Hoffy), manager at the time, did the majority of the speaking for the field staff regarding current player evaluations. Hoffy was an excellent judge of Major League talent, and his evaluations were clear, concise, and persuasive for what he thought of certain players on the Dodger roster.

Hoffy identified one talented player he liked in the field but didn't think he was a positive influence in the clubhouse. The opinions of the group were mixed. Some coaches and front office members wanted this player's talent and offensive production for our club. They didn't care about his negative off-field persona; the team needed his special ability. Others believed the player should not be part of the organization because his attitude wasn't one of a "team player."

We also discussed this player's potential negative impact on our young players.

A Matter of Make-Up

The great debate of talent vs. make-up ensued, and the conversation continued at length. No consensus resulted. The entire group appeared evenly divided. Almost everyone expressed their unwavering opinions, and we seemed to exhaust the discussion without resolving the debate.

I noticed one Major League coach hadn't made his opinions known—longtime Dodger Manny Mota. He'd been a beloved player and a fixture with the coaching staff for many years. In getting to know Manny well while working with the Dodgers, I also knew him to have distinct opinions on players. That day, Manny fidgeted in his seat and seemed frustrated by the proceedings. I believed he had something he needed to get off his chest, so from across the room, I asked, "Manny, do you have something to add?" After a brief stare expressing contempt for calling on him, Manny emotionally replied, "The Dodgers have always had players who were gentlemen. That's been a trademark of our organization for a long time. We have always welcomed good people who respected others and were good teammates. Dodger players are gentlemen."

Manny never made a negative comment or threw the player under the bus, but everyone in the room knew exactly what he meant. Although the O'Malley family was in the process of selling the Los Angeles Dodgers at the time, the owners' legacy of what was required for a Dodger player was still intact. Manny reminded us of that.

Through his years as a Dodger, Manny was guided by the influence of the Dodger DNA that affected his opinions for all of us to witness and from which to learn. The O'Malley family had built the Los Angeles Dodgers into an organization of class and respect by hiring employees and players with those characteristics. Peter O'Malley was Major League Baseball royalty to me, and the time I spent with him until the team was sold was special—one of my career highlights. Both the architect and caretaker for what it meant to be a Los Angeles Dodger, he held everyone in the organization to the highest standard of personal conduct. And it would remain extremely high as Vin Scully was there to emulate the Dodger standard of class and dignity. A man of respect, Peter O'Malley imprinted into the organization the characteristics of what his family wanted for all Dodger employees, players included.

What Do "They" Say About "Us"?

The most successful professional baseball organizations appear to have strong philosophical beliefs regarding what's important for their company and its future. Some employee organizational characteristics may be difficult for casual fans to detect, but specific emphasis of the "on-field" baseball characteristics can be easier to distinguish. The Atlanta Braves and John Schuerholz (president) have long relied on a strong pitching staff. Pitchers Greg Maddux, Tom Glavine, and John Smoltz were keys to their past dominating team performance, and excellent pitching has remained a hallmark of the Braves. The St. Louis Cardinals also exemplify dominant pitching as a consistent, undeniable Cardinals trait prevalent throughout its storied championship history.

Under the leadership of Bruce Bochy (Manager) and his coaching staff, the San Francisco Giants appear to be the toughest, grittiest team in Major League Baseball. Year after year, the Giants have proven to be the better team in close games. Brian Sabean (former GM) and Bobby Evans (GM) have done an excellent job filling the Giant clubhouse with players focused on team wins and championships above individual statistics.

Another example is George Steinbrenner, NYY owner from 1973 until his death in 2010, who ingrained the desire to win into every New York Yankee employee. To this day, all NYY players and staff members understand their responsibility to win a championship—a constant element of the Yankee experience. George Steinbrenner would compensate players and staff extremely well, providing necessary resources for every department to do the job effectively. He was always supportive, *win or tie.* If you receive a paycheck from the New York Yankees, you're paid to win or you go somewhere else to work—that's understood.

The Oakland A's club enjoyed success rooted in its progressive techniques of advanced statistical analytics. Billy Beane (GM) revolutionized the game by endorsing the advanced study of individual player and team evaluations. Even in the face of relentless criticism from many in professional baseball—including old-school disciples and some media members—the A's haven't wavered from the club's philosophy. And this team has changed the game forever, enough to inspire a book and movie called *Moneyball.*

These convey a few classic examples of an organizational identity that lays the philosophical foundation to lead a club to success. It begins with a philosophy that sets guidelines for a plan of action and develops into a dominant strength that other teams can recognize as an organizational identity. Consider this identity the most influential element of a team's DNA—its backbone. The club has an unapologetic posture toward its chosen philosophy implementation. It's a palpable characteristic of the organization, a well-earned reputation. IT IS WHO THEY ARE! Club leaders make every effort to fortify these beliefs throughout the organization.

To complete their duties aligned with the organizational philosophy, leaders are obliged to detail the philosophical priorities and the responsibility of each employee. Appropriate questions for every club would be:

☐ What do we whole-heartedly believe in?

☐ Have we developed the philosophy into an organizational identity?

☐ When a team comes to town, what do they say about us?

Food for Thought

If you were president of a Major League club, what organizational characteristics would be important to implement among the club's employees?

If you were general manager of a Major League club, what "on field" characteristics would be important to implement?

If you were farm director, what departmental characteristics would be important to implement?

If you were manager of a Minor League team, what team characteristics would be essential to implement?

What overall strategies will you adopt to implement your beliefs?

Player Development Perspectives

Every Level Has a Different Perspective

Over the years, I've witnessed dozens of baseball-related disagreements in MLB organizations. Clubs have been confronted with issues necessitating a defined strategy in the face of strong opposing opinions about the right course of action. In all honesty, it's rare to gain a consensus on *any* topic of discussion. Dissenting employee viewpoints exist no matter what the topic.

Most of the opinions I heard were solidly influenced and stubbornly grounded by the perspective of a staff member's role in the organization. Obstinate opinions weren't derived from experience in professional baseball, personal preference, or advanced study. Instead, the varying jobs led to differing opinions—a matter of role perspective.

Each employee level of the organization carries a different perspective on resolving issues. The higher a person was in the organization, the more the opinion tended to favor philosophy. Likewise, the lower the person's position in the organization, the opinion leaned toward the proposed application's practicality (or impracticality). Once I understood the specific predisposition of the individual employee's role within the organization, their opinions became simple to anticipate.

Can I say that my understanding of this concept helped resolve organizational issues? Sadly, I cannot. Still, it helps to recognize various levels of perspective when analyzing issues before meetings as I anticipate questions from employees. My conclusion? Acknowledging and appreciating *all* perspectives in the department help us make reasonably sound judgments.

The Director's Overall Role

Similar to how the Player Development Department falls between the Scouting Department and the Major Leagues, the Director of Player Development is squeezed into an extremely difficult position, as mid-level authorities know. The Director must be the creator and guardian for transforming theory and philosophy into practical, successful applications—and do so without spending too much money. *This is not easy.*

Plus, the Director typically supervises the largest number of employees in the organization. In the Player Development Department, that can be close to 300 employees and players. As such, the person in this position is pushed from above and pulled from below. The Director not only acquires a heavy load of responsibilities but must deal with personal problems employees face, players included. Employee assistance situations might involve the death of a player's family member, a new baby, a child's severe illness, or any other serious issue. Farm directors are very busy people!

The Farm Director's Perspective

A farm director oversees "putting out fires" and in a Player Development Department, there's no shortage of fires from above or below. One after another, critical issues materialize, and most days the flames seem to fly everywhere. To many inside the club, farm directors have been viewed as difficult to reach, short in their conversations, and even distant. Their minds are probably preoccupied, so that perception is understandable; a farm director is possibly the busiest person in the organization. When confronted with an issue, farm directors have to examine it and quickly come up with a strategy for resolution. They know they must deal with issues immediately because the next fire is a phone call away. That's why successful farm directors think fast and make rapid decisions. They want their employees to help rectify situations by providing strategies and a plan of action so they can move on to the next order of business.

Enough people can identify problems. Who will solve them?

The Coordinators' Perspective

Field coordinators, or coordinators of instruction, work directly with the farm director and other front office members. They have authority over the entire player development field staff, and they also oversee and coordinate activities and instruction in the Minor Leagues. Positional coordinators take charge of a specific aspect of the program (e.g., pitching, hitting, infield defense, outfield defense, base running, etc.) within the Player Development Department. They supervise and organize instruction for a particular subset of players in the Minor Leagues. As such, they focus their energy toward an individual aspect of the player development program, assuming responsibility for player performance in that regard. Because they'll be held accountable for their particular aspect of the program, they invest their heart and soul into their work to provide excellent instruction to the players. *They own it!*

Player development coordinators require little motivation to focus on their aspect of the Minor League program. That's inherent with the job. The problem, if any, could be adequately appreciating the organizational philosophies and specific aspects of other programs in the department. By nature of their travel to the Minor League clubs, the player development coordinators are uniquely positioned to act as "quality control" for the entire department.

Throughout the season, they come in semi-regular contact with every player and staff member in the Player Development Department. Ideally, they become the caretaker of organizational philosophies as part of their responsibilities. Coordinators should work closely with the other coordinators to become familiar with aspects of other departmental programs. It's difficult for an individual coordinator to monitor a program in every city when travel to each Minor League city is limited to once every four to six weeks.

Coordinators need other coordinators to be productive resources— additional sets of eyes and ears in Minor League cities. Their primary importance is in their individual specialty but they must act as the quality control component of the organization, which requires them to be in direct communication with the other coordinators. Besides owning their own program, they bring the front office perspective out into the organization, influencing players and staff through their interactions with them.

Many in professional baseball have questioned a coordinator's desire to become involved in issues outside of the individual's normal area of expertise. This is understandable, but as traveling staff members with authority, coordinators should be responsible for upholding the organizational philosophy, with a quality control perspective built into their DNA.

The Manager's and Coach's Perspective

A club's manager and coach live in the real world. They don't have plush offices or the luxury of time to ponder baseball-related theory and philosophy. They're the true laborers of a club, getting their hands dirty with the all-day, day-in and day-out focus on developing championship baseball players.

Managers and coaches tend to take on a pragmatic perspective, often harshly evaluating changes to their routine or new club philosophies. Similar to the players, managers and coaches rely on specific time-tested routines. They possess a healthy skepticism toward any proposed disruption to what's historically been deemed "normal." Their focus is to lead and instruct players. Staff members understand they must maintain a certain level of respect from the players to be successful leaders.

Risk comes into play when altering the routines of players with new ideas and practices. New kinds of preparation increase the chance for having an unsuccessful experience and can result in a player losing respect for the manager or coach. As staff members, they understand the immense physical and mental demands of professional players. They know their time constraints and typically rely on strategies that have worked in the past. According to their perception, philosophy and theory are only as good as their chances for implementation. Managers especially are opposed to whim or experimentation. "Why change habits or routines that have proven to be successful for years?" they ask.

For a manager or coach, having a predisposition of resisting change is understandable and shouldn't be viewed as a negative aspect of the staff's inherent characteristics. Someone has to protect the organization from a crazy theory or philosophy handed down from the front office—yes, certain ideas are utter nonsense. Fortunately, the manager and coach are perfectly positioned to provide a means of checks and balances for the organization.

That said, Major League Baseball Player Development Departments have evolved to become more progressive in their thought process. Staff members throughout baseball have become more progressive as well, adjusting the scale of "normal."

Each new staff member learns on the job in a different environment than a veteran who's retiring from baseball. The circle of employees naturally changes as time passes. Old realistic postures naturally reset to become more advanced processes. Progress is inevitable. The toughest obstacle is when the manager or coach relies too heavily on what they've seen or done in the past. They limit their thinking to "remembering" past strategies and never attempting more advanced techniques. Without the courage to engage in progressive thought or theory, staff members get in the way of progress. As the game changes—and that's inevitable—the manager or coach who resists change can no longer serve as a form of *checks and balances* for the organization and will be expendable.

Summary

The organizational DNA will define the identity of the club and shape departmental strategies.

Every aspect of the Player Development Department is subject to the influence of a variety of perspectives. It needs employee-level quality control to ensure the organizational and departmental philosophies remain intact. Also, the free and open communication as a form of checks and balances. Key questions:

- ☐ Are organizational and departmental philosophies defined and clearly understood by all of the employees?

- ☐ Has the philosophy of the organization developed into a desired organizational identity?

- ☐ What do "they" say about "us?"

CHAPTER 18:

PLAYER DEVELOPMENT—PUTTING
A PRACTICAL PLAN IN PLACE

Applying Departmental Philosophy

MANY VETERAN PROFESSIONAL BASEBALL PEOPLE BELIEVE THE BEST PLAY-
ers don't require a lot of coaching and instruction. They think future Major
League players simply need additional playing experience against high-
level competition to realize their potential, and these players will make the
proper adjustments along the way.

Players develop themselves, and the staff should only facilitate the
proper learning environment without being overly active in the learning process. This opinion reflects a fundamental posture of KISS: Keep
It Simple Stupid!—a laissez-faire "let it be" kind of learning and development. The cream will rise to the top!

This approach suggests that students learn through personal experience and exploration; they don't effectively learn through the direction
of teachers or staff members. Some proponents believe that, more often
than not, player development coaches and instructors do more harm than
good. They tinker with hitters' swings, change pitchers' deliveries, and alter
the players' mechanics away from what made them successful. Instead of
allowing them to focus on the game, they make players think too much
about physical mechanics.

This is a serious indictment of the many caring, attentive, and
hard-working baseball professionals who study their craft for years, yet it

has been a prevalent "below-the-radar" opinion in the game. Let the players play, and stay out of their way.

Of course, I respectfully disagree.

Player development staff members make mistakes on occasion. But I contend that the majority of the mistakes result from the leadership failing to promote a coherent conceptual philosophy. Mistakes can be minimized with a simple understanding of a proper departmental philosophy and how staff members should see the issues that confront them. Managers and coaches should have a predisposed attitude toward every aspect of their jobs and a sense of right or wrong in each circumstance. Key questions:

- [ ] What is the teaching philosophy in Rookie Ball, Single-A, AAA?
- [ ] What are the goals of each level?
- [ ] When can staff members be aggressive? When should they back off?

It's up to the Player Development Department to communicate the appropriate posture that's consistent with the beliefs of the particular level. Staff members need direction. No player development manual can guide employees through every circumstance they'll face developing professional baseball players, especially because the game changes. Players change, technology changes, facilities change. The educational environment is constantly being altered.

I suggest the mistakes of a Player Development Department should not rest on the shoulders of individual staff members. Rather, they should fall on the leaders' inability to educate staff members on the prevailing departmental conceptual philosophy.

The Application Process

The process of philosophy transformed into action can be called "where the rubber meets the road." Successful applications involve the perspective of the managers, coaches, and instructors to ensure they fit a practical need. Not only do staff members help design the application, ideally they build in subjective measures for making proper adjustments within the parameters of organizational philosophy. Employees shouldn't be encumbered by a dubious set of guidelines without latitude or discretion to fulfill their responsibilities for every situation. No employee respects a dictatorship that doesn't allow a voice to affect change, nor is it healthy for advancing new applications. *Objective* guidelines might exist, but staff members also need *subjective* ones to manage certain situations. That way, coaches or instructors can act in the best interests of all involved. They need the freedom to choose the best strategy for the team or player that's also consistent with departmental philosophy. They can make a *subjective* decision so successfully that it evolves into an *objective* guideline, as it did with Tony Diaz and the critiques in Chapter 14.

To apply action to a philosophy, let's examine two examples.

Application Example #1

> *RATE OF SPEED in the instruction of a newly signed Rookie Ball player*

Philosophy:

Both personally and professionally, a first-year professional player must make huge adjustments. The youngest ones feel uncomfortable living away from home at first. They are performing a large amount of physical work. Their every move is constantly evaluated by instructors. They face a higher talent level of opponents than ever before.

During this huge transition, these players benefit from a methodical approach to instruction, recognizing they may have a difficult time adjusting. This requires a great deal of patience. Instructors should focus their teaching on organizational procedures and player routines *(e.g., drills, pregame routine, batting practice, bullpen protocol, weight training, conditioning, and nutrition, etc.)* as the priority instead of the physical mechanics of swing or pitching delivery. In fact, no mechanical changes should be addressed until the players have had ample time to adjust to a new organization, new routines, and a new level of play.

Objective guideline: 30-Day Rule

Staff members including coaches and instructors should:

☐ Allow players 30 days before working on *mechanical adjustments* with a hitter's swing or a pitcher's delivery mechanics.

☐ Allow players 30 days to focus on organizational routine procedures of batting practice, early work, strength and conditioning, work ethic, video, and appropriate behavior.

☐ Schedule player-coach interviews during this time to learn more about the players and start to build a strong bond of trust.

☐ Personally speak to each signing scout for the player's background information, research the player's scouting reports/statistics/video from amateur level play, and study the player's mechanics.

☐ Watch the players in professional games for 30 days to gain awareness of each player's present mechanics, emotional control, baseball intellect, strengths, and lesser strengths.

☐ Form a plan of instruction for each player after consulting with a player development coordinator.

The absence of a 30-Day Rule is why some people form a negative opinion of those in the Player Development Department. Some instructors begin to alter a player's mechanics quickly, and the new mechanics can lead to a player becoming even more uncomfortable with his transition to professional baseball. As a result, any issue of early poor performance is automatically blamed on the staff member and the department. The 30-Day Rule eliminates that excuse. It also affords time for the various perspectives *(director, coordinators, scouts)* to get involved in constructing a developmental plan for each player.

> *Subjective situation in a newly signed Rookie Ball pitcher:*

☐ Pitcher has an injury history.

☐ Pitching coach has grave concerns regarding the pitcher's present mechanics.

☐ Coach believes the pitcher could injure himself at any time based on the way he delivers the ball.

Action:

After consulting with the pitching coordinator, a decision is made to allow the pitching coach to overlook the 30-Day Rule and begin to alter the pitcher's delivery mechanics to alleviate the immediate health concern.

Application Example #2 (Pitchers)

LEVEL TO LEVEL criterion for advancement

Philosophy:

There should be a method of objective analysis to judge whether a pitcher is worthy of a promotion from Single-A to a higher level in the Minor Leagues. The Player Development Department should set a standard objective criterion for advancement. Performance criteria, which reflect the organizational and departmental goals of the competitive use of the fastball and the ability to throw strikes, must be met to be considered a candidate for promotion. If pitchers who fail to meet the standards of their current level are promoted, they're being rewarded when they don't have the skills to compete at the upper levels of the Minor Leagues.

Objective criterion:

☐ 55% successful FIRST PITCH STRIKES

- ☐ 60% strikes with FASTBALL

- ☐ < 4.5 walks per 9 innings

- ☐ < 4.50 ERA

- ☐ < 1.40 sec. time to plate from break of stretch position to catcher's glove with FASTBALL.

Subjective situation:

- ☐ The Single-A pitcher meets all the objective criteria for advancement.

- ☐ The pitcher is dominant at the current level (1.89 ERA).

- ☐ He is easily the best-performing starting pitcher on the Single-A roster.

- ☐ The pitcher continues to distract teammates.

- ☐ Pitcher continues to violate team rules and is punished repeatedly.

- ☐ The pitcher exhibits zero leadership skills.

Extenuating circumstances:

- ☐ The Double-A team needs a starting pitcher because of an injury.

- ☐ The Double-A team is in a push to make the playoffs in their league.

- ☐ The Double-A affiliate agreement expires at the end of the season.

- ☐ The organization hopes to sign an extension with the affiliate team in Double-A.

- ☐ The Double-A affiliate has not made the playoffs in five years.

- ☐ The Double-A front office will only sign an extension if the team makes the playoffs.

Action:

What do you do? Are you willing to risk the loss of a good Double-A affiliate city? Are you willing to risk the loss of respect of players and staff by promoting someone who doesn't follow the public organizational characteristics of leadership and isn't a good teammate? *(I never said it was easy!)*

Because no objective guideline should be inflexible, it's wise to build a way to compromise. Certain subjective situations might call for an action that otherwise wouldn't have been considered. When the philosophy transitions into practice, a simple design leading to an application can serve to recognize differences of players and circumstances.

Assume a Departmental Posture and Create Guidelines

Philosophy is relatively simple to understand compared to the vast complexities and difficulties of the application process. Think past philosophy to assume a departmental posture and create guidelines that minimize mistakes and reinforce the opinion of leadership.

Because no objective guideline should be inflexible, it's wise to build a way to compromise. Certain subjective situations might call for an action that otherwise wouldn't have been considered. When the philosophy transitions into practice, a simple design leading to an application can serve to recognize differences of players and circumstances.

Documentation for Review

One of the most important factors leading to the continued success of any Player Development Department's program is its ability to review. Leaders announce the beliefs or philosophy, create and execute an action plan, and then review the process to understand the positive or negative results. They ask these questions:

☐ What is the philosophy?

☐ What did we plan? What did we do?

☐ What were the results?

Department members need a way to look back on the planning/strategies/results and honestly reflect on their positive or negative impact. It's important to complete a comprehensive review of each part of the program to discern what has happened.

> "There are three kinds of people in this world: people who make it happen, people who watch what happens, and people who wonder what the hell happened." – Tommy Lasorda

No Staff Member is Perfect

Staff members can only surmise what has happened by documenting and reviewing their activities. Similar to evaluating players, it's a given that no staff member is perfect. No one person can impeccably plan and adeptly execute all the complex issues involved in developing Major League players. The variables involved change too often for anyone to be accurate 100 percent of the time. But one thing is certain. Staff members had better know what they're doing *at present* to adjust to changing circumstances. How can leaders properly alter the program to account for changes if they don't know exactly what's been done? Compare this to a chef not knowing the exact ingredients for a signature dish. Similarly, the Player Development Department must know every detail of its development program to repeat success and avoid failure. Documentation helps formulate and execute the best plan to accomplish that.

> "Anyone can have a great year, but can they repeat it?" – Bill Livesey

Mr. Peabody

*In my senior year of college at UC Santa Barbara, we played well
as a team early in the season. After a sweep of the University of
California at Berkeley and beating Stanford University two out
of three games, our record was 19–1. We rose to the rank of #5
in the Division 1 National Collegiate Poll. Our coach was Al
Ferrer, an emotional leader who motivated us to always perform
with our best effort. A tremendous student of the game, Coach
Ferrer had a brilliant baseball intellect and viewed every aspect
of the sport as a potential area of advanced study. He regarded
his baseball field as a performance testing laboratory. Our practices were organized to the exact minute. He rarely allowed devi-
ations from his plan, and he knew exactly how much time we
needed in all areas of the game. Every drill had a purpose. It was
each player's responsibility to be prepared for the day and know
where to be every minute of the practice with the appropriate
equipment. The highly structured plan was laced with a serious
tone of discipline.*

*One day, I arrived at the field to begin my hitting drills before
practice, my usual routine. When I walked into the dugout, I
saw Coach Ferrer sitting with what appeared to be a few college
students. They must have been from one of the classes he taught
in the Sports Management Program at UCSB, I thought.*

*I put on my spikes, grabbed my bat, and headed to the batting
cages. I began with tee drills—hitting balls off the tee at varying
heights and from different spots in front of the plate. Alone in
the cage, I enjoyed the solitude to get my mind right for the day.
It was often a respite between the end of my classes and Coach
Ferrer yelling at me during practice.*

*Suddenly, I caught a glimpse of someone standing off on the
other side of the batting cages a good distance away. I didn't*

think much about this person; I kept banging away in the dusty batting cage hitting dirty old practice baseballs from the tee into a worn-out net.

Periodically, though, I looked over to see if the guy was still there. He was. We never had anyone outside of our team near the batting cages, so who is this guy? I thought he must be a student because he's too young to be a scout.

Then I grew uncomfortable with this unknown person watching me. He was taking my mind away from my practice, but I never said a word. Other players arrived and we started our flip drills to work on our swings. To my frustration, the guy still stood in the distance watching us. He never wavered or took his eyes away from us.

After completing my hitting routine, I headed toward the dugout and purposely walked closer to the guy to get a good look. Skinny and geeky looking, he was obviously a university student. In fact, he looked like the type who'd never received a grade lower than an "A" in his life. He appeared so nonathletic, he probably never had PE in high school. Likely he had the mind of a genius and was a future Nobel laureate who carried a protractor in his pocket. He reminded me of Mr. Peabody, the ultra-smart cartoon dog in the Rocky and Bullwinkle cartoons. (Millennials, google Mr. Peabody.)

As I continued past him, to my surprise, Mr. Peabody followed me to the field. Unable to contain my curiosity, I turned and asked, "Hey, are you following me?"

"Yes," he replied.

"Why are you following me?" I asked.

"Coach Ferrer told me I wasn't allowed to speak to you."

Now I knew what was going on! The scientist, Coach Ferrer, had Mr. Peabody following me around doing some crazy experiment. Using a formula he'd devised from his college internship at NASA, Mr. Peabody would tell the coach that the angle of my bat is a half-centimeter off. Or he would say my weight distribution is too far forward, according to his geometric hypothesis from his physics class.

By that point, I had to find out exactly what Mr. Peabody was doing. I headed right for Coach Ferrer.

"Hey, Coach, what's with Mr. Peabody following me around?" I asked sarcastically.

Ferrer replied, "Don't worry about it; just leave him alone."

"Peabody is following me everywhere, and I don't like it. I want to know."

Begrudgingly, Ferrer looked over to Mr. Peabody and asked him, "How many does he have right now?"

"One hundred thirty-three," said Mr. Peabody.

Coach looked at me and said, "You have taken one hundred thirty-three swings so far today. We are counting how many times a player swings the bat in a day of practice. Is it enough? Is it too many? When we design a day of practice, what should be our goal for the number of swings? Let me ask you this: How many swings do you take in a day, Bill?"

"No idea, Coach," I reluctantly replied,

"Then shut up and leave him alone so he can count."

I felt pretty stupid walking away. How many swings did I take in a day? How many swings did I take in a week? Did I perform better in the weeks when I took more swings than normal? Did I perform worse in the weeks when I took fewer swings than normal? What is normal? How come I never even thought of counting my swings to examine if there was any correlation to my game performance?

Mr. Peabody wasn't using an advanced formula developed at NASA; he was using simple addition. I finished our practice that day with 300 swings. (I made sure I got to a round number.) What an eye-opening experience in documenting my activities to review my process and results.

The lesson learned that day led me to attempt to quantify the activities in the Player Development Department. I would document what's been done and review the results, which is the only way to understand if I'm taking the proper course of action. Key questions:

- ☐ How could you ascertain if your strategy works if you don't know what you have done?

- ☐ How could you repeat success if you don't know exactly what you'd done to succeed?

Having the proper documentation is critical to repeating success. Thank you, Coach Ferrer, and you too, Mr. Peabody.

How Much Time is Invested?

Many corporate leaders attempt to determine their Return on Time Invested or ROTI. They examine their employees' use of time and calculate the associated value of their activities to the company. From there, they aim to direct employees to use their time in beneficial ways.

You can apply this concept of ROTI to the Player Development Department and examine the use of time and its correlation to the success or failure of your organization's goals. Key questions:

☐ How do players spend their time?

☐ What is the result?

☐ Is time being spent appropriately? Efficiently?

When studying ROTI in the Player Development Department, understand two important functions in the equation:

☐ Our time in any given day is limited.

☐ Human beings have limitations to physical/mental stress and need appropriate rest and recovery, especially when the activity will be performed daily for seven or eight consecutive months.

A Baseball Example

Let's deconstruct a day (24 hours) for a Minor League player or staff member when there's a 7:05 p.m. home game. First examine a list of necessary activities in Figure 18.1.

Figure 18.1

REQUIRED ACTIVITIES—TIME EXPENDED	
TIME (HOURS)	**ACTIVITY**
8.0	Sleep
5.0	Game (including game prep; shower/training room)
2.0	Eating (breakfast, lunch, snacks, dinner)
1.0	Travel to and from park (including dressing/undressing)
.5	Restroom activities
16.5 HOURS	**TOTAL TIME FOR REQUIRED ACTIVITIES**

This chart decreases the *time remaining to 7.5 hours* in a given HOME GAME day.

A conservative estimate for a player's proper amount of rest when it's an evening game may be three hours. This decreases the time remaining for prescribed physical activity to a *maximum of 4.5 hours.*

Let's now examine the time needed for generally accepted baseball procedure in Figure 18.2.

Figure 18.2

BASEBALL PROCEDURE—TIME EXPENDED	
TIME (MINUTES)	**ACTIVITY**
40	Stretch and throw
20	Team infield-outfield
60	Batting practice
30	Weight training/physical conditioning
150 MINUTES 2.5 HOURS	**TOTAL TIME FOR PROFESSIONAL BASEBALL PROCEDURE**

This decreases the time available for any other activity to *2.0 hours.*

Now let's examine the instructional phases of the day in Figure 18.3.

Figure 18.3

TIME LEFT AFTER ALL ACTIVITIES	
ACTIVITY	**TIME REMAINING (2 HOURS)**
Early work (30 min)	1:30
Team defense (20 min)	1:10
Video review (20 min)	:50
Team meetings (10 min)	:40
40 MINUTES REMAIN	

Note: Only 40 minutes remain on any given home game day.

Consider player and staff travel time between stations and drills plus field/equipment setup time between activities. This arguably decreases the remaining time to near zero. Add time needed for players involved in supplemental activities such as English and cultural classes, the Employee Assistance Program (EAP) for drug, alcohol, or behavior counseling, vision or virtual reality training, or mental skills training, and we're running into a time deficit.

This deconstruction exercise illustrates the limited time available on a home game day. This example shows the maximum amount of time. On some game days, less time is available because of pregame kids' clinics, Education Day games for young students on field trips, and Minor League promotions. These limit the players' activity time on the field.

The Games Get in the Way!

Because sleep is important for proper rest and recovery, it's critical to *not* demand players arrive at the ballpark early for a day game following a night game. Which decreases the opportunity for instruction.

The situation gets worse for road games. Bus travel (especially overnight) is a concern regarding enough time for rest and recovery. The available time and use of the opponent's facilities can be significantly less than at home. The rigorous game schedule is physically demanding and limits opportunities for instruction and skill development. Maintaining a satisfactory level of player efficiency requires prioritizing and planning instruction times carefully. Key questions:

- ☐ As a team, how are you using your time?

- ☐ How much is solely for game preparation?

- ☐ How much is for repetitive baseball activity?

- ☐ How much is for skill development?

- ☐ How much is for specific instruction?

- ☐ How much is spent in early work sessions to further a player's development?

- ☐ How much is focused on the lesser strengths of individual players?

- ☐ Are traditions of the game dictating how you spend your time?

All MLB organizations strive to teach the game in a comprehensive professional manner. Conscientious staff members prepare and teach their players proper fundamentals in all aspects of the game. They plan presentations, design drills, and execute their teaching strategies. Yet they have only one problem: The games get in the way! Key questions:

- ☐ How do staff members find the time during any given day to instruct without physically exhausting the players?

- ☐ How do they teach without adversely affecting the players' ability to prepare for the games?

- ☐ How do they manage their time given the game schedule and daily pregame requirements?

What a daunting task to manage a heavy schedule and constant travel and still have consistently scheduled sessions with players without wearing them down physically! That's why the front office must set realistic goals for what staff members can achieve daily. The leaders must ask:

- ☐ Is the players' physical workload appropriate?

- ☐ Are the organizational routines designed to maximize efficiency?

- ☐ How much time should be allocated for individual and team defense?

- ☐ How much time should be spent on team offense or situational hitting?

- ☐ How much time should be spent on bunting? Base running? Pitchers' defense and offense?

They must know how the staff spends its time as they quantify the amount of time available, document how it's being used, and evaluate if it's used effectively.

Did We Work Them Too Much?

In my early years in baseball, I was fortunate to be brought up in the game the "right way." I can still remember my Little

League coaches Lloyd Stanley and Alan Oshier barking orders at me during practice. My high school coaches Bob Rodness, Hal Steward, and Nate Harris demanded hard work and settled for nothing less.

In college, the work became increasingly more demanding with coaches Jerry Weinstein, Paul Carmazzi, and Al Ferrer who drove me to near-insanity with their grueling practices and extreme intensity. When I began as a Minor League player, I learned the definition of daily hard work from Rookie Ball Manager Bruce Hines and Hitting Coordinator Rick Down. In Single-A, Manager Tom Kotchman, Instructors Bill Lachemann and Bob Clear, and Field Coordinator Joe Maddon preached hard work and preparation. The California Angels' instructors were exceptional baseball men in terms of knowing the game. They also had a penchant for teaching a strong work ethic and respect for the game at all times. I still owe a debt of gratitude to all of those fine men for teaching me the "right way."

As I transitioned to being a college coach following my playing career, my perspective shifted to the other side. I learned strategies to motivate players to work hard from great coaches such as Dave Snow, Mike Gillespie, Andy Lopez, Jerry Kindall, Wally Kincaid, Bob Milano, Rod Dedeaux, Chris Smith, Auggie Garrido, Mike Mayne, and Mike Weathers. My background as a player and coach were filled with hard-working, successful baseball people. I was fortunate.

When my career path changed from scout to director of player development, I relied on my background as a player and coach. My mentors Bill Livesey, Felipe Alou, Ralph Avila, and Tommy Lasorda amplified what I'd learned previously about hard work. In my role as farm director, I believed our department should strive to be the hardest-working staff and players not only in baseball but in all of professional sports! We would care more, be the most attentive, and work harder than anyone, anywhere. I sought the hardest-working employees to hire, and luckily I found them.

I have the utmost respect for the instructors and players I've been with over the years. They were outstanding in their attention to detail and work ethic. I have witnessed many go well beyond what I had formerly believed was possible in terms of physical workload. At times, I'd be astonished by their endurance and passion for their work. These staff members and players took my hard work to another level. The common philosophy was "The harder you work, the better you will be." It was how I was taught to operate from my earliest mentors in the game, and I felt obligated to continue their legacy.

Even with my extensive background in baseball, early on I didn't have much day-to-day experience at the Major League level. I'd been assigned to evaluate Major League players from a scouting perspective and had watched Major League games, but I'd never been around an MLB club on a daily basis. As my experience expanded and my responsibilities transitioned to the Major Leagues, though, I could witness the highest level of competition consistently.

In all honesty, I didn't fully understand the uniqueness of the MLB level when I arrived. Clearly, I had to gain a better understanding of players' routines and culture. The Montreal Expos' players have no idea that some of their responses to my seemingly innocuous questions have led me to strong convictions on various aspects of the Major Leagues. I trusted Larry Walker, Tim Scott, Gil Heredia, Moises Alou, Jeff Fassero, Kirk Reuter, Roberto Kelly, Butch Henry, Cliff Floyd, Sean Berry, Mike Lansing, and Rondell White, along with coaches Louis Pujols,

Pierre Arsenault, Joe Kerrigan, Jerry Manuel, Jim Tracy, and Tommy Harper. They broke me in. I studied how they went about their craft, observing at full throttle every minute I was fortunate to be around them. That was the mid-1990s. Major League Baseball was starkly different then compared with now.

I have seen many changes over time: no more post-game alcohol in the clubhouse, protein shakes and healthier food options in the player dining room, a prominent strength and conditioning staff, and improved weight rooms. There are now more player workstations: multiple batting cages, indoor pitching mounds, and expansive video and meeting rooms. The changes were parceled out bit by bit in different areas. I don't recall an abrupt renaissance of drastic alterations, but the slightest of changes were happening nonetheless.

Over time, I noticed a worrisome fact: The players were arriving at the stadium earlier than in the past. The Major Leagues had shed the 3:00 to 3:30 p.m. report time to the clubhouse or the standard arrival requirement of 30–45 minutes before team stretch. Players were now arriving as early as noon in preparation for a 7:00 p.m. game! Things had evolved into a competition among the players showing a strong work ethic by arriving at the clubhouse early. These players seemed to show an unwavering commitment to the team, loyalty to the other players, and dedication to their careers—at least it seemed the players thought that way. What was going on?

One day at Coors Field, I went downstairs to the clubhouse for lunch. Game time that day was 7:10 p.m. When I entered the dining room around 12:30 p.m., I was surprised to see four players—Matt Holliday, Ryan Spilborghs, Brad Hawpe, and Garrett Atkins—eating lunch. They weren't wearing their street clothes; they were dressed in workout shorts and T-shirts. They must *have arrived by noon. These players had come up through the Minor Leagues, so I'd known them for some time. They were well respected in the organization for their strong work ethic and dedication to the Rockies. We chatted about baseball, our young prospects in the Minor Leagues, and "Spilly's" contract situation (which he never failed to discuss with me).*

During the entire conversation, I wondered why these players would show up to the ballpark so early before the game. I worried they would wear themselves out. So during our conversation I asked about this routine, saying it was common for past players to arrive at 3:00 p.m. for a 7:00 p.m. game. I said they should spend more time away from the stadium to rest and relax. It would take their minds off the pressures of competition and not physically and mentally tax them to the point of diminished return. After all, the Major League season is a grind. I expressed my opinion in this infamous statement: "You guys are working too hard!"

What did I just say? They were working too hard? What would my mentors say if they heard me accuse players of working too hard? Did I lose my mind? I was trained to believe a player should work as hard as humanly possible! What was wrong with me? Had my diligent observations of the Major Leagues made me disregard the central principle in my baseball upbringing—hard work? In my own defense, the human body does have physical and mental limitations, and these players were pushing theirs to the extreme. I concluded their heavy workload and constant focus on the game would have detrimental effects on their PERFORMANCE.

PERFORMANCE! My new perspective at the Major League level had led me to worry more about performance than skill development. Success in the Major Leagues is determined by performance. It is not a "try hard" developmental league; it's a "do good" league. I thought they could diminish their physical ability to perform in the game that night and future games. That was my logic, yet I still can't believe I said it.

Years later in a phone conversation with Joe Maddon, I told him, "I watch these Major League players every day. They get to the park too early and work too much before a game. It has to be detrimental to their performance to spend half of their twenty-four-hour day at the ballpark. They train too much and think about their play far too long nowadays."

Dead silence. Did Joe think I was nuts? I hoped not, but he was one of my instructors who'd always preached the value of hard work. After a long pause, Joe laughed. Was he laughing at me?

Then Joe told me about the strategies he felt he needed to institute with the Tampa Bay Rays. He had implemented player report times to the clubhouse that moved them to later in the day from their normal routine. The players simply weren't allowed to arrive earlier. For road games, Joe moved the team bus times to the stadium to later in the afternoon to ensure his players didn't spend an inordinate amount of time at the park. He had witnessed exactly what I had suggested.

Players today work harder and longer than they ever have. Yes, the game has changed in many ways. Why? What's the difference in today's player compared to those in the past? As I pondered these questions, it became clear I was asking the wrong ones. I should have been asking, "What has changed around the players to make them work harder and longer?" It suddenly dawned on me. I hadn't reconciled the differences in professional baseball facilities between the past and present. I'd never taken into account how the facilities had drastically improved.

Stadiums of the past offered little in terms of performance areas. Players wouldn't arrive early because they had few options if they couldn't work out on the field. Stadiums of the past had a single-tunnel batting cage, one tee-area to hit, and weight rooms that either didn't exist or had substandard equipment. Today's players have a place for any conceivable baseball activity in their attempt to improve performance.

In addition, today's Major League clubhouses have a dedicated chef to prepare healthy, elaborate individual meals for players. Clubs have poured substantial financial resources into improving workout areas in their stadiums. As a result, players can take full advantage of opportunities to work longer and harder.

Still seeking to understand, I thought about how players of the past spent their time much less efficiently than today. Because they didn't have multiple work stations or batting cages, they had to stand around a lot and wait their turn. Happily, I had proved to myself I could challenge my own upbringing and beliefs. However, I was still upset that I'd failed to recognize the game was changing around me. Professional players of today have the facilities at their disposal to work smarter, not just harder. Joe Maddon was always a little ahead of the curve.

"If you build it, they will come."– *Field of Dreams* movie

Field Staff Duties

The importance of documenting and reviewing activity is indisputable. You need to document all activities to detail what's been done, quantify the time invested, and examine the results.

As shown in the deconstruction exercise, professional players have busy days. Their regular schedule is demanding both physically and mentally. The same is true for the field staff charged with supervising and instructing the players' individual and team activities. They have close to the same schedule as the players except for one difference: *They arrive earlier and stay later.*

Their jobs aren't limited solely to field activity. Following the game, staff members file written and oral reports on the results of team and player performance. They log their players' activities and performances in the various aspects of the game. They plan the players' team and individual early work and other developmental drills. They're also available to counsel any players who require guidance.

Typically, the manager also files scouting reports to the front office on the opposing players. Some organizations require their managers and coaches to file periodic individual player progress reports on the players on their team. They're also involved in phone conversations with coordinators, scouts, Major League staff, or front office staff communicating about issues, offering information, or requesting opinions on strategy. Add to that their time speaking with the media. *They are busy!*

Where's the Time to Manage and Coach?

The ROTI evaluation of the Player Development Department involves a comprehensive study of administrative duties for the field staff. It stands to reason that additional time spent documenting activities and filing reports results is less time spent with their players. Managers and coaches shouldn't be bogged down with administrative office work to the point of limiting their impact and guidance on players. As managers and coaches, it doesn't make sense to spend the majority of their day on the phone or at their desk completing paperwork. Given their passion, talents, and influence, they should be allowed time to manage and coach.

Increasing the time available to interact with players should offer a potentially higher ROTI—something the front office should be cognizant of when designing workload and documentation requirements for their Minor League staff members. The concept of ROTI should lead to making sound decisions on how much time the field staff needs to complete office administrative work during a busy day. Yes, it's advantageous for the front office to have as much information as possible. But at what point does that adversely affect the manager's or coach's impact on the players?

> If managers and coaches don't develop the players, then who will?

Summary

Extreme care must be taken to recognize and appreciate the complexities of developing players. Progressive thought and diligent review should lead to placement at the forefront of the industry. A system of checks and balances bridges the divide between philosophy and practical application in these ways:

☐ Departmental posture shapes the application strategies.

☐ Documentation of activities allows for proper quantification.

☐ Quantification of strategies allows for proper review.

☐ Limited time necessitates wise prioritization.

☐ Today's ever-evolving environment requires constant examination to understand how the change in variables has altered the present landscape and will continue to do so.

Your idea of the best practical plan will change over the years.

☐ Recognize changes.

☐ Think progressively.

☐ Listen to others.

Dedication to philosophy is admirable but rigidity in process or application can be a detriment as situations evolve.

CHAPTER 19:

CONCLUSION

THIS BOOK DOES NOT ATTEMPT TO DEFINE THE *ONLY WAY* TO GAIN AN interview and acquire employment in Major League Baseball—for many ways exist. But it does define critical success factors, including:

- ☐ A personal commitment to a career in professional baseball to uncover any available strategy.

- ☐ A burning desire that inspires the creativity to develop aptitude and skill.

- ☐ A clear brand or identity that sets you apart.

- ☐ Above all else, relentless persistence to gain an opportunity.

It is not a book of details meant for you to remember. Rather, it's a guide to the conceptual thought processes and executive perspective required in designing Baseball Operations programs and procedure. Philosophy shapes the predisposition that promotes a construct with consistent strategies and actions. Quality control is an important element of the construct. A progressive mind then provides the foundation to adjust to ever-changing circumstances. And because change is constant in professional baseball, strategies cannot remain the same as new norms evolve.

To believe one can understand all there is to know about baseball sets up a path for failure. Achieving a mastery level of ability is a never-ending pursuit. That's why it's necessary to assume a student posture throughout your career.

This book is a study of philosophy and practical procedure, and how it's developed, reviewed, and qualitatively analyzed in professional baseball.

In addition, it delves into the human condition and the many variables and complexities that determine performance. It also spells out the role of supportive personnel to drive both individual and organizational success. And most important, it emphasizes the need to build the confidence that will benefit us all.

I hope this book gives you insights that benefit your thought process. Of course the details will change over time, but the ability to solve issues in professional baseball and create successful plans remains the same. Keep it as your guide over the years to come.

Even if you aren't looking for a job in Major League Baseball, I trust you found parallels in your business pursuits through these pages. If you plan on an MLB career, I'm hopeful the lessons conveyed here will guide your journey successfully.

With my deepest sincerity, I wish you the best of luck.

ABOUT THE AUTHOR

BILL GEIVETT HAS 28 YEARS OF EXPERIENCE IN PROFESSIONAL BASEBALL as a player, scout, and front office executive. He has been a member of the California Angel organization, New York Yankees, Montreal Expos, Tampa Bay Devil Rays, Los Angeles Dodgers, and the Colorado Rockies. In 2007, he oversaw the Colorado Rockies Minor League system that featured 16 players who were originally drafted/signed/developed by Colorado. That year, the Rockies were named Organization of the Year. And in 2009, the Rockies' Wild Card team had an Opening Day lineup made up entirely of homegrown players.

Bill has also guided the Montreal Expos' Minor League system, which was named Topps Organization of the Year in 1996. In addition, he was a college baseball coach at Loyola Marymount University (1988-90) and California State University, Long Beach, when it advanced to the 1991 College World Series.

Bill has earned degrees from Sacramento City College (AA), University of California, Santa Barbara (BA) as well as a master's degree in education with an emphasis in physical education from Azusa Pacific University. Drafted four times in the mid-'80s (Los Angeles Dodgers, Chicago White Sox, Chicago Cubs, and California Angels), he signed with the Angels following his senior year at UCSB where he gained All-American accolades as a third-baseman. In 1991, he was inducted as a member of the UCSB Intercollegiate Athletics Hall of Fame.

Currently, Bill is a baseball and business consultant living in Arizona with his wife Bonnie. They have two children, Rachel and Sam. He can be contacted through his website at www.insidebaseballoperations.com.

ACKNOWLEDGMENTS

THE TIME I HAVE SPENT WITH TOMMY LASORDA HAS MEANT THE WORLD to me. He is the greatest motivator I have ever known and he inspired me to write this book. Thank you Tommy, you're the best.

This book would not have been possible without the support and hard work from my sister Patricia, brother Mort, and brother-in-law Randy Hughes. They read my initial rough drafts (some were extremely rough) and offered suggestions to improve the manuscript. My friend John Davis, a UCSB Gaucho brother, gave his insight as a tremendous baseball fan and avid reader. Also, I happened to have the best content/copy editor in the business, Barbara McNichol.

I have mentioned many people throughout this book and feel eternally grateful for all they've done for me and my career. I'd be remiss if I did not also name Phil Womble, Joe Balsinger, David Jackson, Bob Daly, Luchy Guerra, Bob Graziano, Jaime Jarrín, Pepe Yñiguez, Billy DeLury, Rick Monday, Ross Porter, David Kato, Gary Ehrlich, Colin Gunderson, Dave Pearson, Claude Brochu, Bill Stoneman, Mike Scioscia, Chuck Lamar, Al LaMacchia, Don Williams, Edison Lora, Jim Beattie, Matt Stack, John Eugster, Bruce Corwin, Rene and Marcel Lachemann, Marne Obernauer Jr., Keith Dugger, Gary Sheffield, Brian Jones, Scott Gehret, Mike Pontarelli, MaryBea Porter-King, Charlie King, Roy Krasik, Jeff Pfeifer, Bill Schmidt, Dan Jennings, Troy Tulowitzki, Bill Honeycutt, Rick Ingalls, Rolando Fernandez, Lou Holtz, Andrew Checketts, Tom Probst, Bill Ferrari, Joe

Martelli, Jeff Francis, Alan Bossart, Don Welke, Mark Wiley, Jack Gillis, Chris Warren, Drew Goodman, George Frazier, Casey Gorman, Dave Lawn, Russell Wilson, Jay Alves, Mako Oliveras, Paul Egins, Todd Helton, Lori McGregor, Bobby Knoop, Chris Smith, Wayne Morgan, Rafael Betancourt, Clint Barmes, Jon Heyman, Jerry Turner, Mitch Poole, Nao Masamoto, Brian Jordan, LaTroy Hawkins, Matt Williams, Jimmy Tokioka, Ron and Joy Kouchi, Rob Leary, Dave Malpass, Bob Apodaca, Kip Fagg, Michael Cuddyer, Jerry Dipoto, Chris Bosio, Mark Massari, Rick Oliver, Bob Gebhard, Terry Douglass, Pat Daugherty, Jose Mota, Bill Pintard, Trenidad Hubbard, John Drigotas, Pat Gillick, Morrison England, Bill Young, Jim Fregosi Sr and Jr., Paul White, Mark Newman, Tom Runnells, Josh Byrnes, Hervy and Duane Kurisu, Nolan Arenado, Acey Kohrogi, Jim Kellogg, Jim Yogi, Pedro Astacio, Don Logan, Dexter Fowler, Eric Young Jr., Bill Mahoney, Dante Bichette, Don Barbara, Ming Harber, Mark Shapiro, Jimmy Johnson, Eric Anthony, Bob McClure, Nelson Braff, Mark Patton, Derek Vanacore, Sal Nicolosi, Mike and Mandy Coolbaugh, Katie Pavlovsky, Jim Wright, Bo McLaughlin, and Mike Gallego. I have learned many lessons from this group, whether they realize it or not. Others I did not name are equally special to me and have influenced my life tremendously. You know who you are!

Special thanks to Mr. and Mrs. Coop for accepting me into your family and allowing me to marry your daughter and the love of my life.

I'd like to thank my sisters Marji, Jeannie, Jay, and my brother Jim. They have been a wonderful support system throughout my life. Last, but not least, I give the biggest thanks to my late father Morton Jerome Geivett—the career navy man from Kansas City, Missouri, who taught me right from wrong and the meaning of discipline. Love you, Dad.

My dad